Princess, Priestess, Poet

The Sumerian
Temple Hymns
of Enheduanna

PRINCESS, PRIESTESS, POET

Betty De Shong Meador

FOREWORD BY JOHN MAIER

UNIVERSITY OF TEXAS PRESS, AUSTIN

This book has been supported by an endowment dedicated to classics and the ancient world and funded by the Areté Foundation; the Gladys Krieble Delmas Foundation; the Dougherty Foundation; the James R. Dougherty, Jr. Foundation; the Rachael and Ben Vaughan Foundation; and the National Endowment for the Humanities.

Requests for permission to reproduce material from this work should be sent to:
    Permissions
    University of Texas Press
    P.O. Box 7819
    Austin, TX 78713-7819
    www.utexas.edu/utpress/about/bpermission.html
♾ The paper used in this book meets the minimum requirements of ANSI/NISO
Z39.48-1992 (R1997) (Permanence of Paper).

Library of Congress Cataloging-in-Publication Data
Enheduanna.
    Princess, priestess, poet : the Sumerian temple hymns of Enheduanna / [translated and edited by] Betty De Shong Meador ; foreword by John Maier. — 1st ed.
        p.   cm. — (Classics and the ancient world)
    Includes bibliographical references and index.
    ISBN 978-0-292-72353-5
    1. Hymns, Sumerian—Translations into English.   I. Meador, Betty De Shong,
1931–   II. Title.
    PJ4083.E57   2009
    899′.951—dc22

                                                                                                2008049357

Dedicated with love to my grandmothers,
Cora Lee Matthews De Shong and Lena Gilliland Harrell,
and to my mother, Eva Harrell De Shong

CONTENTS

The house of the most powerful goddess in ancient Mesopotamia was described by the world's first known author in poetry that resonates even today, more than four thousand years after it was written, its poetry brought to light for us by Betty De Shong Meador. The house of the great goddess Inanna in Uruk, technically Temple Hymn 16 (of forty-two such poems in the collection), was known as Eanna. The "radiant site" had already been rebuilt some nineteen times before the city of Uruk came into its own. An enormously productive place, with the house of Inanna at its center, Uruk may have been the birthplace of writing itself. The world's first named author, the high priestess Enheduanna, depicted Inanna's house as the very essence of desire, "dazzling" in its "irresistible ripeness."

house of Kullab's cosmic powers
thriving in the radiance of the princess

perfectly shaped fresh fruit
dazzling in your irresistible ripeness
descending from the heart of heaven
    shrine built for the bull

O Eanna
    house of seven corners
    seven fires lit at midnight

seven desires apprehended
your princess   the pure one
she is the whole horizon

As in all the poems in this collection, the poet apostrophizes the site, not its
indwelling spirit, in this case its "princess," Inanna. Both the imagery and the
poetic genre will strike modern readers as exotic. To help us read the poems
Meador provides explanations of individual lines, the organization of the
poems, which fall into no genre that can be readily connected with our own
(unless it is seventeenth-century English topographical poems), and the archi-
tectonics of this most unusual anthology. Developing the poems not through
abstractions and large general principles but through striking images does,
however, resemble high modernist poetics. It takes a while to adjust to the tech-
nique, but Meador makes the poems sing in a way that becomes compelling.

She explains that the poems are addressed to the gods' houses themselves
and that each house has a special character related to the deity and to the community for which it provides a center. Even in Enheduanna's day, late in the
third millennium BCE, Mesopotamian cities contained many small temples,
shrines, and cellas devoted to the hundreds of gods who were worshiped. Enheduanna's selection of forty-two "temples," the modern term for these radiant sites, is a profound theological insight into the powerful forces that organized the city-states.

These residences of the high gods were known to Sumerians and Akkadians of Enheduanna's time. Inanna, who becomes assimilated to the Semitic
goddess Ishtar, probably in Enheduanna's lifetime, is celebrated in three of the
Temple Hymns. Only two other deities, the goddess Ninhursag and the moon
god, Nanna, are similarly highlighted in the collection. In order to translate
the poems and to explain their literary and cultural context, Meador had to
immerse herself in the extensive and highly technical studies of Assyriologists.
She was well aware of the scholarly literature and the difficulties it presents,
as is evident in the first volume of poetry by Enheduanna, *Inanna, Lady of
Largest Heart: The Poems of the High Priestess Enheduanna,* also published by
the University of Texas Press (2001). In this book, as in the earlier work, for
which she won the Gradiva Award from the National Association for the Ad-
vancement of Psychoanalysis, Meador consulted with experts in the Sumerian
texts. To give some idea of the difficulties Meador faced, consider the fact that
the language of Enheduanna's poetry, Sumerian, is an agglutinative language
like Finnish, Hungarian, and Turkish but is unrelated even to those languages.
A project sponsored by the University of Pennsylvania to compile a Sumerian

dictionary has so far produced three volumes on "A" and one on "B." It will be quite a while before nonexperts will be able to work their way through this unusual, long-dead language. Sumerologists themselves must continually update their vocabulary lists as the many thousands of cuneiform tablets are gradually published.

Meador explains that the "cosmic powers" in this poem, a translation of the difficult Sumerian term the **me** (pronounced "may"), are the powers exercised by the goddess, who is strong enough to transform fate. Inanna, "your princess," is capable, among other things, of changing male into female and female into male. Her house in Uruk is pinpointed as lying in the district of Kullab, originally a separate settlement.

Meador further tells us that the poem emphasizes desire, evident in the "fresh fruit" and "irresistible ripeness" of the place. Inanna, after all, was the goddess par excellence of love and sexuality. While the first part of this poem tends to emphasize the sexuality Inanna brings to humanity, the second half, discussed later, introduces the "helmeted" male, who reminds us that Inanna had become a goddess of war as well as of love.

Packed into these few lines are apparent references to Inanna myths that continue to inform us of the goddess's complexity. Her house is said to have "descended" from "the heart of heaven." Urukean thought connected Inanna's seizing of her abode in the heavens and resettling of it on the earth as a consequence of the Flood, which for the Sumerians utterly transformed human life. (Other Sumerian texts claim that "kingship" descended after the Flood.) Bringing her house literally down to earth opened up new possibilities for humans to communicate with her—and for Inanna to interact with humanity.

Likewise, part of the house is said to have been built for "the bull," possibly a reference to Inanna's most famous lover, Dumuzi, the Wild Bull of her youth. The Bible knows him by his Akkadian name, Tammuz. That Uruk contains the shrine built for the bull may be reflected in the famous story of Gilgamesh, who was forced to fight the Bull of Heaven after he had rejected the advances of the goddess.

And finally, the Eanna is described (only here) as having seven corners, with seven lit fires and seven desires. This series of sevens may reflect the idea that Uruk was organized by the Seven Sages, who, according to an Akkadian Gilgamesh story, laid the foundation of the great walls that encircled the city. The city that prospered for many centuries even after it was forced to accept the overlordship of, in turn, Akkadians, kings of Ur, Babylon Assyria, and even Greeks, characteristically maintained its own version of Mesopotamian myths, like that of the Seven Sages before the Flood.

For specialists the Temple Hymns provide very early references to ideas that appear in later texts and attest to the ways in which Mesopotamian culture held onto traditions for hundreds and even thousands of years. For the rest of us, the Temple Hymns offer insights into a culture that profoundly revolutionized human thought and institutions.

Princess, Priestess, Poet is as unexpected a find for readers today as it was for the archeologists who found the original manuscript in the mid-1800s. Of the many thousands of clay tablets that were inscribed in cuneiform, or wedge-shaped, characters, the six-columned tablet that describes forty-two temples is a unique document. But at one time it must have been a very important text. Some thirty-seven fragments of distinct copies have come to light. But what can a modern reader make of a four-thousand-year-old Sumerian poem addressed to forty-two temples in thirty-six cities—now that even the names of the cities are largely unknown to all but a few scholars?

Mesopotamia was polytheistic. Thousands of god names have survived, and a great many more than forty-two temples have been discovered. Most cities had multiple temples. Scholars use the term "temple" as shorthand for buildings that must have served some sacred purpose, since they are closely identified with the gods who "lived" in their houses. Moderns are likely to envision them as Greek or Israelite temples, places where priests performed animal sacrifices—though such rites had little to do with the houses of Sumerian gods. Or we think of them as churches, synagogues, and mosques, structures in which large numbers of the faithful meet for study and worship. Again, the Sumerian houses show little evidence of such uses. Even today, in a society that tries to be inclusive of different faiths and is far more secular than Sumerian society (which probably made no useful distinction between "secular" and "religious"), we have difficulty conceptualizing churches. In the urban area where I live the telephone book identifies hundreds of churches in almost one hundred categories, including synagogues and mosques. *Princess, Priestess, Poet* offers a rare glimpse into the houses of deities at a key moment in Mesopotamian history, when the already ancient Sumerian culture of the southern city-states was encountering a northern Semitic culture of Akkadians, that is, the peoples at the center of a new empire based in the city of Agade, or Akkad. The forty-two temples of the Temple Hymns collection open a window onto the most important sites at a time of a major cultural shift. This may be the best document we have for understanding what a temple meant to the people who built them.

In spite of one hundred years of hard labor by many scholars, ancient Sumer and Akkad are still not very well known to us moderns; but since the Sumerians invented so much that we use today, including (and especially) writing itself, it is worth paying attention to what remains of Sumerian writing. We are not disappointed in picking up the collection of Temple Hymns.

For one thing the collection was unusual in its own time, even though many copies of the text were made over the centuries that followed its composition. An older Temple Hymn does exist, from the earliest period of literature discovered so far, so the collection has at least one prestigious predecessor. Still, we do not find other collections of Temple Hymns after about 2000 BCE.

Even more interesting is the fact that the poems were attributed to the first named author in human history, a woman whose writings were preserved for centuries after her death. The author, Enheduanna, lived nearly two thousand years before Sappho, who is sometimes considered the earliest female poet. Enheduanna was the daughter of the man who defeated the Sumerians and organized the first empire in history, the famous Sargon the Great of Agade. His daughter was installed as the *en,* a largely untranslatable title connoting great political and religious power in Sumer. Enheduanna was selected for the position in the city known in the Bible as the birthplace of Abraham, the city of Ur.

En (or *entu,* as it was translated into Semitic Akkadian) was unquestionably a powerful and prestigious title in the new social order established by the Sumerian city-states. Ur would soon overshadow Sargon's Akkad. Another writer intrudes on Enheduanna's Temple Hymns by including the most famous king of Ur, Shulgi, who was deified, among the gods whose sites are recognized in the collection. The Temple Hymns would eventually outlast the regimes of both Akkad and Ur.

Princess, Priestess, Poet completes Meador's work on the poet Enheduanna. Her earlier volume, *Inanna, Lady of Largest Heart,* studied the poet and three of her remarkable poems in depth. Like the Temple Hymns, the other poems, "Inanna and Ebeh," "The Exaltation of Inanna," and "Lady of Largest Heart," are strikingly original for a culture that increasingly preserved earlier forms. Like the Sumerians, who were great innovators, the author of these poems, herself Sumerian on her mother's side, was what the Romantics would call an original genius. Many writings preserved in Mesopotamia at a time when Sumerian poetry was taught in the schools and new works were being written in Semitic Akkadian are by unknown authors. Even though the name Enheduanna is carefully woven into the text of the final poem in the Temple Hymn collection, a very unusual feature in Sumerian poetry, authorship of the work has sparked a lively debate among scholars. Did Enheduanna, like Homer, actually write the collection of poems attributed in antiquity to her?

As Meador points out in a balanced account of the scholarly debate, the historic Enheduanna apparently grew up in a bilingual home, where her father, the famous Sargon, spoke Akkadian and her mother spoke Sumerian. Some modifications of the Temple Hymns collection, like the later insertion of a hymn to King Shulgi, certainly changed the original plan. And there was, it seems, a certain degree of standardization in the orthography of the later copies of the poems. But it should not be all that surprising that the world's first author was a woman of a social elite.

Enheduanna was not the only woman credited with authorship in those early times. Women in Shulgi's court are mentioned as being authors. In a society that was largely nonliterate, court poets are sometimes mentioned by name, but no writings are attributed to them. The names of many scribes and owners of cylinder seals are known, the reason for this being quite practical: ownership of property and witness to transactions had to be recorded for legal purposes. Many documents that have survived carry no indication of authorship.

And the very idea of authorship in antiquity is complicated. How many hands wrote the biblical book of Isaiah? While we think of authors as individuals working alone—and in "The Exaltation of Inanna" Enheduanna presents herself in that light—in antiquity to a great extent the *authority* behind both the authoring and the copying of texts is foremost. A modern example is the authoring of presidential speeches, frequently managed by a committee of writers that has little interaction with the president. Some years ago the Assyriologist W. G. Lambert brought to light a remarkable document that listed a great many Mesopotamian texts and their authors. While the document itself is from a much later period than Enheduanna's writings, it evinces an idea of authorship very different from the one we have today. There were basically four categories of authors and works. The first, which consists of highly important books for use by exorcists, astronomers, and medical practitioners, were authored *sha pī* the god Ea, that is, "from the mouth of" the god. A second group of texts was authored by the "sages," semidivine creatures who taught humans before the Flood. These two categories might have been considered inspired, as at least one of Enheduanna's poems was inspired by a goddess. The third and fourth categories involved human "experts"—the competent and trained individuals who lived after the Flood. The difference between category three and category four is that one listed men without giving any indication of their family origin, while the other listed men as sons of an ancestral figure. Probably the only work and author known to the general public today—although most of the works listed are known to Assyriologists today—is the "series" *Gilgamesh,* whose authorship is attributed to a certain Sîn-leqi-unninnî.

The debate over the authorship of *Princess, Priestess, Poet* is more than a debate over a name. In Enheduanna's day Sumerian cities were thought to be the homes of major gods: Uruk and Inanna, for example, or Ur and the moon god, Nanna. A city like Nippur might have the divine couple Enlil and Ninlil dominate a site where, as in all the cities, quite a few gods and goddesses were worshiped. The Temple Hymns identify the site and its major deity. Mesopotamia always had major goddesses like Inanna in prominent positions, but there is evidence that the status of some goddesses declined as the status of male deities rose. Kingship, with its heavy emphasis on warfare, may have moved Mesopotamian society toward a more patriarchal culture. In changes that took many centuries to accomplish, the status of women may well have reflected the decline of certain goddesses. Later authors, such as those mentioned in the catalogue of texts and authors, are exclusively male. As the officials who managed both state and temple were increasingly professionalized, fewer official positions were held by women. Inanna's Uruk, which preserved many Sumerian traditions well into Seleucid times (late first millennium BCE), may have been exceptional in this regard.

At any rate, this collection of poems that sheds light on sacred sites and the deities who lived there—a collection attributed to a high-ranking, literate female author—is an important document in social history as well as a striking example of Sumerian aesthetics.

Like the poems in the Temple Hymns collection, the other poems attributed to Enheduanna are extraordinary, and, just as she does here, Meador reveals their exceptional poetic qualities in her translation of them. In *Inanna, Lady of Largest Heart,* she regularly consulted with Assyriologists, as she did for this volume. The Sumerologists who advised her gave Meador the courage to find the Sumerian voice behind (or above) the cuneiform writings, as the example from Temple Hymn 16 shows.

Specialists in cuneiform texts might expect *Princess, Priestess, Poet* to be a new edition of the Temple Hymns, one that would rival the standard edition of the poems from 1969. Both specialist scholars and general readers will find much to appreciate in the translations and commentaries Meador offers. She has captured the nuances of the language and brought out the passion and power of these difficult poems.

These most original poems require a great deal of commentary to elucidate their unusual context. But this is not a new edition of the poems. The 1969 edition by Åke W. Sjöberg and Eugen Bergmann included valuable notes that are used by scholars today. Just as she did in *Inanna, Lady of Largest Heart,* Meador worked closely with an expert in the Sumerian language to produce *Princess, Priestess, Poet.* She has read the extensive scholarly work produced during the nearly forty years since the Temple Hymns were first published and has incorporated it very successfully in the manuscript. Very little work has been done on the Temple Hymns themselves, but the background material has expanded tremendously since the early 1990s. Meador's notes and bibliography show that she has read very widely in that background material—especially in the late fourth- and early third-millennia-BCE materials, which are now essential for establishing the context of Enheduanna's late third-millennium writings.

Sumerology is an international scholarly activity, and it is often difficult to keep up with the latest scholarship since it is published in many languages and, especially, in Festschrift volumes and journals that are difficult to find, let alone read. There is no doubt that Meador has brought to bear the most important scholarship from the early 1990s to the present. On the other hand, Sumerologists themselves know of recent finds that have not yet been published. Thus, while *Princess, Priestess, Poet* does not offer a new edition of the Sumerian poems, it does advance the scholarship on the Temple Hymns in an important way by clarifying many issues that were not resolved when the hymns were published in 1969. Meador's work provides many new conceptions about Enheduanna in light of research on the earliest protocuneiform and early literary texts.

To give just one example of the difficulties in translating and commenting on the poems, recall that the first line in Temple Hymn 16, which I mentioned above, praises the "cosmic powers" held by Inanna of Uruk. The Sumerian term for these powers, **me,** is a plural. No one would dispute the fact that the **me** is a key word in Sumerian, probably more so than its Akkadian equivalent, the *parşu.* To my knowledge the range of meaning and the terms related to the **me** have never been more thoroughly studied than in Gertrud Farber-Flügge's study (1973) of a Sumerian myth, "Inanna and Enki," that lists over one hundred of the **me** that would appear to govern civilized life. (Inanna tricks the wise old god Enki into giving her the **me** and then has to ward off the now-sober Enki's attempts to recapture *them.* He ends up, however, reconciling with the wily Inanna and blessing her city.)

For her part, Meador makes a good case for the **me** as "cosmic powers." Since each of the Temple Hymns describes a portion of transcendental reality, the **me** represent a particular deity's portion of that reality. In Temple Hymn 16, Inanna controls the part of Uruk known as Kullab. The primary **me,** though, involves desire. In discussing the various possible translations of the term **me,** Meador also brings to light an important artistic feature of Sumerian poetry, its dependence upon vivid imagery. Inanna's temple radiates desire. Enheduanna likens the temple to "perfectly shaped fresh fruit, dazzling" in its "irresistible ripeness." In the second half of the poem Inanna is active in one of her most impressive powers, the ability to change male into female and female into male. This is seen in her power to throw "the ever-rolling stone dice." I rather like to think that the Sumerians saw the **me,** which some have likened to Platonic Ideas, much the way we see computer code controlling a vast network of programs. But Meador's "cosmic powers" is better in capturing both the concreteness of the Sumerian poet and the abstractions with which we attempt to grasp those crafty **me.**

It is true that a few shorter poems in the Temple Hymn genre have been discovered from a somewhat earlier period than Enheduanna's, so it is clear, as Meador points out, that Enheduanna's work is not entirely original. One might think of Shakespeare working within the tradition of the sonnet: it takes a bit of care to see how the individual author comes through in traditional forms. One of Meador's arguments is that the Temple Hymns express the individuality of the remarkable princess, high priestess, and poet of the third millennium BCE. Meador had to deal with the scholarly argument that Enheduanna herself may not even have written the Temple Hymns. I think Meador has made the best case that an individual, not just a tradition of anonymous scribes, is behind the writing of the Temple Hymns. Meador adduces solid historical background to show how a woman in an early period of written literature could have made a contribution of such significance that she would be remembered long after her death — even after Sumerian ceased to be a living language.

Meador, as in her earlier book on Enheduanna, is interested in the status of women in the ancient Near East and in the ways in which the status of women is reflected in the religious life of a society that had many powerful goddesses as well as powerful gods in the pantheon. The great goddess Inanna is a major factor in this discussion, since three of the Temple Hymns are devoted to Inanna in three of her major cities. (Uruk was the major site for more than three thousand years; but the city founded by Enheduanna's father, Akkad, had Inanna installed as the great goddess of that city and therefore of the empire; the important conflation of Inanna and Semitic Ishtar occurred during this time.)

First-time readers of these poems may not fully appreciate how much learning and effort went into Meador's commentaries. The forty-two Temple Hymns have to be presented in their original order. That presents a difficulty in the publishing of a modern edition—for both specialists and nonspecialists—because a Temple Hymn addressed to a temple and its deity will in one case be familiar to every Sumerologist (but not to the nonspecialist) and in the next case be unknown even to the specialist. What Meador has grasped is that the sequence of poems is anything but arbitrary. A major deity will be followed by others in the "family," and in any case, as Meador makes clear, the poems follow an intelligible geographical grouping. There has been a tendency to see the Mesopotamian pantheon as a relatively fixed group, but it is increasingly evident that ideological and political forces over many centuries changed the ways in which deities and the keepers of the temples were thought to relate to one another. The most conspicuous example is the rise of the city of Nippur and its main god, Enlil. The religio-political realignment not only affected the earlier cities like Eridu and Uruk; it also exerted even more pressure on the Mother Goddesses whose influence had been slipping for years. The rise of the god Enlil came at the expense even of his "wife," Ninlil, whose myths kept her in memory even as her power in the region was diminishing.

I began these comments with one of my favorite poems in the collection. The second part of Temple Hymn 16, the part that concretizes the divine **me**, captures the Inanna who is both the goddess of love and the powerful fate-transformer, the only goddess to join the highest ranks of the Mesopotamian pantheon: Anu, Enlil, and Ea. Like the other forty-one Temple Hymns, number 16 ends with the formula that identifies the deity responsible for building the house upon its radiant site.

As one who has spent many years reading literature from a variety of cultures and historical periods, I like to think that literature can provide a portrait, if not a documentary snapshot, of a culture. In the lines of Temple Hymn 16 Meador succeeds in presenting highly unusual poetic material in beautiful translation and in providing historical and cultural material that is not well known to modern readers.

> your Lady Inanna
> throws the ever-rolling stone dice
> ever bedecking the woman
> ever helmeting the man
> crowned with lapis lazuli desire
> singular in the sanctuary
> Queen of heaven and earth   Inanna
> has built this house on your radiant site
> and placed her seat upon your dais

Princess, Priestess, Poet goes a long way toward providing readers with a portrait of Enheduanna's complex culture. This is a brilliant and compelling translation of Sumerian poetry. The more we learn about the complexity of Sumerian culture, the more we will value the collection of Temple Hymns. In Meador's translations, each temple and each city stands out in crystal clarity, with their distinctive features highlighted in a way that had never been seen before the world's first named princess, priestess, and poet took up this difficult task.

John Maier
Brockport, New York
January 2, 2008

ACKNOWLEDGMENTS

This work, beginning with the translation of the forty-two Sumerian Temple Hymns, owes its life to John Carnahan, who sat patiently with me for three years, taught me to read cuneiform script, and with his expertise led me word by word, line by line through each hymn.

Friends read and responded to the hymns as they evolved, especially Judy Grahn, who attended every step of the book's evolution. My colleagues at the San Francisco Jung Institute were constant in their support. Tom Singer and Baruch Gould continue to offer a platform for Enheduanna there in the Extended Education program. Tom Singer graciously granted opportunity to put Enheduanna's work in perspective in his valuable books on contemporary culture. I especially thank Jean Kirsch for her friendship and for reading early versions of the essays.

Olympia Dukakis gave me a place in her developing productions of Enheduanna's poems to Inanna. The Assyriologist Ann Draffkorn Kilmer supported this work from its beginning twenty years ago and was always available as teacher, mentor, and friend. John Maier sustained my spirit with his unquestioning endorsement. I am grateful for my editor Jim Burr's patient affirmation throughout and his guidance of the manuscript through the long process to publication. Special thanks to the artist Neil Barton for his drawings of maps and illustrations.

None of this would have happened without the presence of my husband, Mel Kettner, whose constancy added depth to my understanding of what I was doing and why.

A WORD ABOUT THE TRANSLATION

The process of generating a readable script in English from cuneiform writing on the thirty-seven remaining tablets of the Sumerian Temple Hymns involves, first, that the tablets be meticulously hand-copied, then transliterated into alphabetical script. Using photocopies of these hand drawings of the tablets as well as their transliterations, I studied with an expert in the language, John Carnahan, research assistant in the Department of Near Eastern Studies at the University of California Berkeley. We relied primarily on what is currently the only edition of the translation of the Sumerian Temple Hymns by Åke W. Sjöberg and Eugen Bergmann, a complete transliteration and English translation of the text with commentary and photographs of the hand-drawn tablets.[1] In addition, Carnahan brought information regarding the meaning of particular signs that has come to light since the Sjöberg and Bergmann publication in 1969.

The method we used is standard in the field of Assyriology. Carnahan brought to each session copies of the transliterated lines of a hymn in the form of a partitur, or musical score. Thus, the line of a particular hymn, whether partial or complete, might appear on tablets A, D, and G. In a partitur, the words of each line would be printed one over another, like a musical score. From such copies of each of the forty-two hymns, we worked line by line to render the English translation.

In the first several months of our work together, Carnahan taught me the rudiments of reading cuneiform signs. Following this, at the beginning of each of our sessions, we would read the original script, drawn by an expert's hand, of the lines we would undertake that day. It took us three years to complete the translation of all forty-two hymns.

The translation that follows is a literary translation, not a new edition such as that created by Sjöberg and Bergmann. A new edition could be made only by a trained Assyriologist who has spent years immersed in this specialized field studying the intricacies of the language.

Literary translation is a field whose antecedents stretch back to the first written texts, in which Sumerian originals were translated into the language of their northern Semitic neighbors, Akkadian. In literary translation the translator is expected to remain faithful to the original, but also to follow his or her own sense of the meaning, to amplify but not alter, to render a text that is natural in the new language.

In completing the final versions of the hymns, with all the materials and notes from my sessions with Carnahan, I worked alone. I remain grateful to him and to the hundreds of scholars who spend their professional lives uncovering the still-hidden meanings of this ancient language. May my contribution open to others the beauty and intelligence of these our ancestors, the Sumerians.

NOTE

1. Åke W. Sjöberg and Eugen Bergmann S.J., "The Collection of the Sumerian Temple Hymns," in *Texts from Cuneiform Sources*, vol. 3, ed. A. Leo Oppenheim (Locust Valley, N.Y.: J. J. Augustin Publisher, 1969).

ABBREVIATIONS

CANE   *Civilizations of the Ancient Near East*
ETCSL   *Electronic Text Corpus of Sumerian Literature*
JANES   *Journal of the Ancient Near East Society*
JAOS   *Journal of the American Oriental Society*
JCS   *Journal of Cuneiform Studies*
JNES   *Journal of Near Eastern Studies*
NABU   *Nouvelles Assyriologiques Brèves et Utilitaires*
Or   *Orientalia*
RA   *Revue d'assyriologie et d'archéologie orientale*
RIME   *Royal Inscriptions of Mesopotamia: Early Periods*, vol. 2 *Sargonic and Gutian Periods*
ZA   *Zeitschrift fur Assyriologie*

Princess, Priestess, Poet

chapter 1

PRINCESS

Among the thousands of cuneiform-inscribed clay tablets recovered from archeological sites in Iraq in the nineteenth and twentieth centuries, thirty-seven contain the text of a single composition, a collection of Temple Hymns written to forty-two temples throughout the southern half of ancient Mesopotamia, the civilization we know as Sumer. In lines at the end of the final hymn, an individual known from historical records claims to be the author of the text. Her name was Enheduanna, high priestess to the moon god Nanna in Ur. She was the daughter of Sargon, the king who created the first empire in history. Each of the hymns affirmed to worshipers in a particular city their patron deity's unique character and significance. The hymns became part of the literary canon of the remarkable Sumerian civilization and were copied by scribes for hundreds of years after Enheduanna's death. The forty-two Temple Hymns are the subject of this book.

None of the thirty-seven existing tablets is written in Enheduanna's own hand, although unlike most of the population she was an educated, literate individual.[1] All the tablets that contain portions of the Temple Hymns are copies made by scribes. Two of the tablets date from the Ur III period late in the third millennium BCE, one to two hundred years after her death. The remainder were copied even later, in the Isin-Larsa/Old Babylonian period, 2000–1600 BCE. Three of the tablets were found in the ancient city of Ur, where Enheduanna served as high priestess for almost forty years. The others were found in the ruins of the Sumerian religious center, the city of Nippur.

The scant records we have that relate to Enheduanna leave many gaps in our knowledge of her life. Nevertheless, from the remains of the thirty-seven tablets and from three additional long poems attributed to Enheduanna written to her personal deity Inanna, she is recognized as the first author of record, the first individual known to have created a body of her own writing, or, as William Hallo says, "the first non-anonymous author in Mesopotamian history and perhaps all of history."[2] Her name on the tablets discovered and deciphered in the last century is not readily recognized, as are those of the early poets Sappho and Homer. Yet she wrote lyric poetry, hymns of praise, and heroic tales seventeen hundred years before Sappho and sixteen hundred years before Homer.[3]

Her father, Sargon, gained power around 2334 BCE when, tradition says, he overthrew the king of Kish and proceeded to conquer the entire population of southern Mesopotamia, a territory of independent city-states already known for over a thousand years as Sumer. His daughter Enheduanna, at a young age and possibly at her father's urging, moved from her home, Akkad, in the north, the city Sargon built as his capital, to Ur far to the south in the heartland of Sumer near the Persian Gulf. There she became high priestess to the moon god Nanna in his temple complex at Ur. With his daughter in a prestigious position, Sargon may have hoped to calm the unrest rising against him in the southern Sumerian cities.

Legend tells us that before his rise to power Sargon was serving as cupbearer to the king of Kish, Ur-Zababa. The city of Kish was known to be a ruling city in the territory of northern Mesopotamia in the years before Sargon, the Early Dynastic period. Sargon is said to have overthrown this king and assumed the kingship himself. A more likely possibility is that the young Sargon failed in his attempted coup and fled into exile.[4] The scenario that portrays Sargon as a usurper who killed his king and took over the throne of Kish conflicts with the ancient Kinglist, which records several succeeding kings of Kish in the north who followed Ur-Zababa. The Kinglist, a second-millennium, largely fictional document, records impossibly long reigns of certain kings before a devastating flood and more realistic selected tenures of kings after the deluge. Another contradiction to Sargon's legendary conquest was the fact that the contemporary king in the south, Lugalzagesi of Umma, had successfully defeated the territory of Lagash and established his rule over Uruk, Ur, and eventually all the southern cities.[5] Lugalzagesi had even received the coveted blessing of the ruling deity Enlil, bestowed by his powerful priests in Nippur.

Sargon was an upper-class, Semitic-speaking official in a high position in Ur-Zababa's court.[6] After his attempted overthrow of the king, Sargon may have established his fledgling kingdom in the town of Akkad, not far from Kish but out of easy reach of Lugalzagesi's southern army. Eventually, he built a large military force, defeated Uruk, captured Lugalzagesi "along with his 'fifty governors'—i.e., the petty kings of all the separate city states."[7] Tradition says Sargon dragged Lugalzagesi in neck-stock all the way from Uruk in the south near the gulf to the religious capital of Nippur in the center of the alluvium. There, before the great god Enlil (who only recently had blessed Lugalzagesi's kingship), Sargon asked to be named king of Sumer and Akkad. Enlil complied, through his kingmaker priests, and Sargon became king of the land.

The new king created fundamental changes in the centuries-old Sumerian tradition that had existed virtually unbroken from its beginning in the mid-fourth millennium. Hans Nissen emphasizes the contrast between the "Old Sumerian period," or Early Dynastic, 3000–2350 BCE, dominated by "the Sumerian ethnic group," and the "completely different style of the period of the Akkad Dynasty with its new holders of political power, the semitic Akkadians."[8] The changes Sargon made stirred mistrust among the Sumerian-speaking citizens in cities south of Akkad. For the almost two thousand years of these southern cities' existence prior to Sargon's seizure of kingship, the people had lived in relative peace, even during rivalries for hegemony; they were held together by a common pantheon and mythology, by mutual trade interests, and by the Sumerian language. With the evolution of a written script, they could record trade contracts as well as preserve and exchange traditional myths, songs, and stories. Each city's longevity had a sacred history entwined with the specific patron deity. In Sumerian cosmology, each city belonged to its deity, who, it was believed, rose to claim the city the day the world was created.

From the start citizens of the Sumerian cities in the south resisted Sargon's strong central rule and continually fought for their independence. They faced a mighty opponent in Sargon, who with his growing military force sent garrisons in all directions, occupying or establishing outposts throughout most of the known world—south to the Persian Gulf, west to the Upper Sea (the Mediterranean), north and northwest into Syria and Anatolia, and east onto the plains of Iran. In these many locations, far outdistancing the territorial expansion of any previous ruler, he stationed relatives and loyalists to govern the towns and cities, awarding them lands and authority and thus strengthening the centralized government in Akkad to which these governors reported. No such successful seizure of lands had ever happened. Sargon created the first true empire with a successful center holding it together. Citizens attempted revolts, particularly in the autonomous city-states of southern Sumer, but Sargon was relentless and his armies overpowering. With the succession of his sons, Rimush and Manishtushu, and that of his powerful grandson, Naram-Sin, the empire Sargon created lasted over two hundred years. Hallo describes the impact of the empire Sargon ruled:

> When Sargon of Akkad conquered Lugalzagesi of Uruk "together with [his] fifty governors," he laid the basis for a new departure in Mesopotamian political organization and ushered in a complex of social, religious, and artistic innovations that deserve to be regarded as a kind of cultural explosion. Its stimulus spread the norms of Sumer and Akkad far beyond their boundaries, and Mesopotamian influence of varying strength can be detected throughout the Asiatic Near East in what is generally regarded as its last Early Bronze phase.[9]

DAUGHTER OF THE KING — HIGH PRIESTESS OF UR

Into this atmosphere of unprecedented amassing of territory and influence, Enheduanna was born. "Enheduanna" is not the name by which her father or mother, her brothers or nurses would have known her. Like her older brothers, Rimush and Manishtushu, who may have been twins, she would have been given an Akkadian name at birth. "Enheduanna" is the Sumerian cultic name she received on becoming the high priestess at Nanna's temple in Ur.

The palace at Akkad must have been subjected to a constant tumult of activity. Visitors came from exotic places with which Sargon's government traded — the Indus Valley far to the east, cities in the lands of Dilmun (Bahrain), Magan (Oman), and Melukkha (the Indus basin) — beyond the southern gulf. Enheduanna would have heard tales of sailing ships on a vast western ocean, the Upper Sea (the Mediterranean). From inside the palace rooms assigned to the government, she could have learned history as it happened or listened as her brothers were groomed to succeed their father.

Sargon was a Semite whose native language was Akkadian, not Sumerian. He brought his Semitic legacy, whose influence prevailed in northern Mesopotamia and in modern-day Syria and Turkey. By his order the Akkadian language replaced Sumerian in the court, in official documents, and in the interactions of government. Most offensive to the independent southern Sumerian city-states, he established a centralized government with one capital city, Akkad, as the seat of power and authority.

Historians conjecture that Sargon's decision to appoint his daughter to a prominent position in the main temple in Ur was a result of his need to have a strong presence in the traditional Sumerian south, there to stand against the disaffected secular rulers. He knew the temple compound of the moon deity at Ur, Nanna and his wife, Ningal, was one of the most prominent among the southern cities. Furthermore, Nanna had been served in the past by other priestess attendants. The British Assyriologist J. N. Postgate describes Sargon's motives:

> At Ur, Sargon solved his problem by installing his daughter, Enkheduanna, as the high priestess (EN) of Nanna; we don't in fact know if there was an old tradition of placing the ruler's daughter in this role, but it seems likely. It is hardly coincidental that Enkheduanna is named as the authoress of the cycle of temple hymns that celebrate the virtues of all the major shrines of the land: both an acknowledgment of the validity of the local ideologies, and a claim to embrace them.[10]

The all-important head priest or priestess at a city's primary temple carried substantial religious authority in the region. Sargon may have believed that the presence of the royal princess as priestess would counterbalance the unrest in the secular hierarchy of the city. Further, having his daughter as the ruling priestess could extend his own secular authority into the influential officialdom of the temple.

Enheduanna, chosen to be high priestess to the moon god Nanna in Ur, would live in the *gipar,* the official dwelling place, where in ritual acts she would take the part of Ningal as Nanna's earthly wife. Perhaps even more than her father had envisioned, Enheduanna served as an ambassador. For many of the patron deities of the cities north and south, she presented poetic tributes. Forty-two of the hymns she collected survive to this day. In the hymns she is both poet and theologian, as she articulates unique descriptions of the character of each of the primary Sumerian deities.

Enheduanna is thought to have died during the reign of her nephew, Naram-Sin. She would have been buried outside the gipar in Ur where she had lived her long, productive life. The tradition she initiated as high priestess at Ur, daughter of a king, continued for five hundred years after her death. Later priestesses remembered with respect "the resting ones." They were honored in festivals with ritual offerings of cheese, butter, dates, and oil. Within the area of the Ningal temple small shrines were dedicated to certain of the esteemed high priestesses.[11] Because of her preeminence, we can be sure that a shrine to Enheduanna would have been there among them.

chapter 2

PRIESTESS

After Enheduanna was appointed to become the high priestess of the moon god Nanna in Ur, she took at her inauguration the cultic name Enheduanna, thus assuming the title *en*, a title whose origin reaches back to the ancient city of Uruk and the Eanna temple of its main deity, Inanna. Uruk's unique growth and influence profoundly shaped Sumerian civilization. A thousand years before Enheduanna was born, the city of Uruk, located on the Euphrates River a few miles northwest of Ur, was from the mid to the late fourth millennium the site of unprecedented urban expansion.

In the era prior to Uruk's growth, small urban centers, scattered over the landscape, survived by farming, fishing, and tending domesticated animals. By 3200 BCE, the explosive growth of Uruk had far surpassed in size and complexity that of any city before or long after its decline. At its height, its estimated population was twenty thousand, "probably [a] conservative [number]," according to the archeologist Guillermo Algaze.[1] The population in the surrounding villages and towns added another twenty thousand to the Uruk area. Rome, three thousand years later, was the only ancient city that surpassed Uruk in size.[2]

The city's prosperity flourished with its thriving trade network that reached far into the plain north of the alluvium and continued into present-day Syria and Turkey as well as east of the Sumerian alluvium into Iran. The great river systems of Sumer made possible the easy transporting of goods to and from Uruk. Manufacturing, both public and private, supported industrial specializations—the production of pottery, weaving and textile fabrication, and metal smelting. These commodities and agricultural surpluses were traded by the people of Uruk in their search for natural resources, virtually nonexistent in the south. Sumer's only natural resources were clay and reeds, important in the invention of writing and in construction, but almost useless as commodities for trade.

The incremental expansion of Uruk promoted growth that ameliorated the business and government elite. The necessity of record keeping led to the development of writing, and a scribal class emerged alongside the increasing number of officials in the hierarchy of the temple. "The scope of the Uruk 'expansion' is thus overwhelming," says Mark Van De Mieroop, citing not only the number of large-scale buildings, but also "systems of weights and measures, time-reckoning, and numeration."[3] Uruk is credited with the invention of the wheel as well as the domestication of the donkey.[4] Along with the thriving economy in Uruk, the development of true writing enabled a permanent preservation of intellectual activity and supported what Algaze calls "cognitive scaffolding" or "external memory," elements that contributed a valuable framework for the ongoing success of history's first large-scale urban experiment.[5] Algaze continues,

> These "technologies of the mind," so to say, were as much a part of the emerging "created landscape" of early Mesopotamia as the new Uruk Period irrigation canals, noted earlier, and, once developed, arguably became the single most important source of developmental asymmetries between southern Mesopotamia and neighboring areas.[6]

The central temple complex in Uruk was the Eanna, the center of worship of Inanna. It consisted of a number of large ceremonial buildings enclosed by a surrounding wall. During the time of Uruk's prosperity, a royal figure appeared in the art. He was wearing an ankle-length net skirt, and his hair was pulled into a knot at his neck below a rolled-brimmed hat. This figure, many believe, was the *en,* a Sumerian word meaning ruler or lord. Scenes that accompany his image highlight his status as an individual of sovereign authority. He is shown holding a tall spear before tied bodies of a defeated enemy and in a lion and bull hunt pointing his bow and arrow. In other images he is feeding flocks of animals like a good shepherd or standing before a temple presiding over a ritual offering to a deity, or knocking at the door of the goddess Inanna herself. As the ruler/priest he is thought to have lived and carried out his duties in the area of the Eanna known as the gipar. As the principal religious figure, he assumed the role of consort to Inanna herself.

2.1.   The En in a boat with Inanna's emblems on a bull altar—lapis lazuli cylinder seal with imprint, third millennium, Uruk. Courtesy of the Staatliche Museum, Berlin. Photo credit: Bildarchiv Preussischer Kulturbesitz / Art Resource, N.Y.

Many scholars have studied this intriguing figure, and there is no agreement among them who he was. Based on the iconography, some see him as an early depiction of a secular ruler who was also the chief priest—that is, a priest/king.[7] His offices included administrative, economic, and military responsibilities as well as his duties as the primary official in the cult of Inanna in the Eanna. The gipar in which he lived became the administrative and political center of Uruk. His position as the human consort to Uruk's principal deity made the office of en the single most powerful in the territory of Uruk throughout most of the fourth millennium, when the city dominated Mesopotamia. Denise Schmandt-Besserat concludes, "What seems obvious is that the Enship was held in great awe in the early cities. The Myth of Inanna and Enki, for example, features the enship as the first (and probably foremost) of the hundred elements constituting civilization."[8]

A beautiful piece of art from this era, found in the ruins of the Eanna precinct, is the Uruk Vase. It depicts a scene in which the en is being greeted by a priestess at the door of Inanna's temple. This alabaster vase, over a meter tall, is carved in relief and consists of five registers, beginning at the base with the rippling shape of water. Above the water lush plants grow, and above them, animals—sheep and goats—march toward the right. In the fourth register naked men facing left carry offerings of food and drink. The top and widest register depicts the priest/king, the en, presenting to a female figure in a doorway what appears to be a long, woven sash or decorative cloth. A pair of Inanna's stately emblems stand behind the human priestess and specify the presence of the deity. Behind the emblems on an altar resting on the back of a large ram, attendants offer the en a sculpted representation of the cuneiform sign for the written word, en. The priest/king at the door comes with his offerings to receive the title of his office, confirmed by Inanna herself.[9] The scene may also refer to the Sacred Marriage ritual in which the en consummates his marriage to the deity. The depiction in this ritual scene of the sign en in cuneiform script is an example in which the very elements of writing were imbued with numinous meaning. This is also true of the emblems of Inanna in the scene, the tall posts curved into a circle at the top, which designate her presence and are three-dimensional models of the early cuneiform sign (mùš) that wrote her name.[10] Schmandt-Besserat notes that the Uruk Vase is among "the earliest historical documents associating writing and images," suggesting that "scribal art was also an important symbol of kingship."[11]

The en-priest in these early depictions is male, appropriate to his ritual office as spouse/consort to Inanna. No evidence has come to light of a female en in this early period. Piotr Steinkeller suggests a reason for this:

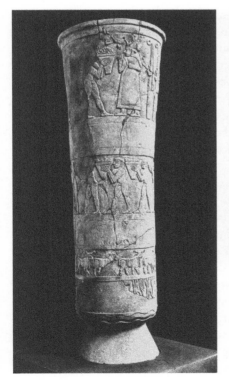

2.2.   The Uruk Vase (a) and detail (b) of priest holding cuneiform sign for en, third millennium, Uruk. Courtesy of the Iraq Museum, Baghdad, Iraq. Photo credit (a): Bildarchiv Preussischer Kulturbesitz / Art Resource, NY; (b): Erich Lessing / Art Resource, N.Y.

It appears quite certain that the earliest Sumerian pantheon was dominated by female deities. As I would reconstruct the situation existing during the Uruk period, most of the city-states (or proto-city-states) had goddesses as their titulary divine owners. Those goddesses controlled broadly all aspects of human and animal life, namely fertility, procreation, healing, and death.[12]

Other Assyriologists question this assumption, given the scant evidence. They do agree, however, that over time the office of the en lost much of its secular authority. At some point a new official, the ensik, appeared in the records, a powerful ruler who, according to Steinkeller, seems to have "appropriated the en's military and political powers," thus leaving the en "with ritual functions only. . . . He continued to reside in the gipar, which, like his office itself, no longer carried any secular significance."[13]

In the earliest literary records from 2600 BCE, the male deity Enlil appears to be the head of the pantheon.[14] The "growing masculinization of the Sumerian pantheon," Steinkeller speculates, "was partly an internal development, reflecting changes in the organization of the Sumerian society, and partly the result of a contact with the Akkadian population of northern Babylonia," where the Semitic pantheon was dominated by male deities.[15] Around 2500 BCE, F. A. M. Wiggerman says, "a northern king Enmebaragesi transformed Enlil's temple in Nippur, exactly between Wari (Akkad) and Kengir (Sumer) into a national cult center, the first step toward the unification of the two cultural provinces under one king deriving his power from Enlil and the national assembly of gods."[16] Female attendants cared for these male deities, although in Sumer they do not appear to have served as earthly wives of the ruling deities.

Enheduanna may have been the first woman to hold the title en, high priestess, earthly spouse of a deity. However, the art historian Irene Winter argues that the office of en priestess existed in the Early Dynastic period and that Sargon's appointment preserved continuity with the past and confirmed his support of Sumerian tradition. Winter presents "visual evidence," including a votive plaque from the gipar at Ur dating to the preceding Early Dynastic period, in which a frontal facing woman in a rolled-brimmed hat similar to that worn by the En at Uruk and by Enheduanna in the disc bearing her inscription (pictured below) takes part in a ritual in which a naked priest pours a libation.[17] Enheduanna's eventual prestige and fame verify that she distinguished the office with her strong intelligence and creativity. Her influence is apparent for the five hundred years after her death during which an en-priestess took the role of Ningal, spouse of the moon god Nanna. Enheduanna's brilliance and leadership drew attention to the temple at Ur. She exerted her influence as the country's defining theologian by distributing the forty-two Temple Hymns to all the major temples, deities, and cities south to north.

THE INSTALLATION OF THE EN-PRIESTESS

Enheduanna's journey from her home in Akkad to Nanna's city of Ur, near the Persian Gulf, required traveling south for days on a boat or barge on one of the rivers or major irrigation canals. For centuries the Sumerians with great diligence had built and maintained the intricate network of connecting canals running the whole length of the alluvium along and between the two rivers, the Euphrates and the Tigris. The system delivered water to crops and was the lifeblood of the entire economy. The canals were an elaborate network of highways stimulating trade, enabling the country to prosper, and fostering communication that reinforced the common religious tradition that cemented the Sumerian identity.

This trip brought the young Enheduanna to the large temple complex of Nanna, the moon god, at Ur. The sequence of events leading to her inauguration is a hypothetical account from the few known facts. Before her installation, not only would she be trained, but she would be chosen by the moon god Nanna himself as suitable to be his human wife. Joan Westenholz has identified two texts by Enheduanna pertaining to her selection and ordination as high priestess. In one of them, Enheduanna refers to herself as "the *en*-priestess chosen for the pure divine offices," referring, Westenholz says, "to divine selection, the knowledge of which is usually obtained through the medium of divination by means of extispicy."[18] The second text "might describe in hymnal discourse the actual ordination and naming ceremony of Enheduanna."[19]

Over a given period of time prior to her selection, the most renowned seers would read portents in the stars and extract the liver from a spotless sheep to determine the omen from the intricate shapes, hills, and valleys of this prized organ. The science of liver divination had been perfected over preceding millennia. If all bode well, the daughter of Sargon, Enheduanna, would be chosen by Nanna to assume the office of high priestess of Sumer.

Nanna's divine selection was crucial. The high priestess would become Ningal, wife of Nanna, and take Ningal's role in the annual Sacred Marriage celebration. The marital union of the high priestess as Ningal with Nanna was the culmination of this traditional festival, enacted to assure the bounty

2.3.   Model of liver used for divination. Courtesy of the Trustees of the British Museum.

of the harvest, the fertility of the domestic animals, and the prosperity and
well-being of the human subjects. Enheduanna made evident the centrality
of her role as Ningal in her inscription on the back of a carved alabaster disk
that displays her portrait leading a ritual procession. The inscription reads as
follows:

> Enheduanna, true lady of Nanna,
> wife of Nanna
> child of Sargon
> king of all
> in the temple of Inanna of Ur
> a dais you built [and]
> Dais, table of heaven you called it.[20]

Some say this inscription is the only remaining text written in her own hand.[21]

During his excavations at Ur in 1927, Sir Leonard Woolley found the disk, broken into pieces, in the courtyard of the gipar. Although the text on the back was in fragments, fortunately it had been copied by a scribe in the Old Babylonian period five hundred years after Enheduanna's death, who used the inscription to fill space left empty on his assigned tablet. Because of this frugal scribe, we know the disc was whole at this time, broken sometime after 1600 BCE; we can compare the restoration made by the excavators with his copy. The inscription contains the first written connection of the title en to a

2.4.   The Disc of Enheduanna. Courtesy of the Penn Museum, object B16665, image #150424.

priestess; the en in her name, En-heduanna, as noted above, signifies her role as consort of Nanna. Dominique Collon describes the scene on the front of the disc:

> Enheduanna is depicted on a disc (the moon?) . . . , facing a stepped edifice (an early ziggurat?). . . . She is accompanied by robed, clean-shaven priests, one of whom pours a libation on an altar from a distinctive, handle-less, spouted vessel similar to actual examples found in Early Dynastic graves in the Royal Cemetery, some two centuries earlier; the second priest carries an object which, on later analogy, is probably a frond or sprinkler . . . while the third carries a bucket. Enheduanna is clad in the flounced robe later reserved for deities, and she wears the distinctive thick hairband of her office—perhaps recalling that of the "priest-king" [the en-priest]—with her hair falling down her back and in braids down the side of her face.[22]

Enheduanna's prominence on the disc corroborates her influential role in the society's religious structure. That the inscription on the back of the disc was copied by a scribe four hundred years after her death testifies to her legacy as a unique public historical figure. Nanna had been served by female attendants before Enheduanna's inauguration. Early evidence, both written and visual, suggests that the tradition of a prominent priestess of Nanna existed prior to Sargon's daughter's installation. Excavators at Ur found a calcite cup inscribed with the name Ninmetabarri, daughter of An Bu, king of Mari, a large city northwest of Sumer in Semitic territory of present-day Syria. Around 2370 BCE, King An Bu conquered large portions of Sumer. Ninmetabarri may have been the first priestess of Nanna, also the daughter of a king, to live in the gipar at Ur.

On even earlier archaic tablets from both ancient Shuruppak (Tell-Fara) and from Ur, 2750–2600, the phrase MUNUS.ZI.(ZI). ^{d}NANNA appears—a phrase suggestively similar to the one that Enheduanna used on the back of the disk: MUNUS-NUNUZ-ZI-^{d}NANNA, "true Lady of Nanna." An eminent priestess of Nanna at Ur may have served even in this period, three hundred to four hundred years before Enheduanna's tenure.

THE GIPAR OF ENHEDUANNA

Woolley and his team from the British Museum excavated at the site of the city of Ur between 1922 and 1934. At the temple of Nanna, they explored the gipar down to the level of the third and last phase of the Early Dynastic period, 3000 to 2350 BCE. In her comprehensive study of this gipar, Penelope Weadock concludes, "It is not beyond the realm of possibility that even earlier *giparus* lie beneath, going back to the beginning of the Early Dynastic period and before."[23] Enheduanna must have lived in the late stage of the Early Dynastic gipar that Woolley discovered. There is no evidence that a structure intervened between this gipar and the next building, constructed on top of it, built in the Ur III period, 2112–2004 BCE — long after Enheduanna's death.

The Early Dynastic gipar that Enheduanna occupied consisted of three separate buildings, each with its own purpose in the ongoing activities of the cult. First and foremost was the temple of Ningal, the moon goddess and wife of Nanna. Built around a courtyard on the plan of a private house, it was Ningal's dwelling. The second building, in a similar building style, the gipar proper, was the home of the high priestess. The third structure was a chapel for the private devotions of the high priestess. These three buildings were combined into one in the later Ur III construction and subsequent reconstructions, but we can assume that Enheduanna and the high priestess Enmenana who followed, the daughter of her nephew Naram-Sin, both lived in the three-building complex.

The most significant of the high priestess's duties was the care of Ningal in her temple near the gipar. Ningal's well-being assured prosperity and abundance for the citizens of Ur and indeed for the country. In her temple she was fed, clothed, and worshiped daily. As in all Sumerian temples, a sacred cella, the room where the deity lived, stood at the heart of the temple. In Ningal's temple, her statue stood on a solid brick pedestal that filled entirely the small room of the cella. Graduated stairs led to the base of the pedestal that supported her statue.

In a separate large room in the Ningal temple there was a low platform that covered half its area. Woolley thought the platform could be for a bed. The room was called the É-NUN,[24] meaning 'house of the queen.' Five subsequent builders also gave the name É-NUN to a room in the sanctuary built for Ningal. An inscription by Nur-Adad, a tenth-century-BCE Aramaean ruler, found on clay cones in the Ningal temple which he built, says, "Nur-Adad built for his own life É-NUN-kug, her [Ningal's] residence, the alcove of the warrior Sin [another name for Nanna]." In 590 BCE, the king Nabonidus, the last builder of the gipar, wrote in an inscription, "The *giparu*, the pure *kummu* in which the rites of *entu-ship* are perfectly carried out, its site was deserted and had become a ruin." The word *kummu* in Akkadian, as reported in Neo-Assyrian religious and literary texts, "is used to mean some part of a house complex . . . in which people spend the night."[25] C. J. Gadd equates *kummu* and É-NUN as "specifically the shrine of the goddess Ningal at Ur."[26] R. Caplice designates the É-NUN as "her holy chamber" related to night and rest, the bedchamber of the deity.[27] Weadock concludes, "This celebration of the sacred marriage between Ningal and Sin [Nanna] was then the supreme purpose of the Ningal temple, a purpose clearly revealed by the plan of the temple and by the inscriptional material connected with the temple."[28]

THE GIPAR AFTER ENHEDUANNA

The gipar at Ur was of such significance that for two thousand years kings in succeeding eras enhanced their prestige by constructing new and more elaborate versions over the ruins of the preceding building. Sacred objects from the earlier building were often buried in the new foundation. Thus, a door socket bearing the name of the high priestess who followed Enheduanna, Enmenana, lay in the ruins of the gipar they both occupied and was carefully placed in the succeeding foundation of the new Ur III building.

In the Ur III dynasty that followed the Sargonic kings, the rulers increased the centrality of the city of Ur and its patron deity, Nanna. Over one hundred years, their large building projects included a new gipar combining the three separate buildings. Later, wars and destruction leveled this gipar until the high priestess Enanatuma of Isin, 1974–1935 BCE, led its rebuilding herself, carving her name on many of the building's bricks and on a statue of Ningal found inside the ruins of the gipar. She and the high priestess who succeeded her, Enmegalana, were venerated after their deaths with "regular offerings of cheese, butter, and dates" and included in offering lists for certain minor gods, found in the records of the Ningal temple.[29] These dead high priestesses, "the resting ones," were elevated to the level of minor deities.[30]

The last of the succession of known high priestesses, Enanedu, who served in the territory of Larsa during the reigns of both of her brothers, Warad-Sin and Rim-Sin, began her tenure by carefully replastering the walls of the gipar. She took pains to restore the cemetery of the dead high priestesses, who continued to be worshiped generation after generation. She described her work in an inscription:

> At that time, as for the "Dining room in which the *urinnu*-symbols are set up," the place of the "fateful day" of the ancient *entus,* the wall did not reach around its site. The breach in it was left pierced, as a wilderness; no watch was set; its site was not cleaned. I, in my great knowl-

edge, sought room for present and future fates. I verily established
a broad sacred area larger than the resting place of the old *entus;* its
ruined site I verily surrounded with a great wall, a strong watch I set
there, and its site I verily purified.[31]

While the sequential records of the high priestesses break off after Enanedu
(1760s BCE), the history of the gipar at Ur continues. The final attempt to restore the gipar was made by a Neo-Babylonian king, Nabonidus. Nabonidus
was the last of the Chaldaean kings, which included the great king Nebuchadnezzar. Nabonidus, like the kings before him, "was a dedicated antiquarian,
who studied old inscriptions, followed ancient rituals, and enjoyed the muse-
ums of antiquities set up in Ur and Babylon."[32] He found the gipar in ruins in
590 BCE:

At the time the Egipar, . . . wild date-seedlings and fruit-trees of the
orchards grew out of its midst. I cut down the trees and removed the
loose earth of its ruins; I discovered the building and ascertained its
foundation-terrace; inscriptions of ancient earlier kings I discovered
within it . . . along side of Egipar, the house of Ennigaldi-Nanna, my
daughter, *entu*-priestess of Sin, I built new.[33]

Bricks inscribed with Nabonidus's name say explicitly that the king
built the gipar for Nanna of Ur and for his daughter the high priestess,
Ennigaldi-Nanna.

Fifty years after Nabonidus, the armies of the Persian king Cyrus II conquered Babylon in 539 BCE, and Mesopotamia was incorporated into the Persian empire. The tradition of the sacred gipar that held significant religious
meaning for almost four thousand years came to an end.

chapter 3

POET

Enheduanna is credited with two major compositions. The first, the Sumerian Temple Hymns, consists of forty-two hymns to the temples of major deities in thirty-six cities. In scribal tradition, copies of all forty-two of the hymns were written on a single tablet. Thirty-seven fragments of distinct tablets have been found, on each of which were originally written all forty-two of the hymns. The second composition, three poems to Inanna, exist separately, exemplars of each one written on its own individual tablet. The Inanna poems are listed in several Old Babylonian literary catalogues from the nineteenth and eighteenth centuries BCE.

THE THREE INANNA POEMS

The poetry attributed to Enheduanna is the first known example in which an author names herself, as she does in the colophon to the Temple Hymns, or speaks in the first person, as she does in two of the Inanna poems. Her work contains the first instance of a poet using her own subjective experience as part of the content depicted in the text. In these poems she portrays herself as well as the deity as they react to external events, some specific, others unidentified in the texts.

A brief synopsis of the Inanna poems provides a sample of the poet's voice. In the first poem, "Inanna and Ebeh," all the characters are divinities, not humans. The protagonist, Inanna, enraged that a stubborn, arrogant mountain, Ebeh, will not submit to her, goes to An, the great god of heaven, to solicit his assistance. She goes as a maiden, "a soft bud swelling," wearing a queen's robe, standing on the back of "a wild lapis lazuli bull."[1] An, afraid of the mighty mountain, refuses to help and twice calls Inanna his "little one." In an instant, Inanna swells into a raging warrior:

> with screech of hinge
> she flings wide the gate
> of the house of battle[2]

Inanna amasses an arsenal of weapons—blinding dust storms, poisoned tongue, arrows, daggers, stones, snakes, fires. The victorious Inanna, "vigor of a young man commanding," "wrestles the mountain to its knees."[3] The poem ends as Inanna builds a temple dedicated to her victory. The poem is thought to be based on actual events in which Naram-Sin, Enheduanna's nephew, defeated a rebellious uprising in the northeastern area of the Jebel Hamrin.[4]

In the next two poems, "Lady of Largest Heart" and "The Exaltation of Inanna," Enheduanna appears as herself. In "Lady of Largest Heart," diary-like laments and supplication before Inanna and her dreaded powers are interspersed with paeans of praise and adoration. Enheduanna is clearly the person who is writing the poem. "I / I am Enheduanna," she says.[5] Her dreadful fate (the particulars of which are not made known) comes about at the hand of Inanna, whom she worships: "I am yours / why do you slay me? . . . My sorrow and bitter trial strike my eye as treachery."[6] Impatient, she demands, "stop I say / enough / moaning unending lamenting / do not cool you down / Beloved Lady of Holy An / look at your tormenting emotions / all the time weeping."[7]

In "The Exaltation of Inanna," Enheduanna recounts her expulsion from the temple by a usurping general. Speaking directly, she describes her torture, exile, and final restoration, telling the story to Inanna, her only hope for rescue. In this poem, too, Enheduanna speaks as the "I," the subjective self:

> stand there
> I
> Enheduanna   Jewel of An
> let me say a prayer to you
>   (flow tears
>   refreshing drink for Inanna)[8]

She says, "I am dying / that I must sing / this sacred song."[9] She suffers "bitter pangs" as she gives birth to this poem "for you my Queen."[10] Finally, in a moment of clarifying insight, she writes, "it is for my sake your anger fumes / your heart finds no relief."[11] Her exile and suffering were not the result of Inanna's inexplicable rage that reverberates throughout the cosmos. Rather, she implies, Inanna's fury was the deity's reaction to Enheduanna's terrible fate of torture and banishment.

The poet struggles in each of the three poems with formidable theological issues. In the poem "Ebeh," a battle of biblical proportions pits Inanna against the great god of heaven, An. Inanna demands before An that all earthly entities submit to her: "wipe your nose on the ground / flatten your lips in the dust."[12] An is terrified of Ebeh, because, he says, of its lush perfection. Inanna, the realist, rises from bent-kneed supplication before An to become the indomitable warrior. She defeats the mountain, "because you puff yourself up / . . . dress up so beautiful /. . . stretch your hand straight to An."[13] She implies that the mountain, where natural enemies lie down together, stretches its hand to An in order to bypass hardship, scarcity, enmity, and suffering. The story of Ebeh is a parable echoed in the biblical Garden of Eden. It tells the story of the collision that occurs when the illusion of paradise—peace, perfection, and happiness on earth—comes up against reality.

The two remaining poems are not parables but real-life situations in which the poet, Enheduanna herself, suffers a fate imposed by the one she worships and adores, Inanna. In "The Exaltation of Inanna," Enheduanna, who with all the authority of the high priestess lauds Inanna as the greatest of the great gods, must flee into the wilderness to escape the torture and torment of a rebel priest or general. Job-like, she cries to Inanna, "what is happening to my fate?"[14] She confronts Inanna: "you allow my flesh to know your scourging!"[15]

Enheduanna does not waver from the shock, the sense of disproportionate injustice over the torment that has come into her life. She articulates her case, astonished that this undeserved, arbitrary disaster could happen to her at the hand of Inanna. In spite of this, her adoration of Inanna does not weaken: "I will praise your course / your sweeping grandeur / forever."[16] She considers why Inanna has abandoned her, imagines that the goddess is distraught for her own reasons, "moaning / unending lamenting," creating a bleak cosmic atmosphere that penetrates into the heart of the one most attuned to her.[17] Enheduanna begs, pleads, scolds, castigates Inanna for her behavior. Only at the end of this poem of exile does she consider that Inanna's resounding fury may indeed be for Enheduanna's sake, a reaction to her forced expulsion from the temple.

As modern readers we can only approach these poems with contemporary insight, conscious that we cannot place ourselves in the minds of their ancient author or of the Sumerians who heard them. Four millennia of literary and theological deliberations separate us. The late British Assyriologist Jeremy Black, in his study of Sumerian poetry, put it succinctly: "A central thesis of this study is that the most ancient poetry cannot be read without the same aesthetic and theoretical presuppositions as we bring to the poetry of the modern Western tradition; and that it can be read by us only in that modern world, with all the multifarious associations and distractions that clutter our minds."[18] Keeping this in mind, we read in the poetry the ancient poet's struggle with the question of human tragedy and suffering imposed by an attentive and supposedly loving deity. The reader can empathize with Enheduanna's suffering, can project into her experience. Out of this imaginative identification, the modern translator attempts to convey the empathic experience in contemporary language.

The two more personal Inanna poems, "The Exaltation of Inanna" and "Lady of Largest Heart," read like long meditations or prayers, uncensored plaints in the most intimate style. The longest sections of these poems praise Inanna's powers, authority, unbridled ferocity, unequaled beauty, and cosmic brilliance. Interspersed are sections in which Enheduanna scolds Inanna as she might scold a girlfriend—"stop I say / enough!"—or questions Inanna as she might question a lover: "I am yours / why do you slay me?"[19] In both poems she implores her deity with accounts of her own suffering. Here is a woman in antiquity who with all the power of her poetic genius railed against the deity, the one with whom she was most personally involved, demanding that Inanna explain the woman's dreadful fate. In the same vivid, aesthetic voice, she expresses her love and adoration and praises the full scope of Inanna's inimitable complexity.

THE TEMPLE HYMNS

The Sumerian Temple Hymns, except for the final colophon, lack the explicit presence of the subjective "I" of the author. Enheduanna, some specialists think, may have collected and redacted existing hymns. If she did work from existing hymns, she crafted their content with the eye and the hand of a mature poet. She was an astute, knowledgeable theologian with a seasoned poetic voice. William Hallo suggests that Enheduanna's mother may have been Sumerian, given Enheduanna's command of the language: "His [Sargon's] daughter Enheduanna used her outstanding command of Sumerian, probably literally her mother-tongue, to create a body of poetry intended to celebrate her father's achievements and make them theologically acceptable to the Sumerian speaking south."[20]

The hymn collection, as Hallo says, may have served to convince the Sumerian worshipers that in spite of the changes the Sargonic regime had imposed, it would uphold their spiritual traditions. Written to deities in thirty-six separate cities, the hymns created a peaceful, unifying arc from south to north by articulating the common beliefs of the ancient Sumerian religion. Temple Hymn 2, written to the Ekur temple of Enlil, the head of the pantheon, says explicitly, "Lord Enlil's divine decisions sired on the high foundation / spread to Sumer and Akkad / right and left through his whole estate." Hallo points out that if one were in Enlil's city of Nippur, located in the north-central plain, facing toward the east, the holy direction, "Sumer lies to the right (south) of Nippur and Akkad to the left (north)."[21] The poet may have included these lines precisely to reassure the public that Enlil embraced both cultures, the Akkadians and the Sumerians alike.

The Temple Hymns articulate the specific qualities and dominions of the portrayed deities. They tell us that the deities alone are in possession of the **me,** a Sumerian concept which Graham Cunningham says, "appears to be translatable as 'essence' (or more basically still as 'being' . . .) **me** being the term used to refer to the prototypes of civilization which are actualized in the human domain by deities, the human world thus being viewed as ultimately rooted in transcendental reality."[22] Each of the Temple Hymns, then, describes a portion of this transcendental reality, the **me,** the portion that a particular deity has under his or her jurisdiction. So the first hymn to Inanna, Temple Hymn 16 (TH 16), in her temple in Uruk says, é me-gal-kul-aba$_4$^{ki}, literally, "house of the great **me** of Kullab"(a section of the city of Uruk), and implies Inanna's possession there of this essence. The remainder of the hymn enumerates the **me** belonging to Inanna of Uruk. The primary **me** articulated in this hymn is desire. That is to say, using Cunningham's description, Inanna brings the element of desire into being in the human realm.

Desire emanates from the temple, "thriving in the radiance of the princess," Inanna. The temple itself radiates desire. The poet likens the temple to "perfectly shaped fresh fruit / dazzling in your irresistible ripeness." These two lines address and describe the temple itself, as do the beginning lines of each of the hymns. Descriptions of its occupant come later, as in this hymn's example, "your princess the pure one / she is the whole horizon." Other of the deity's characteristics or possessions or activities may then be included, for example here:

your lady Inanna
throws the ever-rolling stone dice

In this brief description of TH 16 we detect the sensitive eye of the poet, likening desire to "perfectly shaped fresh fruit," irresistibly ripe. Enheduanna describes what she sees with the immediacy of her photographic eye and the delight of her metaphoric view. She reflects the temple to itself. She imbues the temple, actually made of crude clay bricks, with radiating desire.

Each of the forty-two hymns follows this format. The temple and its deity are given authority over particular elements, the me, which go to make up civilization. They may include simple necessities, water and bread (TH 1 to Enki), or the grand design of cosmic order (TH 2 to Enlil or TH 5 to Ninurta). The temple of the portentous birth deity Ninhursag is "the form-shaping place / spreading fear like a great poisonous snake" (TH 7). Underworld deities provoke terror, like Ningishzida in TH 15: "no one can fathom your mighty hair-raising path."

Other deities command pleasure, beauty, and abundance, like Shuzianna (TH 6), who "sows flowers in profusion on your luminous site." Dumuzi, Inanna's consort, prepares for her: "jeweled lapis herbs fleck the shining bed / heart-soothing place for the Lady of the Steppe" (TH 17). Dream interpreter Nanshe is "laughing in the sea foam / playing, playing in the waves" (TH 22). In the temple of Inanna's hairdresser, Shara, "abundance from the sea's midst / [is] held in the smaller basin" (TH 25). The temple of the sun deity Utu is a "white glowing house" like its owner, whose "lustrous lapis beard hangs down in profusion" (TH 13).

The deities who actualize on earth the elements of civilization make the invisible visible. Thus, several of the hymns allude to the very act of creation. TH 1 to Enki recounts "this first stepped temple split heaven and earth." Enlil's temple (TH 2) is the "navel of heaven and earth." The temple of Asarluhi (TH 10), was "squeezed out of the abzu / like barley oil" "pulling cosmic powers from the dense mist." The abzu, the sweet-water ocean under the earth, is the home of Asarluhi's father, Enki. "All the primeval lords" stand in the temple of Nisaba, the goddess of writing and creative mind (TH 42).

Each hymn is a metaphorical description of the divine incarnate. In his study of Sumerian poetry Black affirms the richness of metaphorical language in Sumerian literature: "There is in Sumerian poetry something particularly striking about the use of imagery," and he continues, regarding the poet's address to the temple itself, "People do not normally address buildings; a hymn is not conversational speech or prose statement but heightened language."[23] The poet transmits not simply the attributes of the temple and its deity, but also the experience the worshipers would have in its presence. Sumerian cosmology elaborates Walter Benjamin's definition of metaphor, which he says gives material form to the invisible.[24] Drawing on the images that occur to Enheduanna as she reflects in the manner of a poet, she creates a picture in words, which enables the worshipers to elaborate their experience of the divine presence. She gives imaginative material form to the invisible.

AUTHORSHIP

Relying on the same criteria for investigating and determining the authorship of the two sets of poems attributed to Enheduanna, specialists disagree. The evidence simply is not conclusive, one way or the other. One issue is the variation in the approaches used by different Assyriologists to assess the question. Black explains:

> Assyriology, as a scholarly activity, has remained (or perhaps even become) a somewhat isolated and esoteric discipline. . . . it has tended towards the style of scholarship which may loosely be called positivist: the view, in its extreme form, that any knowledge not entirely based on factual, historical and extrinsic evidence can be dismissed as fruitless speculation. In the study of literature this approach was explicitly challenged by the Formalists, by the Prague School theorist and . . . by New Criticism, from the 1920s onwards, and by any number of more recent critical approaches, but it still remains a fundamental and lively tradition in much Near Eastern scholarship.[25]

Black clearly excludes himself from those who would refuse to consider "as too subjective . . . those distinctive qualities that make literature 'literary': the meaning and effect of the experience of reading."[26] He appreciated the literary quality of Enheduanna's credited writing but still applied rigorous criteria before assigning her as author.[27] Black, after acknowledging that he is well aware of the tradition that she is the author of the Inanna poems and the Temple Hymns, adds, "Virtually all manuscripts of these works are Old Babylonian—half a millennium later than En-hedu-ana—and the historicity of the traditions of authorship cannot be verified."[28] On the other hand, some of the tablet fragments that contain work attributed to Enheduanna date prior to the Old Babylonian period, from the previous Ur III period, 2168–2060. Hallo dates Enheduanna's lifetime to 2285–2250 BCE; her death, therefore, occurred slightly over one hundred years before the Ur III period began, much closer to her lifetime than tablets written in the Old Babylonian period, five hundred years later.[29] Other scholars believe that the Temple Hymns text originated in Enheduanna's era. Gwendolyn Leick says, "Recent scholarship has revoked earlier doubts about the authenticity of her [Enheduanna's] literary creation and puts it firmly in the context of the Akkadian period under the rule of Sargon's grandson Naram-Sin."[30] J. N. Postgate says, "Although there are some obvious later additions, . . . this is generally accepted as an original composition of the Akkad period."[31] These scholars rely on evidence in the orthography, among other considerations, to make the case that the texts could have been written by Enheduanna.

Black asserts that in general "the degree of variation between some of the [literary] texts militates . . . against the possibility of reconstructing an authentic original text, and moreover argues against the existence of one."[32] A colleague, Piotr Michalowski, who fundamentally agrees with Black, nevertheless reports a consistency in the tablets containing the Temple Hymns, a consistency that, he explains, "is true for the preserved Ur III fragments of the Temple Hymns . . . which differ only in minor orthographic variants from their Old Babylonian versions," copied some three hundred years later.[33] Other investigators might judge this consistency as evidence that tends to establish the authenticity of the text and its tradition, if not its authorship.

The German Sumerologist Annette Zgoll has done the most exhaustive analysis of dating the texts of the Inanna poem "nin-me-šá-ra," best known by the title "The Exaltation of Inanna," the poem in which Enheduanna is cast out of her temple, then restored as high priestess. Although he disagrees with Zgoll, Black credits her for her strenuous argument that the texts originated in the Akkadian period of Enheduanna's lifetime.[34] Zgoll says, "NMS [nin-me-šá-ra] stands out in its much greater similarity to depicting an historical event in the modern sense. Here we have no epic poet who tells us the story after the fact. Here we have the en-priestess En-hedu-Ana, who is struggling with contemporary historical events that are actually happening, and she prevails."[35] Zgoll bases this conclusion on evidence of a revolt against Enheduanna's nephew, the king Naram-Sin, by Lugalane, king of Uruk, who is named in the poem as the rebel who forced Enheduanna out of her temple.[36] Lugalane is mentioned as the enemy king on a Naram-Sin inscription, commemorating his victory after a rebellion in the south which Zgoll equates with the event resulting in Enheduanna's eviction.[37] These historical events occurred during the Akkadian period in Enheduanna's lifetime and convince Zgoll that she wrote the poem after her restoration to the temple in Ur.

In addition, Zgoll presents a thorough analysis of the dating of the actual texts that contain the composition. In her examination of the orthography of the known texts, she reports that 17 percent of the writing is characteristic of that known from the pre–Ur III era, that is, orthography that was used in Enheduanna's lifetime.[38] She also examines the texts using semantic, literary, and historical criteria.

Miguel Civil also considered the orthography of the Inanna poem in-nin šà-gur₄-ra, "Lady of Largest Heart" and concludes that it may be from a later era:

> Usually, one attributes to Enheduanna, the daughter of Sargon of Akkad, all the texts that mention her name. Among these texts is found the hymn in-nin šà-gur₄-ra. . . . The examination of the language and of its vocabulary led me to suspect that the text dates from the Larsa period. If this hypothesis is correct, Enheduanna was in this period a generic name that designated the priestess of Sin at Ur. The implications of this hymn would be very different depending on whether it has reference to a daughter of Sargon or to a daughter of Rim-Sin.[39] (*my translation*)

The name of the high priestess at Ur during the Larsa period is known. She was Enanedu, who served the moon god Nanna/Sin during the reigns of her brothers, Warad-Sin and Rim-Sin. An inscription of her repair to the gipar at Ur, as cited in chapter 2, is extant.[40] Civil's statement is, as he says, a hypothesis.

Hallo, together with J. J. A. van Dijk, was the first to publish Enheduanna's work, translating, as did Zgoll, nin-me-šá-ra, and calling it "The Exaltation of Inanna."[41] At the time of publication in 1968, this connection of a particular author with a body of work from the beginning of the Sumerian era was a new discovery. Hallo writes,

> For at or near the very beginning of classical Sumerian literature, we can now discern a corpus of poetry of the very first rank which not only reveals its author's name, but delineates that author for us in truly autobiographical fashion. In the person of Enheduanna, we are confronted by a woman who was at once princess, priestess, and poetess, a personality who set standards in all three of her roles for many succeeding centuries, and whose merits were recognized, in singularly Mesopotamian fashion, long after.[42]

Thirty years after publishing nin-me-šá-ra, Hallo, in his book *Origins*, continues to hold Enheduanna in high esteem:

> If, then, the three great hymns by Enheduanna in honor of Inanna are taken as forming an integrated cycle, then they constitute a thematic counterpart to her other principal work: the cycle of short hymns to all the temples of Sumer and Akkad. For while the former may be said to celebrate the theme of "the king at war," the latter reflects "the king at peace," solicitously caring for the temples of all the country in a major attempt to satisfy the traditional requirements of Sumerian religion.[43]

Hallo is careful to say that Enheduanna "compiled" the Temple Hymns, agreeing that she collected and possibly redacted hymns that already existed.[44] He makes his position on documentation clear in his presidential address to the American Oriental Society in 1990, titled "The Limits of Skepticism." He chides those who "want incontrovertible proof" for certain aspects of Near Eastern research, who "deal harshly with all who would cross the sacred line between the self-evident and the inferential."[45] He advocates treating the evidence "as a precious resource—none of it to be ignored, or squandered," saying, "However limited that documentation may be, the only limits it imposes on us are to set reasonable limits to our own skepticism."[46]

Joan Westenholz gives a brief survey listing scholars whose opinions regarding Enheduanna's attributed authorship vary in their degree of acceptance or rejection. Their opinions vary, from those who believe that ancient Sumerian poetry must remain anonymous to those who cite evidence that some of the texts of Enheduanna's attributed work seem to have their origin in the Old Akkadian period during her lifetime.[47]

Finally, there is some agreement that the work attributed to Enheduanna has a distinctive, recognizable style, even among those who dispute Enheduanna's authorship. W. G. Lambert has responded to Aage Westenholz's praise of Enheduanna when Westenholz designates her "as the first real author in history." He writes, "The distinctive style of her claimed compositions could be that of a courtier as easily as of the lady herself. And we do not know that other similar texts did not exist from other authors, but they have not survived."[48] Lambert's courtier, then, as well as his undiscovered authors, would, he implies, have a distinctive style, which, one could say, confirms that the writing would belong to one talented person.

In her book, Zgoll cites Claus Wilcke's statement concerning the Temple Hymns, that given "the consistency in the construction and diction of the hymns, we do not go wrong when we speak of the authorship of Enheduanna [with regard to the Temple Hymns]"; he cites particularly the hymn to the moon god Nanna, TH 37, the deity to whom the author of the hymn refers as "my king."[49] The high priestess to the moon god in Ur would affirm her devotion to Nanna with this phrase, "my king." Zgoll praises Enheduanna's writing, saying, "Even after over 4000 years . . . this text is able to cast such a spell on us as if everything were occurring here and now before our very eyes. The descriptions are so inspiring, so vital, so vivid."[50] Hallo and van Dijk agree: "So strong is the stamp of her style and her convictions in the poems that can definitely be attributed to her, that it may one day be possible to detect her authorship also in other, less well-preserved pieces."[51] Westenholz, who says of Enheduanna, "The fire of genius burned in her veins," concurs with Hallo regarding undiscovered works: "We can identify positively those poetic compositions in which her name appears, but she may have written other pieces of poetry not so identified."[52]

ENHEDUANNA THE WOMAN

The appearance of remarkable women in the past few hundred years is not unusual—poets, essayists, artists, heads of state—although whenever one emerges, her self-assured presence and gift of inner authority still capture more than our cursory attention. How remarkable that we would discover Enheduanna speaking her mind over four thousand years ago. She was a brilliant thinker; she was a trailblazer; she was a gifted poet; she was a suffering human being who willingly revealed herself.

Enheduanna writes as an individual who asks life's most perplexing questions: why is life filled with hardship, injustice, and suffering? She writes from her own intense inner experience. From the authority of her unique individuality, she challenges the basic nature of reality—represented by Inanna. Enheduanna is exceptional in ancient literature in the eloquent assertion of her own thoughts and feelings, including a plaintive yet forceful challenge of the actions of the deities.

In the Temple Hymns in the late third millennium BCE, Enheduanna conducts us through forty-two of the principal Sumerian temples. An archaic pantheon comes to life. Her rich imagery and extensive knowledge reach across the centuries to responsive twenty-first-century readers, touching our imaginations and our minds. We recognize the hand of a brilliant poet in her human attempt to comprehend the awful beauty of life, its conundrums, its hidden cosmic creators, and its mysteries.

chapter 4

HYMN TO ENKI

INTRODUCTION

Enheduanna begins her collection of hymns to Sumer's temples with a hymn to the temple of Enki, the god of wisdom, of magic, of the fecund waters. The small city of Eridu was in the extreme south of the land of Sumer in the marshland near the Persian Gulf, a few miles south of Ur where the high priestess resided and, like Ur, west of the mighty Euphrates as it spread its banks before flowing into the waters of the gulf.

While in the order of the Temple Hymns most of the cities cluster into groups according to their geographic proximity, Eridu and its patron, Enki, stand alone. The temple, called Engur, placed first, becomes the mother of all temples. The name of the temple tells a story. Engur is one name for Enki's mother, Nammu. Engur signifies the fertile water out of which Nammu created life. In some versions Nammu *was* the engur, the original swirling pool of self-procreation. The engur also was equated with the abzu, the sweet-water ocean just below the earth, the place of Enki's origin and his home. Over the centuries of myth formation, engur, Nammu, and abzu became interchangeable.

Enheduanna chose to begin at the beginning—with a temple that bore the ancient story of creation. By placing Enki first, ahead of the chief deity, Enlil, she made a political statement. She gave precedence to the mystery of origin out of the dark waters. Mighty Enlil, the fate fixer, the lord of measured reckoning, logically would follow after—on dry land.

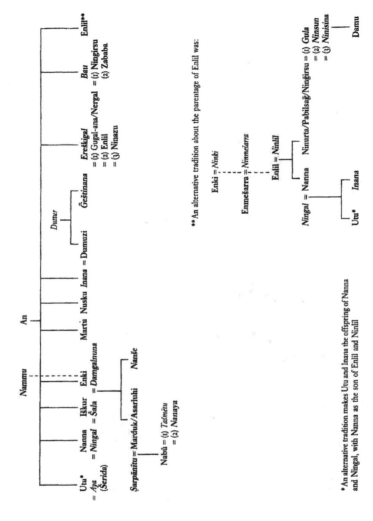

**An alternative tradition about the parentage of Enlil was:

Enki = *Ninki*

Enmešarra = *Ninmešarra*

Enlil = *Ninlil*

Ninurta/Pabilsaĝ/Ningirsu = (1) *Gula*
= (2) *Ninsun*
= (3) *Ninisina*

Ningal = Nanna

Utu* Inana

Damu

*An alternative tradition makes Utu and Inana the offspring of Nanna and Ningal, with Nanna as the son of Enlil and Ninlil.

Genealogical table of Mesopotamian gods and goddesses. Female deities are indicated in *italics*. Dotted lines indicate descent rather than parenthood, or else a variant tradition.

4.1. Genealogical table of Mesopotamian gods and goddesses. Courtesy of the University of Texas Press, Jeremy Black and Anthony Green, *Gods, Demons and Symbols of Ancient Mesopotamia*, Tessa Richards, illustrator, 1995.

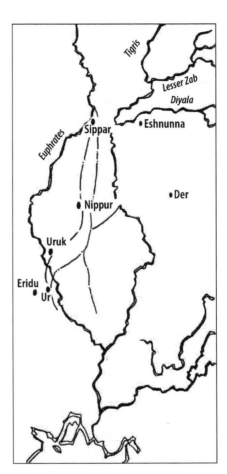

4.2.   Sketch map of Mesopotamia with Eridu. After Postgate, 1994. Reproduced by permission of Taylor and Francis Books U.K.

TEMPLE HYMN I

THE ERIDU TEMPLE OF ENKI
Engur

growing between,
this first temple tower split heaven and earth
    whose roots reach Eridu's dark cella
watery shrine built for a prince
water hauled from his pure canal
pure food gathered from the holy hill
purest mountain scrubbed clean with soap

4.3. Turtle symbol of Enki. Courtesy of the University of Texas Press, Jeremy Black and Anthony Green, *Gods, Demons and Symbols of Ancient Mesopotamia*, Tessa Richards, illustrator, 1995.

abzu   your hymns praise creation's elements

your grand surrounding wall unequaled
and the chamber   where the god lives
whose dining hall lets no light enter
truly from wall to wall
your firm-anchored house has a purity beyond measure

O crowned Eridu   shining crown
sworn by your prince   the great prince
the susbu priest makes the pure plants grow
    where your watery home hits the Great Below
    and voices pour out to Utu
    revered shrine stretching toward heaven

they carry bread from the oven to eat
the oven   brimming over   rivals the holy chamber

words of your prince   prince of heaven and earth
cannot be altered
the creator   the wise one decreed
Lord Nudimmud, the Blood Maker
    O Engur
has built this house on your radiant site
and placed his seat upon your dais[1]

    (23 lines for Enki at Eridu)

THE TEMPLE OF ENKI AT ERIDU

Before Enheduanna could fix the order of her collection of Temple Hymns, she had to make a decision. Which temple should come first? Among the Sumerian scribes, who created encyclopedic lists of the categories they observed, tradition had been established that each list must begin with the most important of its elements. Enheduanna's choice for first place would have significance to the public. Enlil's temple in Nippur would have been the logical choice, given that Enlil was the current undisputed head of the pantheon. The priests at Nippur had declared Enlil the kingmaker, and even Enheduanna's father, Sargon, had received Enlil's blessing at his coronation.

Yet Enheduanna chose to begin her list with Enki of Eridu. The hymn itself offers clues that explain her decision. This first hymn is a paean to creation, and creation, the hymn says, began at Eridu. In the mind of the author, the huge stepped pyramidal temple emerged out of primordial chaos, separating heaven and earth:

> growing between
> this first temple tower split heaven and earth

The primal unity was broken apart by the onset of creation. The force that separated the elements was the temple at Eridu.[2]

Steeped in Sumerian mythology, Enheduanna would have known an early creation myth that described a barren earth, a moonless and sunless sky:

> At that time Enki and Eridu had not appeared
> Enlil did not exist
> Ninlil did not exist
> Brightness was dust
> Vegetation was dust
> The daylight did not shine
> The moonlight did not emerge[3]

The text from a fragment, "one of the oldest pieces of Sumerian mythology, if not the oldest yet known," describes the earth before creation but anticipates the appearance of Eridu and Enki first, then Enlil and Ninlil.[4] This fragment supports the tradition reported in another myth, the Sumerian Flood Story, which tells of the creation of Eridu as the first city and Enki as its god.

The hymn to Enki's temple is one of exalted praise to the god for his bountiful gifts to humanity at the creation of the world. The hymn's first lines name the three essential elements of the cosmos: heaven, earth, and the dark interior of the temple's depths that reach to the underworld. This first temple arrived at the moment of creation, laden with goods to fulfill the needs of the people: pure

4.4.   Archaic Ur sign for engur, abzu, or Nammu. After Labat, 1995. Courtesy of Editions GEUTHNER, Paris.

water essential for survival in this parched land; pure food plentiful on its hillside; its oven brimming over with bread; soap for the susbu priest's purifying rituals; cosmic hymns to accompany worship; a grand protective wall enclosing the sacred space; and a dark inner chamber where the god lives, a reminder of the necessary solitude of contemplation and the deep mystery of the gods.

Enheduanna would have known the long-held Sumerian tradition that Eridu was the first of cities. Even the weighty Sumerian Kinglist gave kingship first to Eridu, saying, "After kingship had descended from heaven, Eridu became (the seat) of kingship."[5] This largely fictional list from the early second millennium depicts kingship as a divinely ordained institution and records the reigns of select kings before and after a great flood. Rarely is it possible, as at Eridu, for a civilization to trace its origin for five thousand years to a particular spot on which its sacred buildings were built, one on top of the other, over millennia. The Sumerians looked to Enki's temple in Eridu as the ancient site of their mythological beginning. The civilizations that followed the Sumerians preserved this tradition at Eridu, until its last temple fell into ruins in the midfirst millennium BCE.

The city of Eridu was in the southernmost part of present-day Iraq, a few miles southwest of the Euphrates, in the marshy area where the Euphrates and Tigris rivers intersect before they flow into the Persian Gulf. At this literal boundary between water and earth the ancestors of the Sumerians developed an origin myth that depicted all living things emerging at Eridu out of the watery abyss they called the abzu. The cuneiform sign for "engur," the temple's name, can also be read "abzu" or even "Nammu," the self-procreating goddess of the abzu who was the source of all life. The original cuneiform sign for engur was a rectangle or square with a star drawn inside. Like many ancient cuneiform signs, the engur sign carries implicit meaning—the star symbol of divinity enclosed in a protected space. This sign, with its enclosure, could have evoked in its viewers a perception of the divine situated in a particular geographical spot, a sense of origin, the source of emerging life.

AN EARLY CREATION MYTH

In Sumerian cosmology, which Enheduanna appears to know well, the abzu is a sweet-water ocean, as noted above, on top of which the earth floats. The tradition that Nammu gave birth to all life from her watery abode in the abzu describes creation emerging from the teeming waters, the fecund womb of the mother deity. This mythology equates Nammu with the abzu. She is the divine source of creation.

In later mythology Enki's home is the abzu, and Nammu is his mother/wife. In an origin myth called "Nammu and Enki," the pair simply "came to life."[6] The couple marry, and Nammu gives birth.

The next section of the myth describes the original awakening and securing of consciousness. Enki is sleeping inside the engur, the watery abzu, "at the place where no god is / where no worship takes place."[7] At this point in the narrative Enki is Nammu's son. She cajoles him to wake up:

Woe! You are lying there
Woe! You are sleeping there.
My son, from your bed,
woe! You don't arise![8]

Nammu is the primeval mother. Yet she has not given birth to Enki. They arrived together. Allowing for the illogic of mythological consciousness, we can envisage that the masculine force must "wake up," become conscious, before consciousness can be secured by narrative and ritual enactment.

After waking Enki, Nammu "held her flesh to the sperm." Enki asks her to "multiply what is in the waters of your belly." "Nammu gave birth to mankind, / the being, out of the waters the head came out." Then Enki "prepared a feast for Nammu, / he ate at the side of the womb together with the newborn princes." The womb is called "the carrying basket of the gods" and "the carrying basket of birth, for the sperm."[9]

In the myth the goddess and the god are mutually dependent; creation requires them both equally. First, they "arrive" together, equal in age and status. Later, the god retreats into a deep sleep within the watery womb of the abzu. The goddess must stir him to perform his part in creation. He obeys "his mother," who, by waking him up, takes the first active step as director of creation.

In this Sumerian version masculine and feminine principles work together. Nammu gives birth through natural female physiology. It is the male, the masculine principle, that has the power to name:

the intelligent, the thoughtful, the researcher,
the god, the omniscient of sacredness, the creator,
the universal, brought forth from the womb,
Enki put his hand therein,
he moved and moved his thoughts.
The god, Enki, the creator,
from his own, from his thinking
from his intelligence, really stamps it.[10]

The act of naming follows creation. Enki's "thought" secures consciousness by naming the elements. His thought is a uniquely human act, one step removed from the natural, physical process of giving birth out of "the carrying basket." He observes natural process from an objective stance. He thinks about it. He gives it a name. Nammu's first task is to awaken the capacity to name.

Enheduanna begins the collection of Temple Hymns with a story of the origin of the Sumerian world at Eridu, watched over by Enki, "the great prince . . . the creator" whose "words . . . cannot be altered." She adds the influential weight of her prestige behind the so-called Eridu theology, in which creation emerged out of the watery abyss, the abzu, and Enki becomes the creator god.[11] This version of creation contrasts in later hymns with that of other important deities.

THE DISCOVERY OF ERIDU

Enheduanna's Temple Hymns contain a firsthand account of a civilization that existed four thousand years ago, a culture whose ancestry reached back another three thousand years before her birth. She speaks to us from long-buried clay tablets only recently discovered.

Although archeologists explored the mound at Eridu in the mid-nineteenth century, they did not uncover its depth until after World War II, when Iraqi archeologists took over the excavation of the many sites. The mound contained a ziggurat, the traditional stepped tower temple, parts of which the excavators could see before they began their work. They discovered it to be a large temple in the traditional style of the Sumerians, dated to 2100 BCE, a hundred years after Enheduanna's death. Gwendolyn Leick describes the further excavations:

Beneath one of the corners of the ziggurat workmen discovered walls of a much earlier edifice, which could on the basis of potsherds be dated to the late Ubaid period (c. 3800). . . . The Iraqi archaeologists decided to remove this late Ubaid layer to see if any earlier remains could be found underneath, and ended up with another sequence of eighteen occupational levels. At the lowest level, "on a dune of clean sand," they discovered the very first building, "a primitive chapel" no larger that 3 meters square. It contained a pedestal facing the entrance, and a recessed niche. The proposed date for this "chapel" is 4900 or Ubaid level 1.[12]

The people of the Ubaidian culture (5000–4000 BCE) were the first to locate in the southern portion of Mesopotamia, although farming settlements had existed in the northern plains for thousands of years.[13] The Ubaid became the most widespread of the Chalcolithic cultures in the north and south of Mesopotamia, reaching even into eastern Saudi Arabia. The archeologist Seton Lloyd, who joined the Iraqi excavators at Eridu, says of the Ubaidians, "These were the Sumerians."[14]

Given its unique origin, Eridu is understandably the first city to appear on Enheduanna's list of Sumerian Temple Hymns. The little chapel at Eridu must have been among the first religious buildings in the south, and Enheduanna was following a canonical sequence that placed Eridu first on the hierarchically ordered list of temples.

The first temple at Eridu was a physical reminder of a continuity of belief, an orienting container of the culture. Only three meters square, it was built on "a pure greenish sand which the excavators believe to be virgin soil."[15] The archeologist Joan Oates is understandably eager to acknowledge Eridu in her article "Ur and Eridu, the Prehistory," written in 1960, before the publication of the excavators' report: "Eridu is of such importance that some comment on its significance cannot be delayed."[16] The finds of the excavators, from the ziggurat on the surface, dating to 2100 BCE, to the small temple built on virgin soil, dating to the beginning of the Ubaid culture, 4900 BCE, confirmed a continuity of culture. The builders of the first chapel, Oates says, "with its cella flanked by lateral chambers, the central free-standing podium or 'offering table' with traces of ritual burning, the burial of ritual objects by the altar, the pilaster-niche facade decoration,"[17] brought with them a religion already substantially formed. Small as it was, the original temple contained architectural elements and furnishings that were frequently reproduced throughout Mesopotamia in the sacred buildings that followed for the next five thousand years.

In Eridu the careful preservation of the old temples on which the new was to be constructed, Oates says, "can only be explained in the light of a persistence of religious beliefs. The ultimate purpose was obviously to protect the earlier foundations from defilement and at the same time to preserve them as 'religious relics.'"[18] As old buildings were leveled to make way for new, the crumbled remains of the old were covered with sand, and votive objects were carefully buried in this sand fill. Eventually, later temples were raised on the growing platform foundation, which became a repository of the sacred remains of the ancestors. The evidence of continuity of the culture convinced Oates that the inhabitants of Eridu were the original Sumerians: "Eridu has now supplied positive evidence of continuity. . . . It is extremely difficult to believe that the location of the temple, its cult, and even its architecture would have continued in an unbroken tradition from al'Ubaid to Sumerian times if there had been during this period any major change in the character of the population."[19]

The swampy marshland surrounding the confluence of the Euphrates and the Tigris rivers as they enter the Persian Gulf has not changed significantly since the Ubaidian people chose the site of Eridu for their first temple. The site suggests the mythical abzu that developed into a central feature of the Mesopotamian cosmos. Leick describes the scene: "The city . . . was built upon a hillock within a depression about twenty feet below the level of the surrounding land, which allowed the subterranean waters to collect together. This swampy place can still become a sizeable lake in the months of high water."[20]

Water was by far the most precious substance. Enki was the god of sweet water, and in a myth supplied water for the Tigris and Euphrates. The myth "Enki and the World Order" tells the tale:

> He raises his member, he ejaculates;
> He [fills] the Tigris with sparkling water.
> . . . he [penetrates?] the Euphrates with all his might.
> He raises his member, brings (his) gift to the bride;
> He fills the womb of the Tigris with joy . . .
> The "water" he (thus) brought was sparkling, and sweet as wine[21]

The availability of water permitted survival.

Water made possible the first plant domestication in the northern mountain valleys of the Zagros late in the Neolithic period, around 7000 BCE. Substantial farming communities arose in the succeeding seventh millennium, three distinct cultures called Hassuna, Samarra, and Halaf, all apparently confined to northern Iraq. At one Samarran site the first small irrigation ditches have

4.5.   Cylinder seal and imprint with Enki, streams of water and fish issuing from his shoulders, accompanied by Inanna standing on a mountain and Utu rising. Courtesy of the Trustees of the British Museum/Art Resource, N.Y.

been found, an invention that became the essential technology supporting Mesopotamian economic growth. Oates describes analogous decorative motifs in both Samarran ceramics and in early Ubaid pottery at Eridu, saying "the basic principles of design underlying these types are so similar as immediately to suggest the possibility of a common origin."[22] No common ancestor of the Sumerians has yet been discovered, but the links in the human community are suggested by the groups that evolved in the fertile crescent over thousands of years, from the Paleolithic gatherers and hunters to the farmers of the Neolithic to the settled Chalcolithic temple builders to the intelligent inventors of a written script that enabled Enheduanna to record in her poem a tradition of origin that stretched back, from her perspective, almost three thousand years.

THE HIGH PRIESTESS AND ERIDU

Enheduanna begins her collection of hymns by reminding the people living between the two rivers, Sumerians and Akkadians alike, of their origin. In Temple Hymn 1 she tells the story of creation in indisputable language. Enki's temple at Eridu becomes the symbolic "carrying basket" for all the Sumerian temples of the hymns that follow. Enki's reckoning of the basic elements of the cosmos forms the structure in which all the gods and goddesses of the succeeding Temple Hymns reside: heaven, earth, abzu, underworld; water, food; temples, gods, worship. The "cosmic hymns" that praise this creation reverberate in the hymns that follow.

Enki appears in the hymn in his late third-millennium guise, "the creator . . . the wise one" in his watery abode, the abzu. But as one of the most ancient gods, he draws ancestral stories in his wake. With the mention of Enki as creator, the listeners would recall the tale of his mother/wife, Nammu, the ancient creator in the abzu. Back before time began, the original small temple at Eridu emerged out of Nammu's primordial waters.

Now, in 2300 BCE, Nammu is seldom mentioned. Although the site at Eridu remains the same, the role of creator in this hymn is assigned to Enki. Almost three thousand years have elapsed since the ancestors of the Sumerians built the first temple here. Nammu played a more prominent role in the past, and she may have belonged "to an older stratum of Sumerian or pre-Sumerian deities."[23] By the Isin-Larsa/Old Babylonian period, 2000–1600 BCE, Nammu had disappeared altogether. Political and cultural changes that favored the roles of male deities in the pantheon may have contributed to her demise.

In the hymn to Enki, Enheduanna draws the reader's attention back to the dark primeval sea before creation. Then, as Mircea Eliade says, the "primordial unity is broken up by creation."[24] A sudden cosmic event marked the beginning of the Mesopotamian world and put the elements necessary for human life to exist in place. In the beginning the temple at Eridu rose out of the primal chaos, separating heaven and earth. The land on which it stood remained below while the sky, the sun, moon, and stars were above. The hymn calls on Utu, the sun god of Temple Hymns 13 and 38, to bind the separate cosmic elements together. Utu passes across the sky and enters the western gate every evening, to sleep in his home in the netherworld. Each morning he arises and begins again his trek across the heavens. His constant divine journey reminds the worshipers that the cosmos is one place and the gods preside in all its parts. Enheduanna ends her hymn by telling the people that Enki's words cannot be altered. He in his wisdom has fixed creation permanently in place.

In this first hymn Enheduanna has stated her purpose. The Temple Hymns together uphold the beliefs of the religion. The careful preservation of their long-held beliefs, she assures the doubtful Sumerians, will continue in the reign of her father and his successors.

In hymns 2 through 7, she presents the gods who would rival Enki's stature as the influential creator god. To meet these gods, we travel north to Nippur, the holy city, the home of the powerful god Enlil and his entourage.

chapter 5

HYMNS TO THE NIPPUR DEITIES

Temple Hymns 2 to 7 are written to temples in and near the Sumerians' holy city of Nippur. The hymns feature the temples of the principal Nippur deity, Enlil (TH 2), his wife Ninlil (TH 3), his minister, Nusku (TH 4), his son Ninurta (TH 5), his "lesser" wife Shuzianna (TH 6), and his sister from neighboring Kesh, Ninhursag (TH 7).

Nippur is the only city of those included in the collection for which more than one temple is honored with a hymn. To understand this exceptional treatment, we look to the cultic tradition at Nippur that developed over the years. The city and its many temples became the religious center for the Sumerians, the Vatican of authority and veneration. Enlil became the chief deity of the pantheon, and his temple, the Ekur in Nippur, was the physical location of religious power. John Robertson sums up the central status Nippur held for the Sumerians:

> From the dawn of history and for many centuries thereafter, the records of ancient Mesopotamia attest the reverence and awe with which the inhabitants of Sumer and Babylonia regarded the venerable city of Nippur. It was for them the pre-eminent sacred city, the home of the great god Enlil and his family. . . . Nippur represented a primordial, yet living symbol of Sumerian identity, a continuing reminder of the underlying shared culture and tradition that was inherent in the term "Sumer."[1]

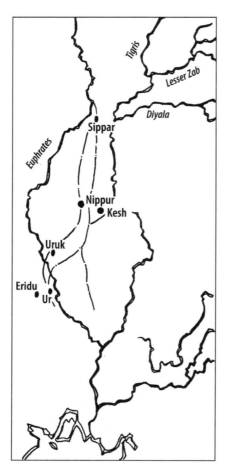

5.1.   Sketch map of Mesopotamia with Nippur and Kesh. After Postgate, 1994. Reproduced by permission of Taylor and Francis Books U.K.

In the sequence of the Temple Hymns, the Nippur gods appear just after the initial hymn to Enki, lending support to the assumption that Enheduanna chose the order of the hymns at least in part to defend the legitimacy of her father's hegemony over his empire. As an Akkadian from the north, Sargon, in his struggle to rule the formerly independent cities of the south, upheld their deities and their religion, sending his only daughter to Ur to serve in the prestigious position of high priestess to the moon god, Nanna. Sargon let it be known that he was appointed king by Enlil, and he worshiped the common pantheon that Enlil led from the Ekur in Nippur.

With its many temples, Nippur had an unusual number of priests and priestesses, bureaucrats, and temple personnel, all of whom apparently had the opportunity to become literate in the scribal schools. Some thirty thousand tablets have been excavated from Nippur, many of these from the third millennium. Of these, up to twenty-one hundred contain literature. Most of Sumer's known myths and tales were included in these tablets. Nippur was the center of a culture of learning and literacy in the third millennium, and the many works written there formed the core of Mesopotamian religious texts. Scholars are able to recognize that Nippur was the source of works copied for many years, not only in Nippur, but tablets found in other cities as well.

While Nippur became known as a religious and literary center, it was also a center for legal expertise. In the Temple Hymn to the Ekur, Enlil is described as the god who determines fate, who dispenses divine decisions, and whose strength is "measured reckoning" and "contemplation." Representatives of the league of cities met in the courtyard of Enlil's temple. Important decisions were made there, and trials took place, all of which contributed to the development of a legal system.

Enlil's ancestry reaches back into the remote past of the Semitic gods of the fourth millennium and beyond. He was a father-god whose impulsiveness and power wielding are familiar features in third-millennium tales as well as in those of his cohorts, Nusku and Ninurta. In his more admirable mode he was the impartial designer of fate and the fair dispenser of divine justice. His wife Ninlil joined him in decision making. Gentle Shuzianna, his second wife, led a house of consecrated women who lived sequestered in her temple, while Ninhursag, Enlil's sister, one of the original three great deities, rivaled Enlil in her prominence as she who oversaw aspects of nature and birth. Enlil's fate led him to Nippur, where the fortuitous conjunction of political expediency, intellectual flowering, and religious ardor elevated him to an unprecedented position of divine authority.

TEMPLE HYMN 2

THE NIPPUR TEMPLE OF ENLIL
Ekur

navel of heaven and earth
O Nippur temple
birthplace of fate

Lord Enlil's divine decisions   sired on the high foundation
spread to Sumer and Akkad
right and left through his whole estate

5.2.   Horned cap of Enlil, Courtesy of the University of Texas Press, Jeremy Black and Anthony Green, *Gods, Demons and Symbols of Ancient Mesopotamia*, Tessa Richards, illustrator, 1995.

house of Enlil
if your dark interior is cooled, refreshed,
your wise knowing heart measures a good fate
your threshold door flung wide
joins earth to the heaven high mountain

the slant wall of your terrace
shoulders a perfect mountain
from whose top comes measured reckoning
     a princely sight
whose base holds contemplation with heaven and earth

great prince Enlil, your prince
the sweet lord
lord to the outer edge of heaven
lord for setting fate
shrine Nippur   the great mountain
and Enlil the fate fixer
has built this house on your radiant site
and placed his seat upon your dais

     13 lines for Enlil in Nippur

THE TEMPLE OF ENLIL AT NIPPUR

Temple Hymn 2 begins with the Sumerian phrase "dur-an-ki," "navel of heaven and earth," the undisputed locus of creation. With that phrase Enheduanna submits Nippur's claim as the holy place of origin. In contrast, the temple at Eridu, TH 1, was itself the live progenitor, splitting heaven and earth with its godly powers. The difference in the two descriptions of creation is notable but leaves no doubt that both temples lay claim to the origin of the cosmos.

Enheduanna wisely includes two traditions of primordial events, both of which have ancient antecedents. The site of Enki's temple in Eridu supported sacred structures as far back as the Ubaid culture, 5000 BCE. Now, in Temple Hymn 2, Enheduanna repeats a phrase used for Enlil's temple at Nippur in one of the first pieces of written literature, the zà-mì, "praise" hymns from ancient Abu Salabikh. This hymn, written some three hundred years before Enheduanna's birth, describes Nippur as "dur-an-ki," "navel of heaven and earth."[2] Like Enheduanna's Temple Hymn, the zà-mì hymn makes Nippur "the cosmic center of the universe," according to W. G. Lambert, who also acknowledges that the tradition of Enki at Eridu may be even older.[3]

Enheduanna came to maturity in an atmosphere in which the literary and religious corpus so permeated the culture that it became the stuff of personal identity for individuals. She was an Akkadian/Sumerian enveloped in a dynamic pantheon and a long cultural history. As a mature woman, a poet, and prestigious high priestess in Ur, she drew on her knowledge of the literature of the past to ground her own Temple Hymns in ancient tradition. "Dur-an-ki," says the first zà-mì hymn written to Enlil in Nippur, and three hundred years later "dur-an-ki" remains for Enheduanna the definitive description of the Ekur in Nippur.

ENLIL'S COURTYARD — UB-ŠU-KIN-NA

Enlil, more than any of the gods, capitalized on the partnership between temple and palace, church and state that permeated Sumerian society. This dynamic interplay became the fundamental political reality of the culture and energized its evolution. The palace was the scene of performances of the growing body of epic literature and myth, songs, and stories, most of which involved deities from the pantheon. On the other hand, the temple sponsored dramatic ritual and cultic performance that shaped the calendar and the cultic year for commoners and elite alike. That Sargon, the king, appointed his only daughter, Enheduanna, to the most important religious office in the land, high priestess to the moon god at Ur, simply confirmed the crucial interplay between temple and state, clergy and king.

Enlil was not always a well-known, powerful god. Indeed, his rise to prominence came from the deliberate act of an Early Dynastic king, Enmebaragesi, in his attempt to unite under one rule the cities on the plain, north and south. A northern king from the area that became Akkad, Enmebaragesi "transformed Enlil's temple in Nippur, exactly between Wari (Akkad) and Kengir (Sumer), into a national cult center."[4] To secure his title, Enmebaragesi had Enlil confirm his appointment as king. The Nippur priests may have taken this opportunity to claim the right to name all future kings "elected" by Enlil. The independent southern city-states, already cooperating economically, began to look to Nippur as their religious center and to Enlil in the Ekur as the most powerful god. Agreement among the major deities of the cities' shared pantheon was essential to their often fragile cooperation. Politics and religion intermingled so thoroughly that, for example, J. N. Postgate reports that oaths taken to secure the peace between two southern cities, Lagash and Umma, "were communicated to the principal deities of the Land by dispatching doves to them at their home cities—Enlil at Nippur, Ninkhursag at Kesh, Enki at Eridu, Nanna at Ur, and Utu at Larsa."[5]

The courtyard of Enlil's temple, the ub-šu-kin-na, was the meeting place of what can only be called a Mesopotamian assembly, the ukkin. Here in Nippur at the will of the king, representatives of the major cities met to make important decisions and even conduct trials. Unlike Enki, who provided civilization's essentials of food and water, Enlil's temple, the hymn says, was the "birthplace of fate." Its gift to humanity was "measured reckoning," "contemplation," and "divine decisions." Enlil's gifts assured justice in the cities and an orderly rule of law. He was a god intimately involved in human politics.

Enlil's temple became the center of legal expertise and the prototypical arbiter of disputes. Its decisions began to form a body of legal precedents. Not only were human decisions pondered, but the will of the gods was sought in the ub-šu-kin-na. The priests of all-powerful Enlil "received" his indisputable will. Leaders from the major cities and temples paid tribute to Enlil in homage and gratitude for his decisions. Kings brought him booty from their exploits, making the Ekur a virtual museum housing valuable objects, gifts the kings collected in their campaigns. Postgate says, "The right to present such offerings to the Ekur would have constituted acknowledgment . . . of a ruler's right to be considered elected by Enlil as 'King of the Land.'"[6]

VENERABLE NIPPUR

The great Euphrates ran through the middle of Nippur as Enheduanna would have seen it. Numerous temples graced its banks on either side of the river. Each temple had its unique tall platform temple or elaborately decorated building, the largest and most beautiful housing the principal gods and goddesses of the pantheon. Enlil's compound consisted of several temples for his family and his favored assistants. Indeed, the site of Enlil's temple, the Ekur, was already a sacred setting at its earliest occupancy in the Ubaid period, 5000 BCE, and may have been even then the central shrine of the ancient city.[7]

Holy Nippur was primarily a city for the gods. It was held in the minds of the Sumerians as their revered cult center and regarded with great reverence as the locale of their religious identity. Unlike the other Sumerian cities, Nippur had no civic government but was ruled by the most prominent priests, those in the temples of the principal deities.

The temples of Nippur were centers of learning. Because so many of the inhabitants were employed in the temples, there was an unusually high level of literacy. Nippur was clearly the center of third-millennium literary culture. These texts, F. A. M. Wiggerman says, "formed the core of the 'Scriptures' of the Babylon stage of Mesopotamian theology" and include almost all the major Sumerian literary works.[8] These works were copied over and over again for many centuries. The scribes were not merely copyists. Their activity evolved into an institution that was the core of Sumerian scholarship. The students came from prominent, wealthy families. Many went on "to become officials in the vast administration of the Sargonic Empire," says Aage Westenholz.[9] During that time the scribes worked closely with singers and performers, as well as maintaining a relationship between the temple and the center of government, the palace. Westenholz describes the Tablet House: "The Tablet House was not just a repository of traditional lore—but a center for research as well. . . . Whatever could be salvaged of the until then largely oral Sumerian traditions, literary and historical, were preserved for the future in written form, and the Akkadians laid the foundations for their sciences of philology and divination. The 'Tablet House' of that time was fully comparable to a modern university."[10] Nippur housed the nucleus of scribal learning and activity. Almost all of the houses archeologists discovered contained "school" or practice tablets belonging to students learning the scribal craft, a constant stream of new scribes entering this esteemed institution. Their work formed the core of the growing library of Sumerian scholarship.

FINDING NIPPUR

The University of Pennsylvania began excavations at Nippur in 1888. The excavation was funded by enthusiastic private citizens headed by a demanding committee at the university. The field director was required to report his progress once a week. Aage Westenholz describes the difficulty of sending and receiving these reports: "It took up to two months for a report to reach the committee, and a similar length of time for their instructions in response to reach the field director; it is no wonder one of the committee remarked that 'by the time our letters reach Niffer, they are already ancient history.'"[11]

It is difficult to imagine the arduous conditions the excavators endured while conducting these early expeditions. Westenholz describes the "unspeakable deprivations" of one of the first directors, R. C. Haynes, the "dangers to his life, and endless difficulties with corrupt Ottoman commissioners and unreliable local sheikhs while he worked at Nippur for three consecutive years, summer and winter."[12]

McGuire Gibson, who became the director of the Nippur excavations in 1972, reports the unusual difficulty of identifying and dating the buildings and artifacts. Hundreds of years of occupation and the digging of large foundation ditches by late occupants, who used piles of refuse (containing valuable identifying materials) to fill the foundation trenches for their new structures, complicated these tasks enormously. Nevertheless, archeologists were able to determine that the site had been occupied in the Ubaid period (5000–4000 BCE). When the great river changed its channel, it left a deep trough through the middle of the city, today called the Shatt an-Nil. Gibson describes the elevated site of the temple area on either side of the river:

> In the Early Dynastic and Akkadian Periods, the city was probably much larger than previously. The Pennsylvania excavators noted that there was an Early Dynastic platform or terrace under the entire sacred precinct. In our work . . . in 1987, we found confirming evidence that the sacred area around Ekur must have been two to three meters higher than the surrounding town in the Early Dynastic period.[13]

As at Eridu, the first sacred precinct at Nippur was built almost three thousand years before Enheduanna collected the hymns to the major temples contemporary with her life as high priestess at Ur. The lofty temple of Enlil she might have seen, the Ekur, rose on its mound almost twenty feet above the city, Nippur, and remained a vital center until 500 CE.

GREAT MOUNTAIN ENLIL

So identified was Enlil with his temple in Nippur, the Ekur—House of the Mountain—that he was often referred to in myths simply as "the mountain." As Enheduanna's hymn says, "the slant wall of your terrace / shoulders a perfect mountain." Enlil's "divine decisions," "sired" high on the temple mountain, "spread through Sumer and Akkad / right and left through his whole estate." Indeed, Enlil's supremacy from Nippur over the entire country was long-lasting. Lambert says, "This prestigious cosmic position of Nippur remained unaltered through most of the second millennium."[14]

Enlil's name in Sumerian combines two elements, en and lil, meaning 'Lord Wind,' or, as Thorkild Jacobsen says, "productive manager of the wind."[15] Enlil is the wind that separated heaven and earth from the original chaos. Or his name may have been Semitic, a "Sumerianization" of the name of a father god, *i-li-lu,* mentioned in texts from the northern Syrian city of Ebla.[16] The root "il" occurs in "such well-known Semitic divine appellations as El and, of course, Allah."[17] Evidence indicates that Semitic and Sumerian peoples lived peacefully together for many centuries. The Sumerian and Semitic roots of Enlil's name bring the two groups together in this one most powerful deity.

Whether or not Enlil was ever a weather god, his moods, like the weather, were unpredictable and his temper volatile. He was "feared and respected rather than loved," according to Gwendolyn Leick.[18] He is the dramatic, uncontrollable subject of a number of myths, and his prominence as the head of the pantheon lasted throughout Mesopotamian history. He blessed the onset of the Akkadian era, "electing" Sargon to be the new king after he defeated Lugalzagesi and brought him in neck-stock to Nippur. Sargon's powerful grandson, Naram-Sin, venerated Enlil but brought the god's wrath down upon his head when in his renovation of Enlil's temple he allegedly committed sacrilegious acts, precipitating his downfall.

So powerful a god as Enlil naturally cast his aura on those around him. His wife Ninlil shared his power, as described in the next Temple Hymn. His minister, Nusku, and his favored warrior "son," Ninurta, basked in his favor. Shuzianna, his second wife, depended on him for her privileged position, while the final goddess of the Nippur group was Enlil's sister, Ninhursag, who rivaled his formidable masculinity with her authority in the female realm of childbearing, while she added prestige to Enlil's Nippur entourage from her city to the south, Kesh.

TEMPLE HYMN 3

THE NIPPUR TEMPLE OF NINLIL
Tummal

molded with grace
    O Tummal

with princely favors
they wrapped you in terror and awe
you the foundation
whose pure cleansing rites stretch
over abzu's sweet waters
ancient city
old reeds and young shoots shape you
your heart, forged in plenty
is a mountain of abundance

in New Year's festive month   you dress in wonder
then the Kiur's great lady outshines Enlil
your own princess
mother Ninlil   Nunamnir's well-loved wife
O Tummal house
has built this house on your radiant site
and placed her seat upon your dais

    8 lines for the house of Ninlil in Nippur

THE NIPPUR TEMPLE OF NINLIL

The hymn to Great Lady Ninlil, Enlil's "well-loved wife," brings her temple
vividly to life. "Molded with grace," the hymn says. By what hand, we ask?
The hymn points to one, amply filled with divine prerogatives—"princely favors"—who dress her "in terror and awe." Reeds, old and young, come alive
and shape her, stretch her ritual foundation across the "sweet waters" of the
abzu. The molding hand forges her overflowing heart; it is "a mountain of
abundance." This is the Tummal, itself a pulsating being, built for its "own
princess," Ninlil.

Unlike her heavenly husband, Enlil, Ninlil and her temple hover over the
sweet waters of the abzu, which floats like a gentle refuge over the deeper,
darker waters of the underworld. Ninlil lives close to Enki's abzu and is
thus connected to Enki's mother of the abzu, Nammu, the origin of all life.
Nammu's is an ancient story, and Ninlil has links to that older tradition. She is
the daughter of Nisaba (Temple Hymn 42), goddess of writing. Nisaba's parents were the original pair of gods, Urash (earth) and An (heaven). Nisaba, as
Ninlil's mother and Enlil's mother-in-law, is considered "the great matriarch
of Sumer."[19] Ninlil's thread reaches back to the time of origin. She is a child of

both worlds, of the earth, her grandmother Urash, and its connection to the underworld, and also of her heavenly grandfather, An.

THE MARRIAGE OF ENLIL AND NINLIL

In two well-known Sumerian myths of the marriage of Enlil and Ninlil, Enlil observes "a maiden so beautiful so radiant" that he is immediately overcome with desire.[20] Ninlil's mother, Nisaba, called Nunbarsheguna in the myth "Enlil and Ninlil," warns her daughter not to bathe in the holy river, the Nunbirdu canal. "His eye is bright, the lord's eye is bright, he will look at you!"[21] The Nunbirdu was a special canal holding waters of purification, possibly where "young women bathe after their first menstruation," says Leick.[22] The maiden Ninlil would have participated in that ritual that imparted the meaning and cultural regulations of her new womanly status.

The canal was named after Prince Birdu, "an infernal deity," says Jacobsen, "so that the shadow of the netherworld already falls over the course of events narrated."[23] Ninlil, in typical adolescent fashion, goes immediately to the place her mother had forbidden, takes off her clothes, and bathes in the canal. Enlil sees the naked Ninlil on the opposite bank of the canal, eventually crosses over and either persuades her or forces her to have sex with him. For this transgression, he is sentenced by the god council to leave the city.

"Enlil went. Ninlil followed. . . . the maiden chased him."[24] Enlil, after his disgrace, disguises himself in his attempt to hide from Ninlil. Even though he has been duly punished by the god council, he succumbs again to Ninlil's advances. Three more times they have sex together. Four gods are engendered in Ninlil's womb: Nanna, Nergal, Ninazu, and Enbilulu. Ninlil and Enlil marry, and she becomes the important queen and mother in the temple complex of the Ekur.

Interpretations of this myth range from hypotheses of male sexual predation, to female passivity, to cravings for a baby, to the instincts connected to primary fertility.[25] One interpretation that has not been mentioned is the adolescent female's strong sexual desire and seductive propensity. She has bathed in the dark waters of the underworld, which wash away conventional mores. She is out of bounds, deliberately disobeying her mother by going against the conventional rules of morality. Despite this inauspicious beginning Ninlil becomes a devoted mother and is worshiped as a mother goddess.

In a second marriage myth, "Enlil and Ninlil: The Marriage of Sud," the proper courtship and marriage customs prevail. Young Sud (Ninlil), daughter of Nisaba, is walking in the street. Enlil makes improper advances to her, assuming she is available because she is in the street alone. He tells her he is "impressed by [her] beauty, even if [she is] a shameless person!"[26] As in the former myth, Sud/Ninlil crosses the boundaries of propriety, tempting the underworld forces by daring to walk alone in the street. This time she rebuffs Enlil. He then follows the marriage custom of declaring his intentions to her mother and giving her gifts. Upon Sud's marriage and entry into Enlil's temple, she is renamed Ninlil.

Both myths depict Ninlil's perilous passage from childhood to womanhood. Both suggest that the peril begins when the young woman dares follow her awakening sexual desire and breaks the boundaries of convention firmly set in place not just by society or by her mother, but by the deities themselves, as they confirm in their sentencing of Enlil. Both myths imply that the danger of unbounded instinctual passion is connected to the influence of the dark underworld gods. In this instance the underworld gods reveal their link to primal sexual instincts, whose force threatens the rules and conventions the culture has established.

The outcome of Ninlil's pursuit of Enlil in the first myth is the conception of four offspring who become significant gods. The first to be conceived is Nanna/Suen, the moon god whose primary temple is located at Ur (Temple Hymn 8). The second son is Nergal (Temple Hymn 36), an underworld god (and atypically also a warrior in the upper world) whom Ninlil hoped would take the place in the netherworld of her beloved first son, Nanna. The third son is Ninazu (Temple Hymns 14 and 34), like Nergal an underworld god and a warrior. The fourth is Enbilulu, a minor god connected to irrigation, responsible for dikes and canals, and not included in the Temple Hymns. Thus, Ninlil gives birth to these important sons and enhances her place as queen, wife of the head of the pantheon, revered goddess of the Tummal. She assumes the role of an appropriate mother goddess and leaves behind the sexually provocative actions that characterized her adolescence.

"IN NEW YEAR'S FESTIVE MONTH"

The Tummal, Ninlil's temple, was located in Nippur in the complex that included Enlil's temple, the Ekur. It was first built around 2600 BCE, in the Early Dynastic era, by King Aka, son of Enmebaragesi, who earlier had established Enlil in the Ekur as the greatest of the great gods.[27] The hymn says, "in New Year's festive month / you dress in wonder." According to widespread tradition, from northwest Syria to south-central Iraq, the beginning of the year was observed in the spring. In Nippur the New Year's festival was held in the month of bára-zag-gar, "throne of the sanctuary" (March–April).[28] The festival was called zag-mu, the border of the year. The celebration at the Tummal in Nippur was the central New Year observance in the country. The festival, as Mark Cohen describes it, "was a time of taking inventory at the temple and for distributing foodstuffs to personnel."[29] Grain was stored throughout the year for distribution at the New Year's festival.

Following the Mesopotamian belief that the equinox was a propitious time, a second major festival was observed at the Tummal six months later, in the seventh month. This was a more somber festival that took place on the Sacred Mound, the du_6-ku. As with Enki in Eridu, Enlil's ancestors lived in the netherworld below the Sacred Mound. Cohen recounts the antiquity of it: "The god pair ^{d}En-du_6-kù-ga and ^{d}Nin-du_6-kù-ga, 'Lord of the Sacred Mound' and 'Lady of the Sacred Mound,' are listed among the ancestors of Enlil throughout the canonical lamentations and in the god list AN = *Anum*, demonstrating the primordial nature of the Sacred Mound, even pre-dating the great god Enlil, himself."[30] The importance of the Sacred Mound is emphasized by J. J. van Dijk, who understood the Sacred Mound as "a hill on the world-mountain on which the gods originally lived and where Sumerian culture originated."[31] The Sacred Mound at Nippur received "special devotion throughout the year, offerings of lambs, sheep, goats, oxen, and especially milk."[32]

The important festivals observed at the Tummal enhanced Ninlil's significance. She was called Mother Ninlil and revered for her motherly devotion as well as for her role in rendering divine decisions. She had the power to decree destinies from the Kiur. She is, as Tikva Frymer-Kensky says, "a perceptive and wise counselor, . . . an august queen who wields power along with her husband, Lord Enlil."[33] In the composition known as "Hymn to Enlil," Ninlil is called "the fair woman / whom you married at sight." The hymn continues its praise of Ninlil:

> In advising she finds the perfect word,
> her word, her assuagement,
>   is the heart's juniper perfume.
> She, for her part too, dwells with you
>   on a holy throne dais,
>   next to the pure throne dais,
> advises with you, ponders with you,
> makes with you the decisions
>   at the (court held at the)
> place of sunrise.[34]

In the four remaining hymns to gods and goddesses in Enlil's entourage, Ninlil's position in the pantheon is both implicit and explicit. Nusku, Enlil's minister, Temple Hymn 4, made possible Enlil's meeting with Ninlil on the bank of the canal; powerful Ninurta, Temple Hymn 5, in one myth is Ninlil's son; Shuzianna, Temple Hymn 6, joins Ninlil as Enlil's second wife; and the great mother goddess Ninhursag, Enlil's sister, Temple Hymn 7, is equated with Ninlil in the Ninurta myth. Thus, the aura of power of those touching Enlil extends its force all through the stories and myths that grew around them.

TEMPLE HYMN 4

THE NIPPUR TEMPLE OF NUSKU
Melam Hush

O house   wrapped in terrifying fire-red glow
   towering shrine   showered with heaven's princely blessings
   storehouse of Enlil shaped a ruler in an ancient mold

counselor of the Ekur
head held at princely height
your house and its horn-capped walls
is a sight close to heaven

here great verdicts are conferred, divine decisions,
where the river ordeal lets the true-walker live
but binds the evil-hearted in darkness
in your great place
fit for ishib's pure cleansing rites
you eat with Lord Nunamnir   your prince
heart-soother of Enlil   welcomed in the exalted shrine
good spirit of the Mountain House
great worker Nusku
house of Enlil
has built this house on your radiant site
and placed his seat upon your dais

   12 lines for the house of Nusku at Nippur

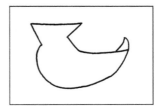

5.3.   Lamp symbol of Nusku. Courtesy of the
University of Texas Press, Jeremy Black and Anthony
Green, *Gods, Demons and Symbols of Ancient
Mesopotamia*, Tessa Richards, illustrator, 1995.

THE TEMPLE OF NUSKU IN NIPPUR

A complicated web of stories and traditions connects the gods of the Sumerian pantheon with each other. In Enlil's group of six deities who cluster around him, each has powers of his or her own, but all bask in their important relationships to Enlil, the venerable head of the pantheon.

Nusku is a typical lesser god, a god of fire and light, who serves his master Enlil as counselor or advisor as well as a minister who is quick to carry out Enlil's commands. His relationship with Enlil is intimate. His hymn addresses Enlil as Nunamnir, his byname. The hymn says they dine together in the impeccable shrine, cleansed and purified by the ishib priest, a purification priest who rids the shrine of all dangers of contamination by contact with witches or sorcerers. There, Nusku soothes Enlil's troubled heart, troubled no doubt because of his immense responsibilities as head of the pantheon.

Such close involvement and familiarity between two gods is fairly unusual, particularly with Enlil, who is frequently portrayed as remote and somewhat harsh in his relationships. Perhaps Nusku brings the softening of intimacy to the great god. Nusku, in spite of his fiery nature, has a capacity to speak from the heart and to foster the same in the revered Enlil.

In the myth "Enlil and Ninlil," the intimacy between Enlil and Nusku plays a part in Enlil's pursuit of Ninlil, after he sees her bathing in the Nunbirdu canal:

> "Nusku, my page!"
> "Yes, Pray!"
> "Great trust of Ekur."
> "Yes, my master!"

"With a girl so nice, so shapely,
with Ninlil, so nice, so shapely,
one gets an urge

> to make love,
>   one gets an urge to kiss!"

The page brought to his master
    the likes of a boat
brought to him the likes of a towline
    of a small boat,
brought to him the likes of a big boat.

"My master willing,
    let me float him down on it,
so he can follow the urge
    to make that love,
    follow the urge to kiss those lips,
Father Enlil willing,
    let me float him down on it,
so he can follow the urge
    to make that love,
    follow the urge to kiss those lips!"[35]

The story unfolds in the myth cited above.

THE RIVER ORDEAL

Significantly, Nusku's temple is the place of divine decision making: "here great verdicts are conferred." The hymn tells us that verdicts in Nusku's temple are decided by "the river ordeal." This method was used in cases in which it proved difficult to determine guilt or innocence. Walter Farber says these cases frequently involved sorcery accusations: "The standard procedure in such cases was not a trial by human judges, but rather an ordeal by immersion into the 'Divine River' who could pronounce the accuser guilty by drowning him, or innocent by letting him survive."[36] Other accounts say the accused was required to swim a certain distance in the river. If he succeeded, he was innocent; if he failed, he was guilty.[37] The river god determined the fate of the accused, and therefore the verdict was in divine hands.

Nusku had other dealings with practitioners of sorcery. As a god of fire, he "at times is called upon to assist in the burning of sorcerers and witches."[38] As Enlil's minister, he is aligned with Enlil's command of justice, he who determines destinies, determines right and wrong. Nusku's symbol as god of light is a simple lamp.

NUSKU IN THE EKUR

The hymn pictures Nusku's temple dramatically as glowing "fire-red," referring to his attribute as a fire god. It is called a "towering shrine," its walls crowned with horn-shaped crenelation. Actually, Nusku's shrine in Nippur was not a separate temple at all, but probably one of a number of shrines inside the Ekur, the temple of Enlil. A. R. George says, regarding the temples listed in the Canonical Temple List, that "probably the majority of sanctuaries listed were not buildings in their own right. Some were certainly only small shrines within larger sacred buildings."[39] Nusku's temple is called é-me.lám. huš, which George translates as "House of Awesome Radiance."[40] His consort is Sadarnunna, whose temple, é-pàd.da.nu.nus, "Chosen House of the Woman," was apparently also a shrine in the Enlil temple.[41] Nusku's temple, the hymn tells us, is Enlil's storehouse or treasury, an essential component of Enlil's ruling position. It was built in great antiquity at the time of the original separation of the elements of civilization, the **me**, its sovereignty established as one of the me-ul, the primeval **me**.

In another hymn to Nusku's master, the "Hymn to Enlil," the ever-obedient Nusku is described and praised:

> His grand vizier, Nusku,
>   leader of the assembly,
> can know and discuss with him
> his commands and the matters
>   that are in his heart—
> most widely he will take
>   directives for him,
> salutes him (in parting)
>   with a holy chalice in holy office[42]

Nusku was "welcomed in the exalted shrine," Enlil's private and intimate quarters. Besides trusting Nusku implicitly, Enlil turned to him with his most pressing concerns. Nusku's capacity as "heart soother" is rare in the relationships of the gods. This very human capacity of relatedness and caring gains divine sanction in Nusku's relationship to Enlil and contrasts with Enlil's great warrior, Ninurta, in the next hymn.

TEMPLE HYMN 5

THE NIPPUR TEMPLE OF NINURTA
Eshumesha

O house
    power-gatherer of heaven
    rising in a big place
strapping hero   you of true cosmic forces
fill the holy throne
you   battle arm
hero's mace   quiver wearer
your foundation strong unending brickworks
conceived by the primeval Lord
will last all living days

decision maker of princely power
holy earth   greater than the mountain
lifting its head among the princes
dawn at your place spreads a glow like daylight
O Eshumesha
Enlil has fixed on your name   a fearsome dread
your prince   a fear force
holds the land in terror to the outer edge
great ruler of Enlil
sovereign   staff-bearer
equal of heaven and earth
who refines the greatness of cosmic order
on the horned crown of father Enlil
mace holder   strong-headed one
Enlil's front-goer   unrivaled
lion given birth from the mountain
he destroys evil-necked rebels for Enlil
    Lord Ninurta
    Lord of Earth
and has   O Eshumesha
built this house on your radiant site
and placed his seat upon your dais

    15 lines for the house of Ninurta of Nippur

5.4.   Bird on perch symbol of Ninurta. Courtesy
of the University of Texas Press, Jeremy Black and
Anthony Green, *Gods, Demons and Symbols of Ancient
Mesopotamia*, Tessa Richards, illustrator, 1995.

THE TEMPLE OF NINURTA IN NIPPUR

The hymn to Ninurta leaves no doubt about his force. His fierce battle-readiness is at the service of Enlil. Enlil's "front-goer," "mace-holder," "refines the greatness of cosmic order / on the horned crown of father Enlil." A daunting assignment, Ninurta is chosen to fine-tune the cosmos at the bidding of the great god Enlil.

His temple in Nippur, like Ninurta himself, is a "strapping hero," collecting "cosmic forces." Its origin reaches back to the en-ul, "the primeval lord," the most ancient of the creator gods, who built the temple to "last all living days." Enlil imbued the temple's very name—Eshumesha—with "a fearsome dread." An uncanny glow emanates from the temple and spreads like a holy aura. Into this temple Enlil placed his "prime ruler," Ninurta.

NINURTA IN NIPPUR

Historical records do not make clear when Ninurta's cult arrived in Nippur. William Hallo says, "In all this long history, there is no evidence for Ninurta at Nippur in the Early Dynastic times, as there is for many other deities."[43] He suggests that the Sumerian myth known as "The Return of Ninurta to Nippur" "celebrates, not the return of Ninurta to Nippur but the effective introduction of his cult there."[44] Ninurta apparently functioned as a local deity in Nippur during the Sargonic era. His influence throughout the country gained in importance only later, from the late third-millennium Ur III period into mid-Assyrian times. His subordination to Nusku (Temple Hymn 4) is apparent in the "Return" myth, Hallo says, when "Ninurta's approach to Nippur is blocked by Nusku."[45] This interpretation is consistent with the order of the Temple Hymns, which places Nusku ahead of Ninurta. At a later period, Ur III, Ninurta and Nusku both receive animal offerings at festivals in Nippur, indicative of Ninurta's growing importance. By this time, Ninurta had shrines and other temples in various parts of the country. In addition, his famous weapons were worshiped in temples in Babylon.[46]

Ninurta is frequently equated with the principal god from the city of Lagash, Ningirsu (Temple Hymn 20). Ningirsu's mother is Ninhursag, further complicating the interweaving of these two gods. Ninhursag is the name Ninurta gives to his mother, Ninlil, in the "Lugal-e" myth, upon her visit to him in the mountains, following his triumphant battle (see below).

Ninurta's consort is Nin-Nibru, Lady of Nippur.[47] Tablets found in later excavations identify his consort as Gula, goddess of healing, although this goddess is not mentioned in the texts until 2000 BCE and therefore probably would not have been his consort in Enheduanna's time. Apparently their temples were not side by side, as would have been expected, but across the ancient riverbed from each other.[48]

A MOTHER'S SON — NINURTA AND NINLIL

In the rich mythology of Sumer striking examples occur of psychological insights not specifically articulated until Sigmund Freud began to identify patterns of human behavior with characters in Greek myths. Ninurta is especially attached to his mother, Ninlil, and she to him, exhibiting perhaps the first written example of the Oedipus complex. This example occurs in Ninurta's myth known as "Lugal-e." In the myth Ninurta battles a rival, the mythological mountain warrior Azag, and proceeds into combat despite dire reports of his enemy's strength. Overwhelmed by a dust storm that Azag spawns, Ninurta has to be rescued by his father, Enlil, who creates rain to settle the dust. In this episode Ninurta is impetuous, like an adolescent. Finally, he defeats Azag.

Ninlil, missing her son during his absence, takes the long journey from Nippur to the northern mountains to see him. The poem says,

> On that day the queen took compassion,
>   in (her bed) where he had been engendered,
>   Ninmah [Ninlil] could not fall asleep.
> She covered [her] back with wool,
>   (looking) like a stately ewe,
> and greatly wailed about the highland
>   In (all) its tracklessness:

[She says:]

"The lord, Enlil's (very) life's breath. . . .
to whom I gave birth for my bridegroom,
>   but who has gone off
>   paying me no heed,
Enlil's son, who has taken leave
>   and not turned his face toward me!"[49]

Ninlil's lament is exaggerated. She bewails the fact that her son simply left, without saying goodbye, much less consulting her. She takes matters into her own hands and embarks on a long, hazardous journey into the mountains to find him.

Ninurta, for his part, is overjoyed to see his mother:

Queen, as you have come to the highland—
Ninmah, as for my sake
>   you have entered
>   the rebel regions,
as you have not shied away
>   from my battle (array),
>   over which hovers its dread aura . . ."[50]

He proceeds to shower gifts upon his mother. He gives her what were formerly Azag's warriors, stones he defeated and piled up, the hursag. He renames her Ninhursag, Lady of the Rocky Mountains, gives her the bounty of the surrounding meadows—herbs, grapes, cedar, cypress, and more; mines of gold and silver, copper and tin; goats and wild asses. Mother and son are equally enamored of one another. Ninurta's neglect in leaving his mother without a goodbye reflects his adolescent self-involvement and bravado.

Another hymn to Ninurta involving Ninlil describes the god performing heroic deeds. Then he praises himself:

As if with a big ax I will pull down a . . . wall,
>   let my mother know it!
As. . . . I will make the troops there tremble,
>   let my mother know it!
. . . . like . . . . I will let a dog eat, let my mother know it!

I, the heroic warrior, ... furious battle, smashes the heads,
I, the En, curse the enemy land which does not obey,

. . . .

> Like a city which I, Ninurta, have destroyed,
> I will turn into ruin heaps.[51]

Ninurta's exaggerated and sometimes impetuous acts are intended, in part, to impress his mother. He seems to beat his chest and roar to get her attention and approval. This description of Ninurta stands in contrast to his second aspect, that of a gentle farmer.

NINURTA THE FARMER

Ninurta was also a god of the earth, as his name implies, nin, meaning 'lord' (or 'lady'), and urta, meaning 'earth': Lord Earth. He is credited with inventing agriculture, with being responsible for the spring thunderstorms that brought refreshing waters to the Tigris and allowed for the essential irrigation of the growing crops.

Ninurta's conflicting aspects work together in the myth "Lugal-e." To defeat Azag, he becomes the ferocious warrior. He piles up the formidable stones of the Zagros Mountains, Azag's "warriors." As the caring en (lord) of his people, he uses the stones to shape a channel for winter runoff to flow into the Tigris. Jeremy Black interprets the myth as follows:

> The Sumerians, starting equally from the premise that the Zagros
> had not always been in existence, could use mythological language
> and make that landscape meaningful by describing it as a heap of
> stones—a heap of dead stone warriors—piled up by a god whose aim,
> ultimately, was to initiate agriculture for mankind: an interpretation of
> landscape which views it as having been shaped in the way that it is for
> human purposes.[52]

Ninurta invented the plow and was called Lord Plow. The second month of the Nippur calendar, ezem-gu$_4$-si-sù, "the month the horned oxen march forth," is dedicated to Ninurta, as the oxen pull the plow to break the soil for planting. Ninurta was the god of the planting festival the month-name designates.[53] The significant ritual involved dropping a seed into the soil below the plow. The plow was the central implement honored in the festival. The king took the part of Ninurta, the farmer, and ritually plowed the seeds into the ground. In Nippur, offerings were made to various temples during the festival.

These two aspects of Ninurta, the fierce and vicious warrior and the gentle farmer, seem, if not contradictory, at least at odds with each other. The complications in Ninurta's history and the contradictions in his character illustrate the difficulty of piecing together an accurate description of any deity who emerged over four thousand years ago. Nevertheless, as we try to understand this god with our present-day tools of interpretation, we find his stories evocative of a whole range of meanings. Above all, Ninurta illustrates the creativity and complexity of the human imagination, no matter what period of history, in its endeavor to make sense of the mysteries of the given world.

TEMPLE HYMN 6

THE NIPPUR TEMPLE OF SHUZIANNA
Egaduda

O Egaduda
set apart on a hill   head lifting above the others
crown of the high plain
holy place   pure place
where women reside
your foundation is the great mast of the prince
your Princess   that uncommon Lady
fills all the house and throne
singular mound   eminent temple
O Dusagash   the princess's house
she sows flowers in profusion on your luminous site
that strikingly wise one   your Princess
    may she never be angry
princely daughter
who showers abundance with the great mountain
Right-Hand-of-Heaven
    Shuzianna
father Enlil's second wife
O Dusagash
has built this house on your radiant site
and taken her seat upon your dais

    9 lines for the temple of Shuzianna
    the lofty closed house for consecrated women

THE TEMPLE OF SHUZIANNA IN NIPPUR

With this hymn to Shuzianna, Enlil's second wife, we step into a world apart from the intrigue and power wielding of the Nippur priests, away from the fateful decision making of the Nippur assembly. Shuzianna's temple was a house for women. In Temple Hymn 6, Enheduanna introduces us to a cloistered group of dedicated women, consecrated to the goddess in their "lofty" and "closed" quarters.

Following each of the Temple Hymns is a scribe's statement of the number of lines written to the named deity. After the hymn to Shuzianna we read, "9 lines for the temple of Shuzianna / the lofty closed house for consecrated women." This is the only hymn that adds a descriptive comment after the line count. The Sumerian phrase used is ǧá-gi-mah—lofty closed house. Åke Sjöberg, who translated the hymns, relates the term to the Akkadian *gagû,* meaning, according to the *Chicago Akkadian Dictionary,* "a building or section of the temple district reserved for the women of the *nadītu*-class."[54] We will hear more about the *nadītu* later in this chapter.

The hymn to Shuzianna is recorded on five separate tablets, five exemplars. One of these, text B, in line number 79, substitutes the Sumerian word ama$_5$, 'women's quarters,' where the other four write é, "house." This renders the translation for line 79 in text B, "where women reside / your foundation is the great mast of the prince." Adding to this evidence, one of the variant names of the Shuzianna temple was é.ama$_5$.du$_6$.dam, "House of Women on a Hill".[55] Text B's insertion of the word meaning women's quarters, plus the variant temple name, reinforces the premise that Shuzianna's temple housed a special group of women devoted to the goddess.

IN THE WOMEN'S ROOMS

The hymn to Shuzianna is not the only reference in Enheduanna's writing to a world of women living in a temple compound. In one of Enheduanna's three devotional poems to her personal goddess Inanna, called after its first line "Lady of Largest Heart," she describes a ritual Inanna performs, a ritual in which she initiates a woman to be an ecstatic priestess:

in sacred rite
she takes the broach
which pins a woman's robe

breaks the needle, silver thin
consecrates the maiden's heart as male
gives to her a mace[56]

The ritual, called the head-overturning, describes an instance of Inanna's dreaded power to turn man into woman, woman into man. The process takes place, the poem says, "within the women's rooms," using the same Sumerian word, ama$_5$, translated in this poem as "women's rooms."[57]

In another verse of the same poem Enheduanna tells of a group of women who live apart, "beyond the river," who devote their lives to the worship of Inanna. They are called "warrior women":

those warrior women
like a single thread
come forth from beyond the river
do common work
in devotion to you
whose hands sear them with purifying fire

your many devoted
who will be burnt
like sun-scorched firebricks
pass before your eyes[58]

The warrior women are explicitly devoted to Inanna in a spiritual practice in which Inanna's hands "sear them with purifying fire." As in Shuzianna's temple, the warrior women are "set apart." The "searing" practice, when compared to historical examples of cloistered devotees, suggests a discipline of self-abnegation, sacrifice, and self-reflection in order for the women to grow in their devotion and service to Inanna.

To the extent that the women were dedicated to a goddess, the practice is in sharp contrast to George's translation of é.ğa.gi.mah, 'House, Exalted Harem,' or é.ama$_5$.du$_6$.dam as 'House, Harem . . . ,'[59] and to Jacobsen's description of Shuzianna as "concubine" to Enlil.[60] Terms such as "harem" and "concubine" are derogatory in the Western world and have questionable relevance to an institution from thousands of years ago, one whose composition and regulations we do not know.

WOMEN'S COLLECTIVES

We have little evidence of groups of women in intentional communities in the Old Akkadian period when Enheduanna lived, other than that mentioned already. In contrast, three hundred years later in the Old Babylonian period, we find numerous records of collectives of women, each group living under its own set of regulations. The most prominent of these groups was the *nadītu,* devoted to the Akkadian sun god, Shamash. Only one mention has been found of a *nadītu* in the Old Akkadian period when Enheduanna lived, the name on a seal—insignia stamped into damp clay—designating the woman as a *nadītu* of Ishtar.[61] The word *nadītu* means 'fallow' and suggests a celibate life.

Rivkah Harris has described the Old Babylonian groups of women in her book *Ancient Sippar.*[62] Hundreds of textual references mention the cloistered group in the city of Sippar, the *nadītu,* consecrated to Shamash. These women lived within a walled complex of the Shamash temple. Evidently most were from the upper classes of society, "daughters of military officials and cloister, temple, and city administrators . . . daughters of wealthy scribes and artisans . . . even daughters of kings."[63] So prestigious was the Sippar cloister that several generations from one family would join, one following the other. These women brought their wealth with them in the form of their dowries. They lived in houses that they owned, employed servants and slaves, conducted their own businesses of buying and selling land, and generally lived independent lives. They were not priestesses but showed their devotion to Shamash and his consort Aja by calling themselves daughters-in-law of Shamash, presenting him food offerings and assuming a new name that expressed their devotion. Upon entering the cloister they took part in a two-day ceremony, first receiving the "rope" of Shamash on their arms, and on the second day participating in a "memorial" festival that included "funerary rites . . . owed to deceased parents."[64] Participating in these rites may have signified the initiates' departure from their parents and their acquisition of a new status in relation to Shamash and Aja.

The *nadītu* of Shamash were not allowed to marry, whereas in the same city another group, the *nadītu* of Marduk, could marry and therefore were not cloistered. These women were not allowed to have children, although they, like the *nadītu* of Shamash, might adopt a child or secure other women to have the child of their husbands. Several other groups of women are reported in the Sippar material. Each group had its own requirements and regulations. Even the prostitutes, the *harimtu,* lived in a group. These groups of "special status" were protected by "many paragraphs" in the Code of Hammurabi, "where laws regarding their dowries and the obligations of their brothers to support them are clearly defined."[65]

It is tempting to connect the few hints in Temple Hymn 6 which suggest a community of women in the Shuzianna temple to the highly developed organization of the *nadītu* and other groups in Sippar. Could the "lofty closed house for consecrated women" have been a precursor of the Old Babylonian groups in Sippar? Enheduanna was well aware of the separation of women from men in the "women's rooms" in the gipar at Ur where she lived. The large gipar compound in Ur was essentially a place for women. She wrote passionately about the warrior women who did "common work" for Inanna and received her harsh purification in return. Clearly, in the Old Akkadian period women had begun the practice of living apart in devotion to a deity. The hymn to Shuzianna says the women in her "lofty" house joined her in devotion to Enlil, "the great mountain," who with the "strikingly wise" Shuzianna showers abundance from the holy temple. For these women, as for the *nadītu*, Shuzianna's temple would have been a safe harbor, removed from the perils of childbearing and relieved of the increasingly restrictive rules and laws governing the lives of women.

DAM-BÀN-DA

Shuzianna is "dam-bàn-da," second or junior wife of Enlil. Ninlil, of course, is Enlil's first wife. Ninlil inhabits Enlil's formidable world of politics. She sits next to him on the holy throne, advises him, and makes decisions. Ninlil, in conjunction with Enlil, partakes of the power in the world of men.

Shuzianna, by contrast, inhabits a world of women. Enlil, of course, is welcome there. The two of them married in the storehouse of Enlil's temple, the é.kur.igi.ğál, 'Mountain House Endowed with Sight.'[66] Their bedroom has a special designation—"Perfect Beloved House."[67] Shuzianna's temple was apparently located within the great compound of the Ekur, Enlil's temple, even though the hymn says it was "set apart on a hill." At least theologically, it stood "above the others," a "crown," "holy place—pure place."

"Dam-bàn-da" she may have been, but Shuzianna's hymn gives us a glimpse into an obscure layer of Akkadian society that opens our minds to an imaginative configuration of possibility, the place of women consecrated to a goddess. Who but a group of women would join Shuzianna as "she sows flowers in profusion on your luminous site"?

"That strikingly wise one / your Princess / may she never be angry," the hymn says of this goddess. In the next hymn another goddess, the great

mother goddess Ninhursag, inspires a similar dichotomy between gentle reflection and potential rage, a pair of opposites particularly characteristic of
certain Sumerian goddesses. Ninhursag joins the Nippur group even though
her temple was south of Nippur in Kesh. Nevertheless, Enlil claimed her as his
sister and assumed under his aegis her prestigious ancient status as one of the
original three great gods.

TEMPLE HYMN 7

THE KESH TEMPLE OF NINHURSAG
The Lofty

high-lying Kesh
in all heaven and earth   you are the form-shaping place
    spreading fear like a great poisonous snake
O Lady of the Mountains   Ninhursag's house
built on a terrifying site

Kesh   like holy Aratta
inside is a womb dark and deep
your outside towers over all

imposing one
great lion of the wildlands stalking the high plains
great mountain   incantations fixed you in place

inside the light is dim
even moonlight (Nanna's light) does not enter
only Nintur, Lady Birth,
makes it beautiful
house of Kesh
    the brick of birthgiving
    your temple tower   adorned with a lapis crown
your princess
Princess of Silence
unfailing great Lady of Heaven
when she speaks, heaven shakes
open-mouthed, she roars

Aruru
sister of Enlil

5.5.   Uterus symbol of Ninhursag. Courtesy of the
University of Texas Press, Jeremy Black and Anthony
Green, *Gods, Demons and Symbols of Ancient
Mesopotamia*, Tessa Richards, illustrator, 1995.

> O house of Kesh
> has built this house on your radiant site
> and placed her seat upon your dais
>
> 13 lines for the temple of Ninhursag of Kesh

THE TEMPLE OF NINHURSAG AT KESH

The hymn to Ninhursag in Kesh is a grand finale to the presentation of the
Nippur gods. Before building his empire, Enheduanna's father, Sargon, wisely
bowed to Enlil in Nippur to receive the god's blessing as the new king. All the
Nippur gods of the Temple Hymns joined to assure Sargon's success and acceptance in the rest of the country. Enlil, with Ninlil by his side and Nusku at
his beck and call, wields political power to make the laws and rules by which
the growing empire will govern. Ninurta waves his battle arm to subdue the
unwilling. Shuzianna reserves a sheltered place for women and stands behind
the power of love to bind connections. Now, mighty Ninhursag appears in
her feared temple, herself the very force of nature that no empire, no king, no
laws, no might can control. Her high-lying temple has in its power the constant and inevitable unfolding of the natural world.

THE ORIGINAL THREE

By the time King Eanatum of Lagash celebrated his victory over Umma (one
hundred years before Sargon) by commissioning the remarkable Stele of the
Vultures, Ninhursag was already one of the three great gods. In the inscription on the Stele, Eanatum claims Ninhursag as his mother: "Ninhursaga gave
birth to him. Ninhursaga rejoiced in Eanatum."[68] She, Enlil, and An were the
ruling triad. An was the supreme god of heaven, the original dispenser of the
apportioned elements that made up civilization that the Sumerians called

the **me** (may). Enlil, as god of wind between heaven and earth, ruled humanity as kingmaker and was intimately involved in law and politics. Ninhursag held double-edged authority over nature, wild and tame. She was the mistress of wild nature. The "hursag" of her name, the stony ground of the foothills, spanned the inhospitable rocky slopes on the mountainous eastern border of the country. Wild animals were her children. She cried when "her sons, wild asses, perished in the inhospitable wilds or [were] lost to human captors," and she bewails their loss: "I am a mother who has given birth. I was mated in vain, was kissed in vain, was delivered of a sound young in vain."[69]

And yet, nature penetrates civilization. As its mistress, Ninhursag presides over human life and death. She is a great mother goddess who attends human birth in all its aspects. All stages of the birth process were monitored by Ninhursag under her various names (sometimes perceived as separate goddesses): Nintur, Lady Birth; Aruru, germ-loosener, who initiates labor; Ninsigsig, the Lady of Silence, who maintains silence around the birthing mother so that a bad omen will not be spoken; Mudkeshda, the blood stauncher; Amadugbad, mother spreading the knees; and finally, Amaududa, mother who has given birth.[70] Of the three ruling deities, Ninhursag commands the mystery of life coming from life, in the human realm as well as the wild world of nature.

A WOMB DARK AND DEEP

Like Shuzianna's in Temple Hymn 6, Ninhursag's temple is women's domain. The temple itself is "the form-shaping place." Its inside "is a womb dark and deep." The very form shaping is made sacred in the dark womb of the temple. The Sumerian word for womb, arhuš, also means compassion. Thus, the instinctual bonding and love of a mother for her newborn became the prototype for human caring and compassion. Ninhursag is called Aruru, the germ-loosener who initiates the labor process: "Princess of Silence . . . / when she speaks, heaven shakes / open-mouthed, she roars." Ninhursag straddles the chasm between silence and the heaven-shaking roar. Silence protects the birthing mother from careless words that might harm the infant; Ninhursag's roar mimics the cries of pain. Her attributes extend over the entire birth process.

In the dark of the womblike temple, Ninhursag as Nintur, Lady Birth, makes this place beautiful. Nintur lends her blessings of a successful birth to what was undoubtedly a terrifying and often deadly process. From the time of the earliest evidence, the Sumerians held human and animal birth sacred. Ancient cylinder seals from Uruk depict a reed birth hut that underscores

5.6.   Archaic Uruk sign for tur. After Labat, 1995.
Courtesy of Editions GEUTHNER, Paris.

5.7.   Sacred byre with beribboned
standard, seal impression, Uruk period.
After Goff, 1963. Courtesy of Berlin-
Brandenburgische Akademie der
Wissenschaften.

the reverence surrounding the birth process. The earliest pictographic sign
for tur (birth), an element of Nintur's name, was a drawing thought to be a
birth hut.[71]

Beatrice Goff, describing an early Uruk depiction of the reed hut, emphasizes its ritual aspect. Of a seal impression, she says, "Two calves emerge from
the byre, and at either side is a beribboned standard."[72] The "beribboned standard" on the seal is the sign of the goddess Inanna (Temple Hymns 16, 26,
40). Drawn on a clay tablet, this symbol is the original pictograph and later
cuneiform sign of Inanna's name. Goff concludes that the inclusion of Inanna's
symbol on the seal confirms that the byre was a sacred area. Hallo and van
Dijk concur with Goff, saying, "The graphic representation of the holy stall
. . . with the symbol of Inanna belongs to the oldest Sumerian pictorial repertoire. This sacred stall may even have served as a kind of 'lying-in hospital' for
women."[73]

As writing developed in the late Uruk period, the sacred byre, originally
depicted on cylinder seals, was among the earliest cuneiform signs on clay
tablets found in the Inanna temple in Uruk. Nintur, as the goddess of birth,
carries the sacred aspect of the birth process even in the original writing of
her name.

GODDESS OF KESH

The city of Kesh has not been located. However, its association with the pantheon at the city of Adab suggests the two cities were neighbors. Adab is known to have been on the large Iturungal canal. Kesh and Adab were connected by water, possibly by a side canal off the Iturungal. Kesh was the more dominant city and the principal site of the Ninhursag temple. In Temple Hymn 29 to Ninhursag at Adab, her son Ashgi is mentioned prominently, as though he resided in Adab. Temple Hymn 39, also written to Ninhursag, praises her as "midwife of heaven and earth" and exalts her ability to give birth to kings. Three hymns to Ninhursag in the collection, a distinction shared only by the goddess Inanna and the moon god Nanna, accentuate her prominence in the pantheon.

A predecessor to Temple Hymn 7 is the ancient "Hymn to Kesh." This hymn is one of the oldest pieces of literature in existence, discovered at the site of Abu Salabikh in the Oriental Institute's excavations in 1964–66. The finds there date to the second half of the third millennium and possibly earlier.[74] The hymn was carefully copied in the Old Babylonian period, c. 1894–1595 BCE, and, according to Robert Biggs, who compared the earlier version with the later, "there is a surprisingly small amount of deviation (except in orthography) between them."[75]

This ancient Kesh hymn is preserved on some thirty-six tablets and fragments from the Old Babylonian period, and three of them contain almost the entire hymn.[76] The hymn is long, 132 lines, compared with the 13 lines of Temple Hymn 7. In the Kesh hymn Enlil praises the temple with metaphor and description. Its complex structure houses vast storerooms and occupies a sizeable number of people. Nisaba, goddess of writing (TH 42), took down the words of Enlil that make up the hymn to Kesh and wrote them on a tablet held in her hands.

The parallels between the Kesh hymn and the Temple Hymn to Ninhursag at Kesh are striking. Nintur figures prominently in both, as a birth goddess, as does her brick of birth, a well-documented accompaniment to the birth process. In the Akkadian myth of *Atrahasis*, according to Anne Draffkorn Kilmer, a brick accompanied the creation of the original deities and "was also prescribed to be present at the subsequent first incidence of the birth of a human baby."[77] Kilmer examines the symbolic significance of the brick and suggests that it was "likened to placental material. . . . The fetus may have been thought of as the product that developed in and from the malleable, clay-like placenta."[78] She concludes, "The *idea* of the brick was a highly significant symbol of the construction of life and of civilized existence as well."[79]

Both the Kesh hymn and the Temple Hymn mention that divination determined the fateful building of the temple, the Kesh hymn saying, "Given an oracle by mother Nintu,"[80] and Temple Hymn 7, "incantations fixed you in place." Both hymns connect the cities of Kesh and Aratta. Aratta was a legendary city often linked with Kesh and renowned for its gold and jewels, particularly its lapis lazuli. It was also honored for its wisdom. In both hymns the temple is crowned, and in both it rises to the heavens as well as reaching to the depths of the earth. Temple Hymn 7 speaks of the inner dark womb of the temple, whereas the Kesh hymn says, "Temple at whose interior is the vital center of the country."[81] The strength of the tradition surrounding the principal Sumerian goddesses and gods is well illustrated in the two hymns, separated in time, but both, with their significant parallels, carefully preserved for hundreds of years after their first appearance.

NINHURSAG LOSES HER PLACE

The three great gods, An, Enlil, and Ninhursag, dominated the pantheon from the time of Eanatum throughout the Sargonic era and well into the Isin-Larsa period, 2000–1800 BCE. At some point Enki's name began to appear among them, so that the three great gods became four. Over time, when the great gods were mentioned, Enki's name preceded that of Ninhursag, and eventually he replaced her altogether.

Why this replacement took place can only be conjectured. Women's influence in the polis may have diminished, along with that of the mother goddesses.[82] Ninhursag was a nature deity. Humans had little control over her domain, and nature with its wild power—floods, drought, and dangers ascribed to the unknown, not to mention the perils of childbirth—threatened the economic structure. The growing state may have allied itself with the gods who commanded aggression and power.

In the next group of hymns the moon god and his cohorts claim their earthly dominion. Divinity is in the moon, is the moon, in the form of its god, Nanna. Divinity enters the high priestess as she becomes the god's wife, Ningal. Enheduanna watched over the divine prerogative from her quarters in the moon god's formidable temple in the ancient and revered city of Ur.

chapter 6

HYMNS TO TEMPLES IN AND NEAR UR

Temple Hymns 8 to 12 are written to temples in and around the ancient city of Ur, one of the few cities in Mesopotamia whose name is commonly familiar today. According to the Bible, Abraham, the revered patriarch of Judaism, Islam, and Christianity, lived in the city of Ur as a young man, as did his wife, Sarah. Five years after the Babylonian king Hammurabi (1792–1750) established his empire and set up his capital city at Babylon, Abraham's father, Terah, moved his entire family north to the city of Harran. Abraham and Sarah lived in the family compound at Harran before moving to Caanan.

Abraham's intriguing origin in the Sumerian city of Ur raises questions of the influence of Sumerian religious beliefs and practices on the founder of Judaism. David Rosenberg, in his imagined biography of Abraham, portrays a devout man, "trained in classical Sumerian," the scribal as well as the theological traditions.[1] At the time Abraham lived in Ur, the daily worship of the Sumerian gods was in decline, and the prominence of the city of Ur was fading. In the earlier Sumerian period, the deities in the temples were the constant focus of worshipers, whose lives were held within the mythological structure of Sumerian religion. The drama of the boundary between the human and the divine was acted out in the Sumerian temples. In his book Rosenberg describes Abraham's motivation: "It was the living boundary between this world and the divine; between the rational and the irrational; between ancient Sumer and his own epoch, that impelled him to move on . . . to Canaan. Here he would restore the old by forging something new, a profoundly new cosmic theater with Yahweh at its heart."[2] The Abraham Rosenberg portrays first transported

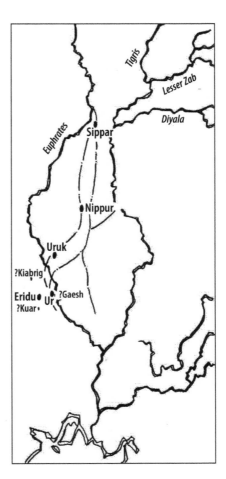

6.1.   Sketch map of Mesopotamia with Ur and neighboring cities. After Postgate, 1994. Reproduced by permission of Taylor and Francis Books U.K.

his intense involvement in the daily enactment in the Sumerian temples, "the daily encounters with the cosmic realm," north to Harran[3]: "His education, his personal and cultural history in Ur and Harran . . . are seeds he is carrying to begin a new history, one whose unfolding is part of the cosmic narrative. . . . It is all portable because it lies within: it is in his education."[4] From Harran, Abraham and Sarah moved east to Canaan, and there, "the Covenant," Rosenberg says, "was established between Abraham and his God in order to keep that boundary clear [between the human and the divine]."[5] He makes the simple assertion, "Judaism had to have a precursor. It was, of course, Sumerian."[6]

The location of Abraham's and Sarah's origin in Ur attracts particular interest in the five ancient Temple Hymns written to deities in and near Ur. Temple Hymn 8 is written to the Ekishnugal temple of the moon deity Nanna. Within Nanna's temple compound, Enheduanna lived her long life as high priestess to Nanna. At the end of Temple Hymn 9 is a statement that it is "the extra one." Temple Hymn 9 was added to the original corpus by the prominent Ur III king Shulgi several hundred years after Enheduanna's death. In the hymn, Shulgi declares himself a god, residing in the Ekishnugal in Ur. Hymn 10 celebrates a temple of Enki's son Asarluhi in Kuar and emphasizes the long relationship between Enki and Nanna. Nanna's son Ningublam is the subject of Temple Hymn 11. Hymn 12 is also written to Nanna, recounting his ritual return from Gaesh back to his main temple in Ur.

The five Ur hymns take us back to a time before the three present-day major religions had been conceived. Ur for the Sumerians was a major center of the practice of their beliefs and ritual and remained a vital center for hundreds of years after Enheduanna. Ur continues to the present day to be a city engraved in our consciousness as a holy place of origin.

TEMPLE HYMN 8

THE UR TEMPLE OF NANNA
Ekishnugal

O Ur
    breed bulls standing
    in the watery reed brake

white stone Ekishnugal
    calf of a great cow
    grain-eater of holy heaven

Wild Cow   a snare sprawled over a nest
Ur   first-fruit-eater of all lands
shrine in a pure place   An's first piece of earth
O house of Suen
    "princely" fits your front side
    "kingly" suits your back

at your feast, the adab hymns
holy drums   metal ub and leather-covered ala
fill your banquet hall

6.2.   Crescent moon symbol of Nanna. Courtesy
of the University of Texas Press, Jeremy Black and
Anthony Green, *Gods, Demons and Symbols of Ancient
Mesopotamia*, Tessa Richards, illustrator, 1995.

your emanating light
your faithful lordship
(are) precious things

(in) the gipar   the priestess' rooms
    that princely shrine of pure creation's elements
they track the passage of the days

Ekishnugal
waning moonlight spreads over the homeland
the sweeping light of midday fills every country
house   your shining face is
the great snake of the reed marsh

O shrine   your foundation
    the fifty abzus
    the seven seas
has plumbed the inner workings of the gods

your prince
    decision maker
    crown of wide heaven
he   Ashimbabbar   king of heaven
O Ur shrine
has built this house on your radiant site
and placed his seat upon your dais.

    17 lines for the house of Nanna at Ur

THE TEMPLE OF NANNA AT UR

Temple Hymn 8, written to the moon god's temple at Ur, carries a significance
beyond the others. First, this particular manifestation of the moon god around
2300 BCE is a single instance in a long tradition of moon worship, dating

back to the preliterate Near East and beyond. Second, Sargon, the northern Akkadian-speaking king, combating the antagonism and sometimes open rebellion of the southern Sumerian cities, chose the moon god's temple at Ur as the place to send his daughter, Enheduanna, as the honored high priestess of Nanna, to be the earthly manifestation of Nanna's spouse, Ningal. His appointment of Enheduanna respected the Sumerian cultural tradition whose entire ceremonial year was based on the progression of the moon.

THE HIGH PRIESTESS AT UR

The moon god Nanna was the firstborn son of Ninlil and Enlil, engendered when Enlil met Ninlil by the Nunbirdu canal.[7] In this hymn Nanna is called "calf of a great cow," a reference to his venerable mother, Ninlil. The prestige of the moon god was widespread in the Sargonic period, made even greater by Sargon himself when he appointed Enheduanna to be the moon god's high priestess.

Enheduanna lived in the temple at Ur for the almost forty years of her tenure as high priestess. The temple was the site of her life as she took on the role of Ningal. She called herself nin-dinger, godly lady. While there may have been priestesses in Ur before her, Enheduanna virtually created the office of the en, or high priestess, during her tenure. Mark Hall, in his study of the moon god, emphasizes her importance: "The most significant activity undertaken by the kings of Akkad and their successors for the cult of the moon-god was the installation of the En-priestess at Ur. The first and foremost representative of this priesthood was Enheduanna, the daughter of Sargon, founder of the Akkad dynasty."[8]

For five hundred years after Enheduanna's death, a daughter (or sister) of the king was appointed to the position of high priestess to the moon god at Ur, a position and a tradition that Enheduanna shaped during her Ur residence. After Enheduanna's death, the high priestess who succeeded her was Enmenana, the daughter of her nephew, the powerful king Naram-Sin. As tribute to his daughter's importance, after she was chosen by oracle, Naram-Sin gave her name to the year of her appointment. That Enmenana's appointment was the most significant event of the year bears witness to the prestige of the office of the high priestess that over her tenure Enheduanna had established. A clay tablet found at Ur bears the following inscription:

Naram-Sin, king of the four quarters:
En-men-ana, *zirru* priestess of the god Nanna.

spouse of the god Nanna,
entu priestess of the god Sin at Ur,
is his daughter[9]

TRACKING THE PASSAGE OF THE MOON

In addition to being the most influential religious personage in the country, the high priestess in Nanna's temple inherited the important role of reckoning time. The Sumerians tracked the moon's course daily and monthly and marked its position in relation to the sun and other celestial bodies. The calendar and all that it implied, the seasons, the designation of planting and harvesttime, the festivals connected to agriculture and to religious beliefs, were calculated by the position of the moon in its cycle. The beginning of every month was fixed by an individual or individuals charged with sighting the new crescent at twilight on the western horizon. Only then did the month begin.

The long history of Sargon's Semitic ancestors' worship of the moon deity enables us to understand the respect he showed toward the moon god's temple in Ur. In the first recorded calendars throughout the Near East, time was set according to the cycles of the moon. These moon-determined calendars were widespread from northwest Syria to south-central Iraq. The archeologist Hildegard Lewy, speaking of the moon god, says, "He was worshiped and had sanctuaries wherever Semites settled or traveled. . . . In the Lebanon, the moon was worshiped as Laban, 'The White One,' . . . In Palestine, one of his holy cities was Hazor, in the Arabian peninsula among others, Tema and Hureidha."[10] For the Assyrians the moon, visible everywhere to all peoples, had the prominence of a universal god, and the cycles of dominance of the various planets, they believed, would eventually end with "the moon-god's rule which then would last for ever."[11]

By 2600 BCE, the three names of the moon god in Mesopotamia, Nanna, Suen (Sin), and Ashimbabbar, were all in wide use, evidence of the popularity of his cult. Hall suggests that the power and influence of Sargon's empire gave the final impetus to the fusion of the three, "involving what were probably three separate local moon gods and a long period of syncretism and historical development stretching far back into the pre-literate phase."[12] Given Nanna's long association with cattle and herding, the antiquity of moon worship, Hall says, may reach to "the pre-settled stage of Mesopotamia when nomadic groups made their living by grazing their herds on the steppe."[13] By the time of written records, the complex and well-established traditions in the Ur temple and the number of personnel serving the moon god bear witness to its great antiquity.

The Mesopotamians at this early stage were well aware of the difference between sun time and moon time. Major festivals marked the sun-determined equinox. The year began at the spring equinox, and a significant midyear celebration at the autumn equinox came six months later. Many communities, acknowledging the equinoctial passage, held major festivals in the first and the seventh months.

The Assyriologist Mark Cohen postulates that the Mesopotamians' reliance on the moon to denote the passage of time stems from their need to define a period shorter than a season or a year, periods controlled by the sun. Cohen says, "This was a somewhat contrived means — man could not intuitively sense the moon's effect upon him as he could the sun's — but the moon was a dependable means for reckoning elapsed time."[14] With the necessary intercalation to fit the lunar year with the solar, Cohen remarks, "the Mesopotamian year was, in effect, a solar year squeezed into a lunar strait-jacket."[15] "The Mesopotamians," Cohen continues, "unswervingly adhered to fixing all annual festivals to the lunar cycle, even if this meant that the observance would not coincide exactly with the solar or seasonal event being celebrated."[16]

THE MOON AND SYMBOLIC CULTURE

The moon god was worshiped throughout the Near East. For the Assyrians he was "the prototype of a universal god," who in the recurrent movement of the stars would eventually rise to a position of dominance that would last forever.[17] Some understanding of the ancient history of moon worship in other cultures may shed light on the moon's prominence in the ancient Near East.

Evidence of the moon's significance in ancient cultures appears as early as the Upper Paleolithic period, 28,000–10,000 BCE. Alexander Marschack deciphered archeological evidence of markings on hundreds of animal bones, tusks, and horns as "calendars" tracking the procession of the moon's phases over months, sometimes years of time. The widespread Paleolithic occurrence of the moon calendars across present-day Europe led Marschack to conclude that the moon and its phases were central to these ancient people and the basis of a cultural belief and a story that revolved around the phases of the moon.[18]

A number of writers, archeologists, and anthropologists have taken a step further in an attempt to explain the evidence of the prominence of the moon in early cultures. These authors speculate that the human acquisition of the ability to symbolize may have been focused on the moon, particularly on its correspondence with women's menstrual cycles. The poet and philosopher

Judy Grahn[19] and the British anthropologist Chris Knight[20] both describe the moon-related ritual of menstrual seclusion practices as a crucial building block in the securing of symbolic consciousness and the creation of culture. Because these rituals are almost universal in the groups studied in the past few centuries, they are thought to have very ancient origin.[21]

Knight places the human acquisition of the capacity to symbolize within the past seventy thousand years. Both Knight and Grahn painstakingly describe the creative influence of menstrual seclusion on culture formation. Knight says, "Women's menstrual self-identity was the generative source of all culture's other basic categories, polarities and rules."[22] Grahn leads us carefully through the logic of the taboos imposed by menstruation as well as the cultural constructs such as dress, body markings, the proscribed use of everyday utensils, tools, and weapons, and the foundation of cultural institutions that are connected to menstrual observances.

While the influence of "menstrual logic" on the formation of culture may have been long forgotten by the Semitic moon worshipers in the Near East, its presence is implicit as a factor in their reliance on the cycles of the moon to form the cultic year. The moon in Mesopotamian culture was the key to their conceptualization of the division of time. Each month began at the first sighting of the new crescent at sunset. On the first, seventh, and fifteenth days of every month, days corresponding to the phases of the waxing moon, they held observances called the eš-eš festival or "all temple" celebration. These and other observances were constant reminders that they lived inside a natural rhythm whose ebb and flow was dictated by the moon.

In Mesopotamia Nanna was worshiped as a god of fertility and generativity. The dependable cycles of the moon, the light that returns month after month from three days of darkness, were celebrated as assurance that Nanna would shower his blessings of cyclic favors on all people. The widespread occurrence of moon worship pertains to an experience of a reliable cyclic rhythm in which human beings are held: menstrual cycles recur; human and animal gestation proceeds; crops grow, flourish, and die. Human beings respond to the given rhythms by marking these tidal events and celebrating the fluctuations with festivals and observances that organize culture inside the larger world of nature. Nanna is the one god who alone exerts his profound influence on the calendar to set the year in motion. He is the one, as the Sumerians say, iti u_4-sakar gi-né mu ki-bi-šè an-[gar]: "[Nanna], fixing the month and the new moon, [setting] the year in its place."[23]

THE MOON GOD'S TEMPLE

Temple Hymn 8 begins with a salutation to the temple, calling it "Ur." "O Ur," the hymn says, as though city and temple are one. Following this greeting, the poet recites epithets of the temple that equate it to the moon god. Temple, city, and god are treated as interchangeable divine beings. The moon is implicit in the temple's name, Ekishnugal. While the name is obscure, it relates to alabaster, which glistens like the white light of the moon. The temple is characterized as bull, calf, and wild cow, evoking Nanna's role as guardian of the herds and perhaps his role in preliterate time as protector of the nomadic shepherds.

The city, Ur, is singled out as "first-fruit-eater of all lands" and "An's first piece of earth." These epithets refer to Ur as the city of the first gods, the primeval city from the dawn of cosmology. An is mentioned here in his role as one of the original god pair, An and Ki, heaven and earth. In other literary texts An is portrayed as the father of Nanna.[24] The moon god is not referred to in the hymn by his Sumerian name, Nanna. He is called Suen and Ashimbabbar. The house of Suen, his Semitic name, is princely and kingly. His Sumerian name, Nanna, is used only in the line count at the end of the poem. This seemingly arbitrary use of his three names suggests that the three once-separate moon gods are now one.

Typically in the Temple Hymns, a section of narrative descriptions follow the initial epithets. The narratives in this hymn describe both festive activity in the temple and cultic duties in the gipar. First, a banquet is held in an atmosphere filled with music. The adab hymns praise the temple, its precious light, and its faithful lord.

Mention of the gipar and the activities there suggest Enheduanna's hand in this hymn. The high priestesses were the dominant figures in the moon god's temple from the time of Sargon. Their residence in the gipar established it as the center of cultic activity. The hymn describes the gipar as "that princely shrine of pure creation's elements," èš-nun-me-kù-ga. There, the hymn tells us, "they" watch or track the passage of the days, $u_4z[al]$.[25] Then, intriguingly, the next two lines mention the moon and sun, the two heavenly timekeepers. Moon and sun are the crucial arbiters of time. Their cycles must be carefully observed and somehow reconciled in order to honor them equally and contain the cultic year. These lines suggest that astronomical observations took place in the gipar, that the high priestess and her cohorts, steeped in the knowledge of the heavenly cycles of creation's elements, kept track of the moon's phases, in this hymn the waning moon. And they note the sweeping light of

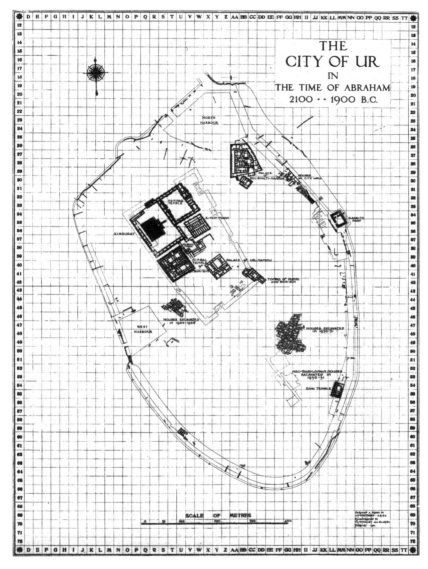

6.3. City Plan of Ur. Courtesy of the Penn Museum, image #149968.

the sun that dependably shines throughout the land and beyond. The lines emphasize the role of the high priestess in maintaining order as decreed by the **me,** the cosmic elements that constitute the universe. With her connection to the divinity, she was the intermediary between earth and heaven and led the proper observances that pleased the gods.

The temple is the great primordial snake. In some mythology this is the world snake that supports the universe. The shining face of the house is the awesome snake itself. Nanna is not typically associated with the snake, although he is sometimes called ušumgal, a mythical snake that is connected to the great archetypal snake in other literature.[26]

The hymn says that the temple's foundation reaches "the fifty abzus / the seven seas." At this unfathomable depth the temple touches the very heart of the gods and understands them. Nanna travels to the underworld for three days of each month, leaving the night sky dark, lightless.

Finally, he is Ashimbabbar, who holds the auspicious power of deciding fates. He is "crown of wide heaven," an epithet related to the crescent moon at first sighting. In Mesopotamia the crescent appears to be horizontal, like the horns of a bull or the double-horned crowns seen on depictions of their deities.

The Mesopotamian calendar was embedded in the ebb and flow of the moon's cycles. Even though the Sumerians had, by Enheduanna's time, constructed an impressive urban culture, they continued to live their lives inside the beliefs and rituals that had developed from an earlier relationship to the natural world. It was the moon's cycles they followed throughout the ritual year. This essential understanding set the moon god Nanna apart from the other gods, since moon time, as noted above, was fundamental to the structure of their lives and culture.

TEMPLE HYMN 9

THE UR TEMPLE OF SHULGI
Ehursag

O Emumah   house [of the] lofty name
high-lying mountain of heaven

precious is the holy base   pure, your great foundation
the heart inside fills with measureless princely forces
glows a shining light

O shrine
your outside a verdant height
your visible facade (touches) all people
binding the land in a single path
a mighty river   opening wide its mouth
gathering widespread cosmic powers

at your root is great terror
faithful mountain raised in the broad plain
your lofty dwelling is a mighty thing
(with) all cosmic powers of princeship
a broad and central mountain
a vast gathering storm rumbles

O house, flowing luxuriance
the sight of you gladdens the inhabitants

O house, your prince Shulgi
has made it great among the princes
the noble one on the throne   imposing strong wind
graced (with) cosmic powers for deciding fates
O Ehursag, heaven's own Shulgi
has built this house on your radiant site
and established his seat upon your dais

    14 lines, the extra ones, for the Ehursag house of Shulgi at Ur

THE TEMPLE OF SHULGI AT UR

A reader with knowledge of the ancient Near East would pause over this hymn. Shulgi? The Ur III king? A statement at the end of each of the Temple Hymns tells the reader the number of lines in the poem. At the end of Hymn 9 we read, "14 lines, the extra ones, for the Ehursag house of Shulgi at Ur." Only for this hymn does the line count include a descriptive identification of the hymn: the lines of Temple Hymn 9 are "extra ones." Shulgi lived in Ur and worshiped the moon god Nanna, but he was a mortal who lived and died several hundred years after Enheduanna put together the corpus of the Temple Hymns. This hymn, as the line count states, is a later addition.

THE KING WHO WOULD BE A GOD

Some years after the fall of the last Old Akkadian king, a local governor of Ur successfully expanded his territory into a kingdom and made Ur his capital. His name was Ur-Nammu. When he died an early death, his young son Shulgi became king. Gradually, Shulgi built a flourishing state, expanding its economic prosperity and enhancing its religious and cultural institutions. Several hundred years after Enheduanna's death, during the Ur III period, or the Third Dynasty of Ur, 2112–2004 BCE, Shulgi came to rule as king over a large territory in both southern and northern Mesopotamia.

Shulgi's first twenty years as ruler were dedicated to building the prosperity of his empire, and in the years following he embarked on military campaigns to enlarge his territory. His accomplishments were phenomenal. He increased the agricultural yields at the temples and encouraged industrial production. He divided the areas of production into regional specializations and had the products collected into large depots for distribution. These changes were overseen by a huge bureaucracy that reported to the central government in Ur. He standardized weights and measures and established a unified calendar. He organized a judicial system and a banking system. The empire was thriving, and the changes these innovations required were felt throughout the culture. Significantly, the temples now came under the domination of the royal government, thus losing much of their independence and power in the culture.

In his tenth year of rule Shulgi built an elaborate palace he named Ehursag, which later became the temple where he was worshiped as a god. Possibly his addition of this hymn to the Temple Hymns occurred at this time. Jacob Klein says, "Indeed a Third Dynasty edition of the ancient Collection of Temple Hymns, probably composed by Sargon's daughter Enkheduanna, was augmented by a new hymn dedicated to the Ekhursag, which became now a temple."[27]

Shulgi may have been imitating Naram-Sin, the Sargonic king and Enheduanna's nephew, who was the first Mesopotamian ruler to declare himself a god. Being god and ruler in one necessitated changes in the religious practices and beliefs. However, following the tradition initiated by Sargon, in the fifteenth year of his reign Shulgi appointed his daughter high priestess to the moon god Nanna. Her priestly name was Ennirzianna, which means "trustworthy, faithful priestess of heaven." The Sumerian word nir incorporated into her name means 'sovereign' or 'trust' and is a frequent epithet of Nanna. This high priestess's name, like that of Enheduanna, "jewel of heaven," refers to Nanna in his celestial aspect and relates him to An, the god of heaven.[28]

As Shulgi promulgated his divinity, he said his parents were the goddess Ninsun and the legendary hero Lugalbanda. Since these two were the parents of the hero Gilgamesh, Shulgi claimed Gilgamesh as a brother. He further took the place of the semidivine Dumuzi, spouse of Inanna, in the sacred marriage ritual (Temple Hymns 16 and 17). As Inanna's husband, Shulgi became as well the tutelary god of Uruk, Inanna's city.

LITERATURE IN SHULGI'S UR

The period of Shulgi's long reign was one of a literary flowering. Even though the Sumerian language was no longer spoken, it was esteemed as the language of literature and continued to be learned and used by the literate elite. The court scribes copied and carefully preserved Sumerian literature from the past, and the court poets created many outstanding works for the kings. En-heduanna's Temple Hymns were among the corpus of valued works copied by the scribes.

Shulgi's insertion of his own hymn into the corpus of Temple Hymns, a hymn praising himself, tells us, first of all, that the Sumerian Temple Hymns were part of the literary canon at that time. Numerous copies must have existed, probably from the curriculum of the scribal schools. The learned of the society would have been familiar with them. Second, it tells us that Shulgi had the power to insert a creation of his own court poets into a well-known ancient and revered composition. His motives, we can surmise, were to enhance his prestige, to augment his potential legacy, and to add one more bit of evidence to his claim of divinity.

The flourishing of literature that developed in Ur III supported Shulgi's claims. Klein notes, "The ideology of divine kingship also gave rise to a varie-gated corpus of royal literature in which this ideology was based and ex-pounded. It included votive and historical inscriptions, royal hymns, royal prayers, and all kinds of Wisdom literature."[29] Klein counts some twenty royal hymns of Shulgi so far discovered, written by Shulgi's court poets. In these hymns, "the king proper is the principal object of the praise and is addressed as a divinity."[30]

SHULGI'S TEMPLE HYMN

The Shulgi hymn, Temple Hymn 9, stands out as markedly different from the other hymns. While the hymns vary from one to another, they tend to follow a certain pattern that is absent from the Shulgi hymn. This usual pattern gives the hymns an expected rhythm that the reader begins to anticipate in moving from hymn to hymn. The pattern has three parts. The beginning lines tend to be addressed to the é, the temple itself, "O house" frequently being the first words of the hymn. This section offers a description of the temple, its purpose, reciting what is unique there. Section two frequently calls the city or the temple by name and continues with a description of the building, using its epithets. The third part may begin 'your prince' or 'your princess' and then describes the god's unique identifying characteristics and says how he or she relates to other gods. Each hymn ends with recognition that the god or goddess built the house, concluding with the familiar colophon.

The Shulgi hymn begins "O Emumah," which translates as "house of the lofty name"; it does not use the name of the temple, Ehursag, until the end, and it does not mention the city Ur at all. The majority of the lines describe and praise the temple and its powers. The lines include many of the elements used in the other hymns, descriptions of its foundation, its formidable interior, its facade, the terror it inspires. The lines that describe the influence of the sight of the temple on the inhabitants are striking, particularly the following verse:

> your outside a verdant height
> your visible facade (touches) all people
> binding the land in a single path
> a mighty river   opening wide its mouth
>   gathering widespread cosmic powers

These lines and the phrase "the sight of you / gladdens the inhabitants," portray Shulgi's mesmerizing influence on his people. The lines and the closing adulation — "the noble one on the throne," "imposing strong wind," "cosmic powers for deciding fates" — elevate the king to the heights of the deities in the other hymns.

While the assignment of authorship of the Temple Hymns is disputed, the Shulgi hymn unquestionably was not written by Enheduanna. Even though other hymns, such as the hymn to Nanna at Gaesh, are unlikely to be hers, this hymn is the only one whose style is markedly different.

TEMPLE HYMN 10

THE KUAR TEMPLE OF ASARLUHI
    O city
        squeezed out of the abzu
        like barley oil

a plain   heavy with clouds
pulling cosmic powers from the dense mist

in Kuar   true sanctuary of your foundation
the Lord   not hoarding his bounty
goes about in wonder
the Seven Wise Ones
made it grow in your name
top to bottom

your prince most treasured prince
Asarluhi   all-powerful one
hero born to be a prince
young lion who snatches his prey
like a battering storm he gores the traitors' land
as long as they rebel he spits on them   all over
Asar-alim-nunna   bison of the prince by name
son of the abzu
O house of Kuar
has built this house on your radiant site
and placed his seat upon your dais

    11 lines for the house of Asarluhi in Kuar

THE TEMPLE OF ASARLUHI IN KUAR

The hymn to Asarluhi's temple in Kuar appears as number three in the sequence of temples connected to the moon god Nanna at Ur. Shulgi inserted his
hymn into the honored second place following the Temple Hymn to Nanna.
King of Ur, Shulgi bowed only to the prestigious god of Ur, declaring himself
a second god in the capital city of his empire. The hymn to Asarluhi, now in
third place, must have followed the hymn to Nanna in the original sequence.
Disregarding the hymn to Shulgi, we ask, who was Asarluhi to merit the honor
of second place to Nanna?

NANNA AND ENKI

Asarluhi is best known for his relationship to his father, Enki. His temple is
in Kuar, a village just south of Eridu, Enki's home. The placing of Asarluhi
among the gods connected to Nanna strengthens the tie between Nanna and
Enki, a relationship apparent as far back as the pre-Sargonic Early Dynastic

period. In an early calendar from that era, one of the months bore a name that included both gods, Nanna and Enki.

Ur, Eridu, and Kuar are not far apart geographically. Mark Hall says, "It is known from many attestations in literary texts, inscriptions, and offering-lists that there were considerable cultic connections between Ur and Eridu."[31] Before the legendary flood in Mesopotamian history, the seven antediluvian sages "were originally linked with Eridu," William Hallo says, the same Seven Wise Ones who appear in this hymn as creators of the temple in Kuar.[32] The archeologist Max Mallowan reports that in the excavations of the Early Dynastic Ehursag, Nanna's temple at Ur, an "abundance of vertical terra cotta ring-drains, far in excess of the requirements of any one building, may represent ritual arrangements for libations to the god Enki through the *apsu;* some of these drains contained deposits consisting of clay cups filled with animal bones."[33] In that era, Enki may have been an integral part of the ritual worship in Nanna's temple. Hall also presents what may be a hymn to the moon god in which Enki has a significant role performing cleansing rites for Nanna from the abzu.[34]

In this Temple Hymn Asarluhi is "born to be a prince" and has a byname, "bison of the prince," the prince being his father, Enki. The village of Kuar is near a sweet-water, marshy lake sometimes known as the abzu. The abzu is Enki's dwelling place, and Kuar is "squeezed out of the abzu," as though it barely found ground to stand on. The Sumerian verb *sur,* "squeezed," describes the process of pressing oil from barley. The temple of Asarluhi rises out of the fertile waters of Enki's domain. The placing of Asarluhi with Nanna aligns the important god Nanna with the Eridu theology that claims Enki as the creator god, shaping and naming the original abundant life that emerged from the abzu (see THI in chapter 4).

MAGIC AND INCANTATIONS

Asarluhi is best known as a master of magical powers that he acquired from Enki. In pre-Sargonic times, this power belonged to a goddess, Ningirim, an important deity in the Abu Salabikh and Fara texts. In her Temple Hymn 19, incantations are chanted in Ningirim's temple by the ishib priests, known to lead rites of exorcism. While Asarluhi is mentioned in the Early Dynastic period in relation to incantations, his prominence came later when he and Enki usurped these magical powers from Ningirim. Tikva Frymer-Kensky says the shift in power to Enki and Asarluhi from Ningirim is representative of "a constant direction to the movement, one in which the areas under goddess control are shrinking, with more and more occupations taken over by male gods."[35] The process of change in the Mesopotamian pantheon continued after the Sargonic period. With the rise of the Babylonian empire (1800–1600 BCE), Asarluhi became identified with Marduk, the god of the city of Babylon. To enhance his prestige, Marduk's priests distinguished him as the son of Enki, so that his name became interchangeable with that of Asarluhi, and he absorbed Asarluhi's characteristics.

Asarluhi and Enki were frequently called upon to perform their magic in relation to problems of love and potency and even over difficult births. One Old Babylonian incantation follows a typical pattern of Asarluhi calling on Enki for help, in this case for a young man who desires the affection of a young woman. "I do not know what to do in such a case," Asarluhi cries to his father. Enki, impatient, says, "What I know, you know too." Nevertheless, Enki proceeds to give the magic formula to his son, the formula being that the man sprinkle holy milk from a white cow on the breast of the maid. This type of dialogue between Asarluhi and Enki, later Marduk/Asarluhi and Ea (the Akkadian Enki), became a distinctive format of question and answer in magical incantations.[36]

THE GOD OF KUAR

Asarluhi's temple in Kuar is not given a name. Rather the hymn is written to the city itself and its surroundings in a plain. The Kuar sanctuary rises among heavy clouds. Its potency astounds as it pulls "cosmic powers from the dense mist." Asarluhi is connected to clouds and storms. Thorkild Jacobsen calls him a rain god.[37] In the hymn he is "like a battering storm." In his cloud-strewn temple in Kuar, "the Lord . . . goes about in wonder."

Although Asarluhi found prominence as Enki's son and cohort in magic and incantations, he is not listed in his temple in Kuar in the gazetteer of ceremonial names of temples. He is mentioned, however, in the gazetteer in four temples or chapels, three in Babylon and one in Assur.[38] In a pre-Sargonic hymn from Abu Salabikh (2550 BCE), he is praised as "ᵈasal-lú-KAL", deity of Ku'ara and son of the abzu.[39] Temple Hymn 10 also calls him nin-kal-kal, "most treasured prince," the repetition of the word kal providing emphasis on his quality of being precious, treasured, mighty, and strong. The use of the same phrase to describe Asarluhi and the location of the temple in Kuar in the Abu Salabikh hymn suggests that Temple Hymn 10 was following an old tradition.

As the Temple Hymn describes, Asarluhi's temple was made to grow in his name by the "Seven Wise Ones," creatures said to have "lived before the Flood"; they are sometimes pictured in "fish-garb" and sometimes as "winged figures with birds' faces."[40] These figures appear in later eras carved in stone as creatures conveying magical protective powers. These and other aspects mentioned in the hymn establish Asarluhi as a powerful, beneficent, and treasured god in the pantheon.

After the interruption of the Shulgi hymn, the hymn to Asarluhi and the remaining two hymns in the moon god's group from Ur fit an expected pattern. Ningublam in Temple Hymn 11 is Nanna's son, while the fourth hymn is to Nanna himself, in his neighboring temple in Gaesh.

TEMPLE HYMN 11

THE KIABRIG TEMPLE OF NINGUBLAM
Gabura

O house
   teeming with unblemished bulls
   whose king stands on precious stones
a towering trap   crown of the princely son
its finest oil is pure   preserving its sweetness
O Gabura   pure cattle pen
cows moving around the juniper plants

your prince   great wild bull
horned wild bull exulting in his vigor
wild cow growing horns   basking in his radiant horns
an incantation priest   knows different tongues
makes clouds go around in the sky
a storm roar in the heavens
sunlight strikes the earth

Ningublam   son of Nanna
has, O Kiabrig,
built this house on your radiant site
and placed his seat upon your dais

    10 lines for the house of Ningublam in Kiabrig

THE TEMPLE OF NINGUBLAM IN KIABRIG

Ningublam is a son of the moon god Nanna. He makes his appearance in the Temple Hymns among the gods of Ur, just after his "brother" Asarluhi. Ningublam is an even more obscure god than Asarluhi. His long and continuous association with Nanna goes back to the pre-Sargonic period and lasts throughout the Mesopotamian era.

COWS, BULLS, AND MAGIC

Nanna features prominently in the Temple Hymn to Ningublam. Surely he is the "king" who stands on the "precious stones." And he is the father of the "princely son" whose temple is the "crown." Nanna is the patron of the "pure cattle pen," the owner of the many cows.

Ningublam's temple in Kiabrig is lauded as "house / teeming with unblemished bulls," é.gu$_4$.du$_7$.šár, Egudushar. Unblemished bulls are unaltered bulls, those that have not been castrated. Ningublam is the "great wild bull" himself, "exulting in his vigor," "basking in his radiant horns." Obscure though he may be, Ningublam comes alive in the force of the poet's voice. The dominance of the bull alongside his herd of docile cows strolling among the juniper evokes a scene of placid order. Bounty and fecundity rest in the hands of the gods.

Ningublam became a protective deity of the Ekishnugal, his father Nanna's temple. Like his father, Ningublam is associated with herding. On a single tablet from ancient Abu Salabikh, a hymn to Ningublam follows immediately after a zà-mì (praise) hymn to Nanna. The Nanna hymn includes a long list of his livestock. The sequential placement on the tablet of the hymn to Ningublam again associates him closely in the earliest written literature with the care of Nanna's cattle.[41]

Ningublam, like Asarluhi, had magical power as an incantation priest. The hymn calls Ningublam a maš-maš priest. This type of priest took part in healing, in purification and exorcism, and in ritual incantations. Records of this priest occur from the Early Dynastic period all the way to Seleucid times in the third century BCE.[42] In the Temple Hymn Ningublam is said to know "different tongues." Did he understand a variety of languages? Or does this unusual capacity refer to his understanding of the language of magic or the silent language of animals and of nature? In a further enumeration of his uncanny powers, he is able to pull the clouds around in the sky and cause storms and even sunlight to fall on the earth. While Ningublam is not a well-known deity, he may have held more prominence as Nanna's son and as a divine incantation priest than the sparse records show.

THE WORSHIP AND CARE OF NINGUBLAM

This Temple Hymn is written to Ningublam's temple in the village of Kiabrig. In the ancient temple lists, his temple is known both as é.gu$_4$.du$_7$.šár, "House of Numerous Perfect Oxen" and as ğá.bur.ra, "Chamber of Jars."[43] In the first lines, the typical place in the hymns for the temple's name, it is called "house / teeming with unblemished bulls," egudushar. A few lines later, it is referred to as "Gabura," chamber of bowls or jars, a reference to offering or dedicatory bowls. Both names must apply to the temple at Kiabrig.

During the reign of the powerful nephew of Enheduanna, Naram-Sin, Ningublam received the king's honor in the form of two inscriptions. One praises Naram-Sin's widespread and unique territorial conquests, and the other includes his daughter, the en-priestess of Nanna at Ur, Enmenana; both inscriptions were created in devotion to Ningublam. Naram-Sin is named for the moon god, "Sin" being a form of the Akkadian name of the moon god Suen. To praise Ningublam would have been to praise the son of the moon god, which Naram-Sin, the king who declared himself a god, considered himself as well.

All the deities received daily offerings, called sá.du$_{11}$. On one accounting tablet, Ningublam was scheduled to receive flour and barley. On another he is to receive a "barley-fatted sheep" during the month called "ezen-an-na," month of the feast of An.[44] Indeed, the care and feeding of the gods must have occupied much of the time of the workers assigned to this task. The many tablets involved in recording the daily ration distributions are evidence of how time-consuming an occupation it was. The detailed records attest to the importance attached to this work. For example, one tablet says figs, honey and ghee, "a sá.du$_{11}$ . . . regular maintenance ration taken [as a cultic expenditure] for the purification ritual of Nanna [and] the minor deities and for the requirements of the great festival."[45] Ningublam was probably included in this offering as one of the minor deities connected to Nanna. One has only to multiply this record by the thousands of daily offerings and monthly festivals to imagine the enormity of effort that was put into the careful tending of the gods.

The "great festival" whose "requirements" are mentioned above would have been the akiti festival at Ur, held twice each year at the time of the equinox. The festival celebrated Nanna's triumphant return to his city of Ur from an outlying temple in Gaesh. Ningublam, Asarluhi, and all the gods of Ur would have made offerings to Nanna at this celebration, marking the grand reentrance of Nanna into Ur, a symbolic act of renewal. The cyclic new beginning came at the equinox, when night and day shared equal time. The next Temple Hymn is dedicated to Nanna's reentry into Ur from his akiti temple in Gaesh.

TEMPLE HYMN 12

THE GAESH TEMPLE OF NANNA
Karzida

O shrine   great princely house
firm, solid by the cattle pen
town Gaesh   Suen's shining amber

Karzida   the Good Wharf
your inside is a mighty place
your foundation   pure and clean

shrine
your gipar   [the high priestess's house]
readied for purifying rites

your copper door   a strong thing
set up in a great place
cattle pen house
you lift your horns high   bellow like a young stud

your prince lord of heaven
standing in joy
radiating the heat of noon
keeps on running [across the sky]
to the forefront

O Karzida   good wharf house
Ashimbabbar has built this house on your radiant site
and placed his seat upon your dais

     10 lines for the house of Nanna in Gaesh

THE TEMPLE OF NANNA AT GAESH

From the first written records in Sumer, a great festival celebrated the two auspicious days of the year when the moon and sun shared equally the hours of night and day. In the archeological record of Gaesh from the Sargonic era, excavators found evidence of this tradition, one that was already several hundred years old. This tradition confronted one of the most ancient human dilemmas: in the reckoning of time, how is it possible to reconcile the disparity between the two heavenly deities, the moon and the sun. In Sumer the vernal equinox in the spring when the two bodies had equal time marked the beginning of the calendrical year. Six months later in autumn, the auspicious day came again. Day and night were equal, and a second celebration marked the event. Each equinox was a beginning point in the year, not only in Mesopotamia, but throughout the Near East. Cohen says, "In many locations there were parallel major festivals in the first and seventh month[s]—suggesting that rather than considering one of these festivals as marking the beginning and the other the half-way point of the year, the ancients viewed each as a beginning, the onset of this 6-month equinox year."[46]

THE AKITI FESTIVAL

The celebration that was held for the equinox, both in the spring and in the fall, was called the akiti festival. The first mention of the term á-ki-ti occurs on a tablet from Shuruppak, ancient Fara. These Early Dynastic III tablets (2600–2350 BCE) are among the first readable texts that have been found and indicate that the akiti festival was observed in pre-Sargonic times at Ur and at Nippur.[47] In the Sargonic period during Enheduanna's lifetime, the akiti was celebrated "at Ur, Nippur, Adab, Uruk, and probably Badtibira."[48] Every indication suggests that the festival originated in Ur and was copied by the other cities. The festival began at the sighting of the new moon crescent on the first evening of the first month. This vernal akiti focused on the planting, while the akiti of the seventh month was a festival of harvest.

The spring akiti festival occurred at the beginning of the calendrical New Year. It lasted for five days, while the autumn festival lasted eleven days. Cohen speculates that the longer fall festival celebrated the onset of longer nights, increasing the time of visibility of the moon.[49] In Ur, cultic offerings in both spring and fall took place in three locations, at the Karzida temple in Gaesh, at the Ekishnugal temple in Ur, and also at the sanctuary of the Sacred Mound in Ur, the du$_6$-úr, the mound of origin "from which the gods and civilization sprang."[50]

The festival began with Nanna traveling by boat on a canal from his temple in Ur to the temple in Gaesh. Nanna traveled by night in the Boat of Heaven, the high-prowed má-gur$_8$ boat, shaped like the new crescent moon. This type of boat has been used continuously from ancient times to the present, being the chief means of transportation for the marsh Arabs of Iraq. He arrived at Karzida, "the Good Wharf." At daybreak the priests, priestesses, and others presented him with offerings.

Offerings were featured events in the celebration. Their presentation was frequently made at night, particularly "the Great Offering (sízkur-gu-la)."[51] Oxen, sheep, goats, lambs, various plants and reeds, dates, beer, ghee, cheese, flour, and confections of all kinds embellished the festivities as offerings to the gods as well as contributed to lavish meals for the participants. The elaborate festivities included official clothing for the oxen drivers and, as one tablet says, special garments for young girls who were singers.[52]

The culmination of the festivities came on the third day, when Nanna traveled back from the temple at Gaesh to his primary temple, the Ekishnugal in Ur. The entry of Nanna into his city from a location outside the gates gave the Gaesh temple its reason for being. The god returned triumphant. The arrival of Nanna at his city signified a new beginning at the turn of the year, a renewed dedication to order and prosperity. Cohen describes Nanna's "glorious reentry into his city":

> The statue of the god had to be escorted into the city with great pomp and circumstance. . . . [T]he god has just entered his city and been declared chief god of the city. And it was this procession, bringing the chief god into his city, that so captured the minds of the Mesopotamians and enabled the *akītu*-festival to proliferate, each city observing it for its own chief god . . . a procession . . . [that] captured the imagination of an entire civilization for over thirty-five hundred years.[53]

The Sumerian tradition of a deity embarking on a ritual journey is reported in numerous records. In his study of Nanna's travel to and from Gaesh, A. J. Ferrar refers to "a sizeable body of non-literary evidence" that refers to such journeys, saying these rituals "were a central and meaningful practice of the Sumerian cultus and ritual journeys of divine images or emblems are well-attested in offering lists of the Old-Sumerian [Akkadian] and Neo-Sumerian periods."[54]

The akiti festival was celebrated throughout Mesopotamia. Each city organized the festivities according to its needs, and the principal god of each city was the focus of the reentry. Whatever celebratory differences there were among the cities, the essence of the festival was based on the original Ur model. The concept appeared also in the cultic year of other Near Eastern cultures, the autumnal and vernal equinoxes, for example, being observed by the Hebrews as "the time when the year turns."[55] The significance of the observance kept it alive throughout the Mesopotamian era. One tablet records its celebration in Uruk in the third century BCE.

THE TEMPLE AT GAESH

The sole purpose of the akiti temple in Gaesh was to provide a temporary home for the god Nanna from which he could then make his journey back into his city. Gaesh may simply have been a suburb of Ur. Originally it seems to have been the location of Ur's stockyard. As the hymn says, the temple was "erected [or founded] by the cattle pen," as though the area grew around the activity of caring for and trading cattle.

Because the Ur III king Shulgi built a temple in Gaesh, he may also have instigated the insertion of this hymn into the corpus of the Temple Hymns. Records from the ninth year of the reign of Shulgi at Ur report the construction of the Karzida temple and the installation of Nanna in the temple. The name of the temple, Ekarzida, the "good wharf temple," indicates that it was built beside a canal. If this was the first temple of Nanna at Gaesh, then Enheduanna could not be the author of this hymn. Cohen remarks that the Shulgi document may record a major restoration of the temple; the temple may already have been in use. Records do show that the akiti festival was celebrated in Ur several hundred years before Sargon came to power. In that case, if Shulgi was merely restoring the temple in Gaesh, Enheduanna could have written or edited this hymn. However, another Ur III king, Amar-Suen, Shulgi's son, built a gipar for the temple in Gaesh and installed an en-priestess there. Temple Hymn 12 mentions the gipar in the shrine at Karzida. If the reference to the gipar in the hymn refers to the work of Amar-Suen, then Amar-Suen may have written the hymn.

In form the hymn fits the pattern of the other Temple Hymns more accurately than, for instance, the Shulgi hymn, Temple Hymn 9. We know that by Enheduanna's lifetime the akiti festival was the major festival of the year. The high priestess surely would have been a participant in the ritual festivities.

Nanna was not considered a netherworld god in spite of the fact that he spent three days each month in that unsavory place. His mother, Ninlil, made sure that one of her other sons would take her precious firstborn's place there, allowing him to return each month after his sojourn. All the gods in the next group of hymns spend significant time in the underworld. The shadow of the underworld falls upon them in varying degrees. They include Utu, the sun god; Ninazu, Ninlil's son, therefore Nanna's brother; Ninazu's son Ningishzida; and the famous pair Inanna and Dumuzi, who both have fateful stays in the Great Below. This group of hymns gives us the first, but not the last, exposure to the world below the flat earth.

chapter 7

HYMNS TO TEMPLES IN THE CENTRAL LOWLANDS

Each of the seven deities of this group of Temple Hymns has spent mythological time in the netherworld, the land of the dead. Utu, the sun god (TH 13), enters the underworld through the western gate each evening and rises from his sleep every morning to ascend into the world above. Ninazu (TH 14) and his son Ningishzida (TH 15) have dual traditions. They are among the young dying fertility gods who disappear into the underworld at the time of the barley harvest, but they also ascend with the new growth in the spring. Nevertheless, both are also gods of the land of the dead, identified with the great snakes of the underworld.

Inanna makes her way to the underworld in the myth "Inanna's Descent to the Netherworld," but in this group (TH 16) she is described as a goddess of great cosmic powers and enticing sensual allure. Dumuzi (TH 17), Inanna's spouse, is banished to the underworld by Inanna as ransom for her release. In this particular hymn he is only her adoring spouse. However, the shade of death falls on Dumuzi with the mention in the hymn of the Arali, the sheep-grazing plain where, at Inanna's bidding, underworld demons finally catch him in his sheepfold and kill him. Ninshubur (TH 18) is the trusted minister of Inanna. Before Inanna's descent into the netherworld, she gives Ninshubur the task of securing her rescue. Ninshubur had other clear underworld connections, sometimes as wife of the underworld god, even at times equated with its queen, Ereshkigal. In Temple Hymn 19, Ningirin, an incantation priestess, sprinkles flour and barley as food for the dead in the Great Below.

The seven cities that harbor these temples cluster near the Euphrates, a

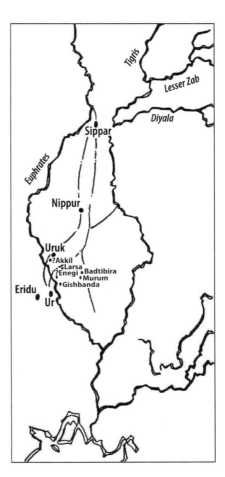

7.1.   Sketch map of Mesopotamia with Larsa and neighboring cities. After Postgate 1994. Reproduced by permission of Taylor and Francis Books U.K.

short distance across the river from Ur and Eridu. The cities, Larsa, Enegi, Gishbanda, Uruk, Badtibira, Akkil, and Murum, were served by large irrigation canals, part of the extensive system that drew water from the Euphrates before it emptied into the Persian Gulf.

Originally, Sumerian belief placed the land of the dead in the rugged, seemingly uninhabitable mountains that lay on their eastern boundary. The earliest cuneiform sign for the word mountain, kur, consisted of a triangle of three half-moon-shaped figures, stacked to represent a mountain. The word kur became a designation of the netherworld. This concept was based on the early Sumerian view of the cosmos as being horizontal. Looking east from the fertile plain, the Sumerians saw the impassable Zagros Mountains. There,

7.2.   Solar disc of Utu. Courtesy of the University of Texas Press, Jeremy Black and Anthony Green, *Gods, Demons and Symbols of Ancient Mesopotamia*, Tessa Richards, illustrator, 1995.

among strange barbarians and demons, they imagined the dead would enter the netherworld. Gradually, a second concept gained prominence, seemingly from the Semitic-speaking peoples of the north of Sumer. This concept placed the netherworld far below the surface of the earth. In the earlier version, the entrance to the underworld would have been in the east. The "road of no return" stretched from the grave of the deceased eastward to the mountains, where he or she entered the land of the dead. With the advent of the concept that the netherworld lay below, the gate of death moved to the west, following the path of the sun god, who closed and locked the western gate each night. Nevertheless, the word that designated the underworld continued to be written with the original cuneiform sign for mountain, kur.

TEMPLE HYMN 13

THE LARSA TEMPLE OF UTU
Ebabbar

> O house sent from heaven
> visible from Kullab
> shrine Ebabbar   white glowing house
> white young breed bull   lift your neck to the sky
> close to Utu who tends you
>
> your shining horns   silver and lapis lazuli
> mound on your shoulders
> your lustrous lapis beard hangs down in profusion
>
> your prince   lord of soaring light
> is lord of the faithful word
> who lights up the horizon
> who shines on heaven's vault

7.3.   Archaic Uruk sign for kur. After Labat, 1992.
Courtesy of Editions GEUTHNER, Paris.

Utu
sovereign of Ebabbar
has built this house on your radiant site
and placed his seat upon your dais

  9 lines for the house of Utu in Larsa

THE TEMPLE OF UTU AT LARSA

The sun god Utu was the principal deity in two important Sumerian cities,
Larsa in the southern alluvial plain and Sippar in the north (Temple Hymn
38). Utu was son of the moon deities Nanna and Ningal, a twin born with his
sister, Inanna (Temple Hymns 16, 26, 40). Larsa was located ten kilometers
east of the city of Uruk, Inanna's city, which dominated the southern plain
throughout the fourth millennium BCE. The first lines of this hymn locate
Utu's "white glowing" Larsa temple in its relationship to Uruk, mentioning
the Uruk suburb Kullab. The large, imposing temple of the sun god, the poem
says, can be seen all the way from Kullab.

LARSA AND THE FIRST CITIES

Although 2300 BCE, the time of the collection of the Temple Hymns, may
seem to be ancient history, that date marks the culmination of one thousand
years or more of the development of Mesopotamian cities. During that long
one-thousand-year period Utu was the city god of Larsa. A number of so-
called city seals have been found in the archaic southern cities of Ur and Uruk,
Jemdet-Nasr and Urum. The oldest of these from Jemdet-Nasr and Urum date
from 3100–2900 BCE. A seal from Urum lists almost twenty cities, although
only five or six of the archaic cuneiform signs can be read. Among these is
Larsa.[1]

7.4.   Imprint of the city seal of Larsa. After Postgate, 1994. Reproduced by permission of Taylor and Francis Books U.K.

The topograms that designate each city frequently contain a symbolic depiction of the city's main temple and its patron god. A topogram on a city seal from the beginning of the Early Dynastic period depicts Utu in Larsa with the image of an altar holding the rising sun.[2] While there is disagreement on the significance of these city seals, most specialists concur that they reveal the beginning of a common cultural identity among the then-independent city-states. Others find evidence that the seals suggest a cooperation among the cities in support of a common pantheon and may indicate military and political alliances as well. The most ancient of the seals are unique in that, as Piotr Steinkeller says, "this is the only evidence of a potentially historical nature that survives from late prehistoric times."[3] Interpreting these city seals, Thorkild Jacobsen suggests the possibility of an alliance of southern Mesopotamian cities.[4] While Kengir, the name Jacobsen proposed for a league of cooperating cities, has not generally been accepted, his thesis has kept the possibility of a league alive, and later intriguing discoveries add weight to the general evidence of important state-building interactions among the early cities.

The city seals confirm that Larsa and its principal god, Utu, were an ancient pair, at least one thousand years old at the time of the writing of the Temple Hymns. The image of the temple altar crowned by the rising sun, the insignia of Larsa, is evidence of the centrality of the temple in the city's identity. The city in some important way existed because of the god and his shining temple, Ebabbar.

The archaeological site of Larsa was first dug by W. K. Loftus in 1854. His soundings discovered cylinder seals and inscribed bricks that identified the ancient city.[5] Loftus was followed by a number of distinguished archeologists, Walter Andrae in 1903, and André Parrot in 1933. Following World War II, in 1967 J. Margueron began to excavate the temple Ebabbar. Although the temple remains incompletely explored, it was central to the work in 1972 of J. L. Hout, T. Jacobsen, R. McC. Adams, and H. J. Nissen.

The old city of Larsa was crisscrossed by irrigation canals, as were many southern Mesopotamian cities. Between the multiple mounds of the city, archeologists found large depressions that followed the route of the ancient watercourses. Elizabeth Stone says these watercourses divided the town into sections, zones for administration, for religious purposes, and for habitation. While the canals connected the city to the outside world as they linked all the major cities, they also divided and stratified the population of Larsa in significant ways.[6]

UTU IN MYTH AND POETRY

Utu in his role as god of justice appears in early myths and prayers. He is able to shine his bright light, illuminating difficult situations brought before him. As purveyor of justice, he brings a consistent sense of order, reinforcing tradition and custom.

Utu's strong sense of fairness is reflected in his bighearted compassion. He is called upon to guard and to guide pilgrims through the night. His compassion directs his response to the plight of sufferers:

> Utu you are their mother
> Utu you are their father
> Utu, for the widow you are like her mother
>   bringing her again into custody[7]

Another prayer to Utu calls upon him to help a woman in childbirth: "may Justice stand to your right; may Law stand to your left . . . ; may this woman give birth safely."[8] In the myth "Lugalbanda in the Mountain Cave," the sick hero Lugalbanda prays to Utu:

> Utu, I greet you! Let me be ill no longer! Hero, Ningal's son, I greet you! Let me be ill no longer! . . . Don't make me fall like a throwstick somewhere in the desert unknown! . . . Let me not come to an end in the mountains like a weakling!
> Utu accepted his tears.[9]

In his response to the suffering Lugalbanda, "the youth Utu extended his holy, shining rays down from heaven, he bestowed them on holy Lugalbanda in the mountain cave."[10]

The hero Gilgamesh received the divine protection of Utu, as did Dumuzi (Temple Hymn 14). Utu made certain that Gilgamesh successfully battled the demonic guardian of the Forest of Cedars, Huwawa, and ensured that he returned safely to Uruk. In another myth, Dumuzi begged for Utu's help after his wife, Inanna, threatened to banish him to the underworld as punishment for ignoring her loss while she herself suffered in the underworld. Dumuzi pleads to Utu:

> Dumuzi cries out
> turns pale
> raises his hands to heaven
> to Utu
>
> > O Utu
> > you are my wife's brother
> > I am your sister's husband
> >
> > I am spouse of a goddess
> > I am not mortal
> > I carried oil
> > to your mother's house
> > I carried milk
> > to Ningal's house
> >
> > I have danced
> > on Inanna's knee
> >
> > make my hand the hand of a snake
> > make my foot the foot of a snake
> > help me escape these demons
> > don't let them hold me[11]

Utu obligingly turns Dumuzi into a snake, who slithers away from the pursuing demons. Utu is moved by the plight of the weak, the downtrodden, the ill, sufferers in all situations. He uses his power to dispense equal-handed justice.

UTU IN THE UNDERWORLD

The Mesopotamians, like other ancient peoples, struggled to conceptualize what the sun god did at night. Where did he go? Like the Greeks, the Mesopotamians believed Utu traveled into the underworld, traversing the distance from west to east each night in order to initiate the morning light with his rising. In the evening he entered heaven's interior, "the invisible part of heaven below the earth."[12] Wolfgang Heimpel notes that various texts describe heaven's interior as "invisible to the human eyes, being located as it is beneath the horizons" and "far off in heaven but still in direct communication with the surface of the earth, unobstructed by the horizons and doors that shut it off from view."[13] Some texts describe the sun god as having the human needs of a man returning home from a long day's work, his wife greeting him with a fine meal, his bedchamber ready for his rest.

The sun enters heaven's interior through the western gate, which he shuts and bolts behind him. Does his light then shine in the underworld? The texts give conflicting reports. Some say the sun is asked to cast light in the underworld.[14] In Temple Hymn 38 Enheduanna tells us that Utu binds a crown around his head in order to dim his light. Heimpel summarizes the beliefs:

> The sun god opens the western door of heaven. . . . He brings his light to the previously dark places below the horizon and to the Annunakku who dwell there. Because of the lack of draft and being shut off from the atmosphere above, his light dims gradually. He proceeds to the "level place" and concerns himself with the matters of the dead. He then goes home to his residence, the White House, where his wife has prepared his dinner. Later he enters his chamber and sleeps.[15]

Utu is a benevolent god to those who ask for his favor. His consistent rising and setting, Lugalbanda says, are gifts essential to humankind:

> Utu, shepherd of the land, father of the black-headed, when you go to sleep, the people go to sleep with you; youth Utu, when you rise, the people rise with you. Utu, without you no net is stretched out for a bird, no slave is taken away captive. To him who walks alone, you are his brotherly companion; Utu, you are the third of them who travel in pairs.[16]

This unusual text reveals the personal relationship the Mesopotamians developed with their gods, seeing Utu, in this case, as a "brotherly companion," a presence unseen but caring and substantial.

The poet in the Gilgamesh Epic describes the sunrise: "With the flowing light, with heaven's foot brightening, with the birds giving voice at the flowing light, Utu emerged from the chamber."[17] Lugalbanda describes the setting sun as "Utu setting his face toward his house."[18] His house, described vividly in the Temple Hymn, the white gleaming house, waits for Utu in heaven's interior, while it manifests itself on earth in the temple in the city of Larsa.

Later texts from the Isin-Larsa/Old Babylonian period, 2000–1600 BCE, cast Utu in the role of judging the dead in the underworld. While this belief may have existed in Sargonic Mesopotamia, it is not evident from the existing texts. In Sumer he was known to be a god of justice who traveled to the underworld at night, but his role as judge of the dead, even one who could revive the dead, developed in the centuries following the decline of the Sargonic empire.

THE PASSAGE OF LIGHT

Temple Hymn 13 begins with the sunrise, as the temple, Ebabbar, appeared "sent from heaven," referring to heaven's interior through which the sun passed at night and from which it emerged at dawn. The house/temple is vividly described as a young bull lifting its neck to the sun, and Utu as the master who "tends" the shining house. The crenelation on the "shoulders" of the house become the jeweled horns of the young bull, whose lapis beard is lush and flowing.

The image of the sun moves then to midday, when his soaring light reaches the zenith of the vault of heaven. The hymn leaves us there in radiant light, although mention of the horizon reminds us of the "western gate" that waits on earth's horizon for the setting sun to enter again into the netherworld.

Like Ningublam's in Temple Hymn 11, Utu's temple is a young breed bull with shining horns and the lustrous lapis beard of a youth. The Lugalbanda myth calls Utu a youth, and in the myth "Inanna's Descent to the Netherworld," Utu is the age of his twin, the maiden Inanna. The god of light appears young and vigorous and above all compassionate in rendering justice. His eternal return to the land of the living offers empathetic companionship to his subjects, who ultimately face the entrance to the underworld themselves.

TEMPLE HYMN 14

THE ENEGI TEMPLE OF NINAZU

Egidda

O Enegi
great waterway of the underworld
gutter of Ereshkigal

Gudua of Sumer
gatherer of humankind

Egidda
Your shadow spreads over all the princes of the earth
even into the netherworld

your prince   seed of the great lord
shita-priest of the underworld
born of Ereshkigal
plays his lyre loudly
a calf resounding in its voice   very sweetly
Ninazu   who hears words of prayer
    O Enegi
has built this house on your radiant site
and placed his seat upon your dais.

    7 lines for the house of Ninazu in Enegi

THE TEMPLE OF NINAZU AT ENEGI

In the third millennium when the Temple Hymns were joined together by
Enheduanna, Ninazu was a significant Sumerian god of the netherworld in
Enegi, a village on an irrigation canal that connected it with Utu's city, Larsa.
We learn of this connection of the two cities from a literary text that describes
the ceremonial journey to Nippur of the moon god Nanna. The text identifies
his first stop as Enegi, followed by Larsa.[19] This text not only lets us know
of the waterway connection between the two cities, but also accentuates the
importance of Ninazu's temple in the small town of Enegi. The revered Nanna
chose to stop here.

KING OF THE SNAKES

Ninazu's significance extends back several hundred years into the Early Dynastic period. The earliest literary reference comes from a zà-mì (praise) hymn from Abu Salabikh. The hymn connects Ninazu with his powers over cattle, excluding any reference to his later identification as a snake god.[20] His character as an underworld deity evolved so that in the Sargonic period he was known as "King of the Snakes." In Sumerian description, the netherworld "was a sort of mirror image of the inhabited world," as described by Volkert Haas: "The center of this city was a palace, which was occasionally called the 'Mountain of Lapis Lazuli.' Here, deep in the earth, the god Ninazu was enthroned in the temple Egidda in the city of Enegi."[21] In this intriguing image the deep-blue palace of lapis lazuli, far below in the underworld, mirrored the palace in Enegi, Ninazu's dwelling on earth. The Sumerian word for Enegi, IM[ki], means clay or earth, making the city "Earth Place," "earth" being strongly connected to and sometimes a synonym for the underworld.

Ninazu's name means "Lord Healer," possibly referring to the mythological healing capacity of snakes. His wife, Ningirida, is equated with the goddess of healing, Gula. He is called "shita priest of the underworld," the Sumerian shita priest being one of the highest officials in the temple. His son Ningishzida in the next Temple Hymn is also a shita priest, both apparently performing their duties in the Great Below.

As king of the snakes, Ninazu is familiar with the snakes' living quarters in long burrows, similar to the waterway and gutter pipes that connect his temple to the underworld. His temple is the "great waterway of the underworld" and "gutter of Ereshkigal," Queen of the Great Below. Dina Katz describes the importance of water to the dead: "The main obligation of the living toward their dead relatives was to supply them with water to prevent the spirits from suffering thirst in the netherworld and thereby secure their peaceful rest."[22]

F. A. M. Wiggermann thinks that the snake character of Ninazu and his son Ningishzida in the next Temple Hymn, both clearly Sumerian gods, developed outside of Mesopotamia, in Elam and Iran. Ninazu was not originally a snake deity. Wiggerman says of this "Iranian substrate," "as has been repeatedly shown, a religious interest in snakes in these regions goes back deep into prehistory."[23] The snake aspect of the two southern Sumerian gods, Ninazu and Ningishzida, may have been imported from the important northern city of Eshnunna, near the Iranian border, the city that housed the other major temple of Ninazu (Temple Hymn 34).

NINAZU'S PARENTS

Several accounts identify Ninazu's parents. Even the two Temple Hymns to Ninazu (14 and 34) differ, emphasizing the dissimilar traditions surrounding the two temples, one in the south of the country and one in the far northeast at Eshnunna. The temple in Enegi was clearly connected to the underworld and to the tradition that Ninazu was the child, or in some cases the spouse, of the great queen of the underworld, Ereshkigal. This hymn says he was "born of Ereshkigal." The mention in the hymn of the city Gudua, "often a designation of the Nether World," says Åke Sjöberg, and equated with Enegi, locates Ninazu's temple on the spot from which clay pipes or gutters carry water and ritual libations to the dead into the Great Below.[24] Ninazu is sometimes described as the ruler of the netherworld. Haas says he was replaced by Ereshkigal at the end of the third millennium.[25]

In Ur, Nanna's primary city, Ninazu was the young dying god, a mythological role usually belonging to Dumuzi, Inanna's spouse. Somber festivals for Ninazu were held at Ur, as he descended into the underworld, and, given his clear association to the underworld in this Temple Hymn, festivals may have been held in Enegi as well. Ninazu's tradition in Ur is based on his being a son of Enlil and Ninlil, and the purpose of his passage into the underworld was to free their son, the moon god Nanna of Ur, to return each month to the upper world. Ninazu was the third son born to Ninlil, during her pursuit of Enlil described in Temple Hymn 3 (see chapter 5). Ninlil, troubled that her precious firstborn might remain in the dark of the underworld, connived to get one of her other sons to take his place, thus releasing Nanna to return after three days to the world above.

THE YOUNG DYING GOD

The myth of the young dying god portrays the death, passage to the underworld, and eventual resurrection of the god. Ritual observances of the myth follow the agricultural year and occur at the time of the drying up of crops, the subsequent fallow land, and the rejuvenation of growth in the spring.

In this role, two consecutive months at Ur, the fifth and the sixth months, were named for Ninazu. The festival in the sixth month may have involved a celebration of Ninazu's return from the netherworld. Later texts indicate that funerary rites for dead kings were observed in these months. Mark Cohen writes, "The obligatory offering of water and strewing of flour occurred throughout the year. However, during this month special elaborate ceremonies were observed at these funerary shrines," when participants poured water for the dead through the waterway pipes in Ninazu's temple.[26]

Ninazu is mentioned as one of the dying gods in the laments that make up the composition known from its first line as "In the Desert by the Early Grass." Jacobsen's introduction to the piece identifies Ninazu as "a netherworld god who seems to have been a god of the rains of spring which seep down into the earth."[27] Ninazu's burial is described in the text:

> by flowing waters
>   of holy-water fonts,
> [amidst the water conduits]
>   of the young [anointed ones,]
> the war[rior Ninazu]
>   is laid to rest[28]

SNAKES, GRAINS, AND NATURE'S CYCLES

Ninazu's snake character, so evident in this Temple Hymn, may have been a later accretion. He is first known as a god of agriculture. In a text called "How the cereals came to Sumer," Ninazu and his brother Ninmada bring barley to Sumer. Frymer-Kensky reports a myth in which the people originally "ate only grass, as do sheep."[29] The god of heaven An gave them cereal, barley, and flax, which Enlil then put in the mountains. Eventually, Ninazu and his brother brought the grain down to the Sumerians.

As a young dying god, Ninazu's dual aspects come together: the god who brings barley and flax to his people and the snake god who lives in the underworld. His seasonal cycles of death, descent, and resurrection follow the rhythms of nature. The young god dies after the time of harvest and enters the netherworld when the earth is bare. With the spring rains the land is planted, and the young shoots of barley and flax grow. The god is resurrected.

Nevertheless, Ninazu of Enegi as depicted in the Temple Hymn is a chthonic god. Gudua, as the world of the dead, is the eventual gathering place of all humanity. Its shadow spreads, the hymn says, over prince and commoner alike. Ninazu plays a particular instrument, one shaped like an ear; he plays it sweetly like the cry of a calf, but very loud.[30] His music may be somber, given his location among the dead. Still, the hymn tells us, as a god of the underworld he hears the prayers of the many petitioners above who pray for their deceased relatives and pour libations for them from Ninazu's temple above, down the great waterway to his lapis palace below.

TEMPLE HYMN 15

THE GISHBANDA TEMPLE OF NINGISHZIDA

ancient place
set deep in the mountain   artfully
dark shrine   frightening and red place
safely placed in a field
no one can fathom your mighty hair-raising path
Gishbanda
 the neck-stock   the fine-eyed net
 the foot-shackling netherworld knot
your restored high wall is massive
 like a trap

your inside
the place where the sun rises
yields widespread abundance

your prince   the pure-handed
shita priest of Inanna   heaven's holy one
Lord Ningishzida
his thick and beautiful hair falls down his back
O Gishbanda
has built this house on your radiant site
and placed his seat upon your dais

  10 lines for the temple of Ningishzida in Gishbanda

THE TEMPLE OF NINGISHZIDA AT GISHBANDA

Ningishzida is the son of the god Ninazu of the preceding hymn. Like his father, Ningishzida is a god of the netherworld. His temple is known simply as "House of the God Ningishzida." His hymn vividly portrays the stark and contradictory aspects of the land of the dead. The first words of the hymn, ki-ul, locate the netherworld at the beginning of time, ul meaning "primaeval," and ki meaning "place," "location." The temple of Ningishzida is an ancient place, and its identity with the netherworld later in the hymn suggests that the land of the dead existed at the moment of creation.

PARADOX IN THE NETHERWORLD

In the imagination of the poet, Ningishzida's temple is deep within the mountain. The word kur, "mountain," is also a designation of the underworld, since the first location of the underworld was thought to be far east of Sumer in the distant mountains. This first image of the temple, "deep set in the mountain," places the temple inside the netherworld. Later, the poet says the sun rises from the temple's interior, suggesting that Ningishzida's temple encompasses the whole of the land where the sun spends the night and from which it rises each morning. The sun in the hymn is said to spread abundance with its rising. The bounty that the sun god brings contrasts with the mystery of the land to which he, Utu, disappears, down Ningishzida's "mighty hair-raising path." The sun's daily passage exhibits the epitome of the paradox Ningishzida houses in his underworld temple domain.

Paradox dominates the second verse — "dark shrine frightening and red place / safely placed in a field." The juxtaposition of the safe field and the frightening place startles the listeners and prepares them for the harrowing descriptions to come. The poet spares no words in describing the terror and finality of being a captive of Ningishzida's devices — "the neck-stock — the fine-eyed net / the foot-shackling netherworld knot," the trap of its massive wall. By contrast, in the world of the deities Ningishzida is a "pure-handed" prince, a high-ranking priest of holy Inanna.[31] Who can resist as "his thick and beautiful hair falls down his back"?

In this hymn the poet draws on the intense human emotions surrounding death. Ningishzida becomes the object of human terror of death's finality as well as of human longing for an afterlife. Death is inescapable like the "foot-shackling netherworld knot." On the other hand, how can the traveler not soften to pure Ningishzida with his abundant dark hair? The emotions that the poem's imagery evokes — more than in many of the hymns — demonstrate that the Sumerian deities embody a conflated mix of human longing and experience.

NINGISHZIDA'S MYTHOLOGY

The complex development of the gods of Mesopotamia is apparent in Ningishzida's rich mythology. While he was not among the most prominent of the gods, he did have family ties, iconography, a mythology and was named on a number of god lists that survived through the ages. He first appeared on a mid-third-millennium god list from Early Dynastic Fara, and he remained a significant god through the Old Babylonian period, to 1600 BCE.[32] Two conflicting traditions emerge around Ningishzida. In the first, he is, as in this hymn, a god of the underworld, while in a second current of myths and laments he, like his father, Ninazu, is one of the young dying warrior gods who are condemned to the underworld but return.

The young dying gods seem to have originated in the fourth millennium. Jacobsen traced laments dedicated to them to that early period. These young heroes all were doomed to descend to the netherworld. Jacobsen located them "on the lower course of the ancient Euphrates" in a region "of orchard-growers in towns along the river and of oxherds who grazed their herds on the green reeds in the nearby marshes."[33] Ningishzida was among the most prominent of these early gods.

In a singular myth of Ningishzida's Descent to the Netherworld, the god is condemned to that unsavory place, then taken before Ereshkigal, queen of the netherworld. His mother, Ningirida (Lady of the Woman's Hair Clasp), wife of Ninazu, intervenes and persuades Ningishzida's guard to bring her son back to life and release him. She offers the guard enough silver to construct a statue of her son. For good measure, she tells the guard how to trick Ereshkigal into letting Ningishzida go, since no one is allowed to return from the netherworld once sentenced by Ereshkigal.[34] In another collection of texts known as "In the Desert by the Early Grass," both Ningishzida's mother and sister pursue him to the netherworld. His mother clearly prefers to follow him, even if it means she will die.[35] Sometime in the second millennium, the young dying gods all seem to have been assimilated into the most revered among them, Dumuzi.

Ningishzida's role as a strictly netherworld god is a tradition separate from that of the dying god who returns. W. G. Lambert says, "Ningishzida is most commonly an underworld official and would neither need nor want to be released."[36] In the Old Babylonian period, several hundred years after the collection of the Temple Hymns, Ningishzida assumed the important role of "chair-bearer" of the underworld. Presumably he was assigned the task of carrying the king and other important dignitaries upon their entry into the Great Below. His wife, Geshtinanna, was assigned the office of scribe; she "checked the names of new arrivals against a master list so that extraneous visitors from the upper world . . . could immediately be recognized and turned away."[37]

Ningishzida's name complicates his dual identity of being a strictly underworld god versus one of the young dying and resurrected gods. His name means "Lord of the True Tree." The name of the village where his temple was located, Gishbanda, between Lagash and Ur, means "Little Tree." In one of the god lists, the name Ningishzida appears twice, the second one, ᵈgiš-banda, meaning "God Little Tree." Is he, like his father, Ninazu, a god of agriculture as well as a god of the underworld? Jacobsen describes him as "a god of trees, particularly of the roots from which the tree grows up. . . . Since . . . the ancients assumed tree roots and serpents to be identical and wrote the word for roots with a picture of crossed snakes, Ningishzida was also king of serpents."[38] Lambert identifies the tree as the grapevine, since his wife was Geshtinanna. The word geštin is composed of the signs giš (tree) and tin (life) and means "vine." Geshtinanna was a goddess first attested in Early Dynastic Lagash and Ur. Lambert discusses the difficulty of the identification, given that grapevines "did not grow in Sumer, nor indeed in most of Mesopotamia."[39] He suggests that the cults of Ningishzida and Geshtinanna originated in the Semitic-dominated north of Mesopotamia, where there was grape cultivation. Sumerian incursions into the north occurred during the fourth and third millennia (Uruk and Early Dynastic periods), resulting in an exchange of cultures.

The influence of northern religious ideas on Ningishzida's character is apparent in his iconography. Ningishzida is associated with the snake constellation Hydra, as is Ereshkigal. In his study of snake gods in the area east of the Tigris near the Iranian border, Wiggerman says their origin reaches "deep into prehistory and through the ages remains quite visible in the iconography of Elam and the Iranian mountains."[40] He asserts that Ningishzida's "ophidian traits were developed under the influence of transtigridian religious ideas," ideas originating east of the Tigris.[41] Like Geshtinanna, his wife, Ningishzida assimilates traits in his southern location from prominent religious ideas that originated among the Semitic population of northern Mesopotamia and Iran. While Ningishzida was clearly a Sumerian god with his temple in the south at Gishbanda, he, like Ninazu, has as his dragon the northern mušhuššu, in its earliest representation, a lion-headed snake with front paws. In the period following the end of the Sargonic empire, his snake iconography appears in the southern city of Lagash on a dedication bowl from the prominent ruler Gudea, who revered Ningishzida as his personal god.

Ningishzida, clearly a god of death and the underworld, gathered conflicting traits and traditions over the ages. The Temple Hymn ends with an image of him as "pure-handed"—perhaps referring to his dealings with the dead. Next, he is called a high priest of Inanna, "heaven's holy one," a shita priest like Ninazu. We have no record of how he served Inanna, the sensuous god-

dess of erotic pleasure, conjugal love, and fierce battle. That he served Inanna
suggests that Inanna, primary among the goddesses, was superior in rank to
Ningishzida; that is, life is superior to death. Inanna visited the netherworld
in a myth; she is beaten, killed, brought back to life, and resurrected, a cycle
of transformation that might account for Ningishzida's service, he who was
consigned to the netherworld interminably. The poet of the Temple Hymns
significantly placed Inanna's hymn next in the sequence.

TEMPLE HYMN 16

THE URUK TEMPLE OF INANNA
Eanna

> house of Kullab's cosmic powers
> thriving in the radiance of the princess
>
> perfectly shaped fresh fruit
> dazzling in your irresistible ripeness
> descending from the heart of heaven
>   shrine built for the bull
>
> Eanna
>   house of seven corners
>   seven fires lit at midnight
>   seven desires apprehended
> your princess   the pure one
> she is the whole horizon
>
> your Lady Inanna
> throws the ever-rolling stone dice
> ever bedecking the woman
> ever helmeting the man
> crowned with lapis lazuli desire
> singular in the sanctuary
> Queen of heaven and earth   Inanna
> has built this house on your radiant site
> and placed her seat upon your dais
>
>   11 lines for the house of Inanna in Uruk

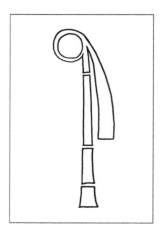

7.5.   Ring-post symbol of Inanna. Courtesy of the University of Texas Press, Jeremy Black and Anthony Green, *Gods, Demons and Symbols of Ancient Mesopotamia*, Tessa Richards, illustrator, 1995.

THE TEMPLE OF INANNA AT URUK

If Sumerians were to travel from Ur to the third-millennium city of Uruk, they might board one of the magur reed boats and head northwest along the Euphrates. As they came near the city, the oldest, largest, and most renowned of the original loosely knit confederation, they would have seen it rising above the horizon long before the boat docked at the busy wharf. Inanna's temple, the Eanna, covered some three thousand square feet and was first built a thousand years before Enheduanna's birth.

Enheduanna would have traveled this same route from Ur to Uruk, as evidence suggests she served as high priestess in Uruk as well as Ur.[42] In three long devotional poems to Inanna, she had written a diary-like account of her love for and struggle with the unpredictable, emotionally volatile goddess.[43] We do not know the time sequence of the appearance of the devotional poems in relation to the Temple Hymns. Nevertheless, her intimate account of their personal relationship confirms that Inanna was the center of her spiritual life. "She is the whole horizon," Enheduanna writes in this Temple Hymn, and her three personal accounts of their relationship leave no doubt that Inanna was indeed Enheduanna's whole horizon.

WHO IS INANNA?

Enheduanna's portrayal of Inanna in the three devotional poems is a unique ancient documentation of an individual's private relationship to a deity. Inanna was a multifaceted goddess held in high esteem by the Mesopotamians as far back as the fourth millennium BCE and forward to the Common Era, a period of three thousand years. She was a chief deity of the pantheon, the most prominent goddess of the Mesopotamians, and, some say, of the ancient world. She is often described aphoristically as a deity of love and war. While these characteristics do indeed apply to Inanna, her troubling complexity is not captured in a two-word description. Her many myths, hymns, poems, and stories portray a strong-willed goddess who exercised her prerogatives across a wide spectrum of circumstance. Rivkah Harris sums her up as follows: "The highly elusive yet essential aspect of the goddess's configuration . . . [is] paradox. . . . [She is] a deity who incorporated fundamental and irreducible paradoxes."[44]

Ancient Near Eastern specialists attribute her complexity, which is unmatched by that of any other Mesopotamian deity, to a variety of reasons. Harris says her "traits and behavior . . . confused normative categories and boundaries and thereby defined and protected the norms and underlying structure of Mesopotamian civilization."[45] H. L. J. Vanstiphout argues similarly that Inanna's character served to "incorporate" strife in opposition to the "well-ordered world" of the Mesopotamians, thus enabling the opposites of chaos and order to be contained and portrayed.[46] Harris describes Inanna's festivals as "institutionalized license": The festivals "celebrated and tolerated disorder. They were occasions when social rules were in abeyance and deviance from norms was articulated. Through symbolic inversion they attacked the basic categorical differences between male and female, human and animal, young and old."[47] Among other characterizations of Inanna, Jacobsen calls her "a goddess of infinite variety,"[48] while J. Bottéro believes her "marginality . . . derived from her association with the prostitute."[49] Others understand her contradictory complexity as the result of a syncretism between the Sumerian Inanna and the Semitic Ishtar.

Three of the Temple Hymns are written to Inanna, hymn 16 as well as hymns 26 and 40. While other deities have two hymns in the collection, only Inanna, Ninhursag, and Nanna have three, an indication of the three deities' high status in the pantheon. This first hymn to Inanna focuses on her as a goddess of allure and sexual desire. The theme of number 26 celebrates her astral aspect as the morning and evening star we call Venus, while number 40 presents her warlike capacities, appropriate to the location of that temple near the capital of Sargon's empire, Akkad.

Enheduanna was well aware of the spectrum of Inanna's characteristics. Her three devotional poems, unlike the Temple Hymns, are paeans to her goddess that include touchingly personal entreaties and chronicles of the priestess's life in relation to Inanna. Enheduanna calls herself "child of yours / . . .

bride of yours."[50] She reminds Inanna that she, Enheduanna, was called to be the high priestess by Inanna herself and says to her, "rightfully you are High Priestess." That is to say, Inanna is high priestess in heaven; Enheduanna is her counterpart on earth.[51] In her distress, she cries,

> I plead with you
> I say STOP
> the bitter hating heart and sorrow
> my Lady
> what day will you have mercy
> how long will I cry a moaning prayer
> I am yours
> why do you slay me
>
> * * *
>
> Your storm-shot torrents
> drench the bare earth
> moisten to life
> moisture bearing light
> floods the dark
> O my Lady
> my Queen
> I unfold your splendor in all lands
> I extol your glory
> I will praise your course
> your sweeping grandeur
> forever[52]

These poems include the whole spectrum of Inanna's complex attributes, just as the Temple Hymns focus separately on Inanna's sensuous, astral, and war-like characteristics.

DESIRE AT THE HEART OF THE COSMOS

Temple Hymn 16 combines Inanna's cosmic authority and originality with images of sensuality. The temple, the Eanna, descends "from the heart of heaven" and corresponds to Inanna in its "irresistible ripeness." Implicitly, she transports the fundamental force of desire from heaven to earth. The poet places sensuality and desire at the heart of the cosmos. The life force itself is energized by desire.

Inanna's temple, Eanna, is the house of "cosmic powers," the dwelling place of the **me**. "**Me**" refers to inherent essence, for example, of the categories of civilization. This essence belongs to the divinities. Divine energy, at the will of the deities, enlivens the earth and all the elements of human life as we know it. Divine enlivening confers characteristic being to everything that is. Thus, this inherent essence, the **me**, imparts sacred essential character and gives each share of civilization its existential nature.

These categories of civilization originated in Kullab, the hymn says, originally a village near Uruk. The two joined into one city at the beginning of the Early Dynastic period, around 2900 BCE. Kullab may have been the center of Inanna worship even before her temple in Uruk. Archeologists discovered that in the period preceding the Early Dynastic, the fifth millennium Ubaid period, the village of Kullab contained a high terrace that supported a temple. The fact that the hymn cites the origin of the **me** of Inanna in Kullab may refer to a very ancient tradition of the worship of Inanna in this village. This origination would extend the worship of Inanna back another thousand or more years.[53]

Inanna's temple in Uruk is built from a divine plan, carefully designed around the sacred number seven, the number of wholeness, completion. It is a house of seven corners, seven fires, seven desires. "She is the whole horizon." Fundamentally, everything in existence is mobilized by the energetic movement of desire, and Inanna is the epitome of that force.

For Inanna, desire is personal. Her temple is "built for the bull," a reference to her consort/husband, Dumuzi (Temple Hymn 17). There they will live in the sensual bliss of a sacred marriage. She, like the temple, is "perfectly shaped fresh fruit." She bestows the essence of desire, "lapis lazuli desire," on humankind, forever bedecking the woman, placing a handsome helmet on the man, rendering them sumptuous and sensually alluring, the better to foment desire.

On the other hand, Inanna's darker aspects enter the poem, acknowledging her role as a deity who dispenses fate. She "throws the ever-rolling stone dice" whose portentous fall determines the destiny of the individual.

INANNA'S MYTHOLOGY

Inanna's character as we know her is derived from the discovered myths, poetry, hymns, and laments that tell her story. The Sumerian Love Songs emphasize her sensuality and willfulness and are consistent with the sense of this hymn. In a myth known as "Inanna's Descent to the Netherworld," she visits the underworld but returns transformed and does not become an underworld deity. However, her famous visit to the dark realm of her older sister Ereshkigal warrants her inclusion in this group of hymns related to netherworld gods. In another myth, "Inanna and the God of Wisdom," she accepts the gifts a drunken Enki generously offers, his precious **me**. Inanna transports them by boat to her home in Uruk, driving off all of the efforts by the now-sober Enki to stop her.

Inanna's warrior character is evident throughout Enheduanna's devotional poems to her, portraying her as queen of battle:

> fighting is her play
> she never tires of it
> she goes out running
> strapping on her sandals[54]

This Temple Hymn portrays Inanna as the cosmic love goddess. The Sumerian Love Songs most often link her to her consort, Dumuzi. These songs were an integral part of Sumerian culture and were sung and recited in the ritual of the Sacred Marriage.[55] In the love songs Inanna is the initiate of lovemaking. She entices Dumuzi:

> listen!
> I will scrub my skin with soap
> I will rinse all over with water
> I will dry myself with linen
> I will lay out mighty love clothes
>   I know how exactly
> I will look so fine
> I will make you feel like a king[56]

Two myths depict Inanna exercising her will with potential lovers. The first "victim" is Ishulanu, a gardener. She invites him to make love to her, saying,

> "let us enjoy your strength, put out your hand and touch our vulva!"

But the man rudely refuses:

> "Me? What do you want from me? Did my mother not bake for me? And did I not eat?
> What I eat [with you] would be loaves of dishonor and disgrace.
> Rushes would be my only covering against the cold."

Upon which Ištar [Inanna] hits him and turns him into a toad."[57]

In the myth "Inanna and Shukalletuda" Inanna again is involved with a gardener, who risks taking Inanna while she is sleeping. She is enraged. "As far as the goddess is concerned," says Gwendolyn Leick, ". . . intercourse during a deep sleep is not what she would call an erotic experience worth having."[58]

Erotic sensuality is a given in Inanna's character. Inanna enjoyed her sexuality and sought ways to express it. One of Enheduanna's poems to Inanna describes her attempt to soothe Inanna's temper by saying, "I have readied your room in the tavern," the tavern being the locale of prostitutes.[59] Inanna was the goddess of prostitutes. Enheduanna hoped to cheer her distraught goddess by enticing her to the bedroom.

On the other hand, Inanna counted in her domain the joys of marriage. In a recitation of Inanna's domain, Enheduanna relates the following: "to have a husband / to have a wife / to thrive in the goodness of love / are yours Inanna." Another verse conveys the same intent: "allure ardent desire / belongings households / are yours Inanna."[60] Allure and ardent desire, according to this text, belong in ordinary life. Inanna, the hymn says, is "crowned with lapis lazuli desire." Inanna is the energetic force of desire at the heart of the cosmos.

INANNA AT URUK

Inanna remained the prominent goddess of Uruk throughout its long history. In the center of the city was the compound known as the Eanna, the large area that included buildings and temples, public courtyards and squares. Inanna presided over the Eanna. In excavations archeologists discovered nineteen building levels dating from the fifth and fourth millennia BCE. On top of these were the levels built and continuously occupied almost until the Common Era. During this long period, surviving social and political evolution, Inanna remained the central goddess of Uruk.

Uruk was not only the first inhabited settlement that contained all the elements of a city, but in the fourth millennium grew to be the largest city in antiquity. Only Rome at its peak rivaled Uruk in size. These phenomenal developments originated in the fourth millennium. The Urukeans created trading colonies all across the northern plains and montane valleys of present-day Syria and Turkey as well as east of the Tigris in Iran. Well-worn trading routes crisscrossed the area east and west and followed the Tigris and Euphrates riverbanks north and south. The Uruk traders developed an organized system of long-distance commerce as they sought essential resources that were lacking in the southern alluvium. Guillermo Algaze discovered "evidence for close contacts between societies in the southern alluvium and communities in the plains of northern Mesopotamia predating the emergence of Uruk [period] city-states by a millennium or so."[61] This expansion was "momentum toward empire" in the fourth millennium, a momentum that was fully realized by Enheduanna's father, Sargon.[62]

The dire need of the Urukeans for resources gave impetus to the creation of organized structures in the culture that grew to accommodate the increasing complexity of the trading system. This led to the need for record keeping and bureaucracy. The beginning of writing developed in Uruk, as did a well-organized civic government. In the 1930s, German excavators in Uruk first discovered cuneiform tablets dating from around 3300 BCE. The tablets were written in an archaic script, but specialists who have studied them have determined they are to be read in the Sumerian language.

Not only did the Urukeans invent writing, but they also were the first to use the plow, the bow, and the cylinder seal; in addition, they were the first to develop a literate, intellectual elite, the scribes, who in the process of their record keeping not only learned to write, but also learned grammar, vocabulary, mathematics, science, law, and business. Eventually, the scribes recorded literature, beginning with the traditional myths and stories already alive in the folklore. This highly developed culture influenced other Mesopotamian cities, who appointed officials similar to those of Uruk. Many of the cities also adopted Uruk's preeminent goddess, Inanna, whose stature remained exceptional throughout Mesopotamian history.

Kullab was a ceremonial site for the worship of Inanna as well as of other deities. It was built on a high mound in the western section of Uruk, and in this flat desert country it could be seen for miles around.[63] In the Temple Hymn to Inanna's twin brother, the sun god Utu, Enheduanna locates his temple in the city of Larsa "visible from Kullab," thus relating him to Inanna, another instance of the centrality of her temple complex in Uruk in the pantheon.

In 2300 BCE, when the Temple Hymns were collected, Uruk came under the domination of Sargon and his empire. Inanna's prominence in the city endured. Enheduanna's poem "The Exaltation of Inanna" tells of the high priestess's exile from her position in Ur by a Urukean leader named Lugalane. Enheduanna laments, "he eats away at my life / I wander through thorny brush in the mountains."[64] She begs Inanna to restore her rightful place in the temple, which Inanna eventually does.[65] This story reflects a rebellion in Uruk against Sargon's rule. Inanna's loyalty, however, remains with the high priestess in Ur, not with the secular leader from her city Uruk.

Inanna maintained a long tenure as the principal goddess of the Sumerians and the civilizations of ancient Mesopotamia that succeeded them. Enheduanna in her personal poems repeatedly elevates Inanna above all other gods, saying, for example, "SHE of the gods has power / SHE executes their verdicts / before her matchless word / the great Annuna crawl / ever sneak away."[66] While the selection of one deity above all others (called henotheism) is not unusual in Mesopotamian literature, it takes on a special cast with Inanna and her Semitic counterpart, Ishtar. Simo Parpola traces the evolution of monotheism through the Assyrian deity Aššur. Inanna/Ishtar is the voice of Aššur, paradoxically identical with him while being entirely separate, the female aspect of the one deity, she who connects the earthly humans to the divine.[67] The role Inanna/Ishtar played among the Assyrians in their version of monotheism occurred a millennium and a half after the collection of the Temple Hymns. The author of this collection portrays Inanna in all her complexity as it was understood in the third millennium.

TEMPLE HYMN 17

THE BADTIBIRA TEMPLE OF DUMUZI
Emush

O house
    jeweled lapis herbs fleck the shining bed
    heart-soothing place of the Lady of the Steppe
Emush   brickwork glistening and pure
its burnished clay placed firmly [on the earth]
your sky-rising wall sprawls over the high plain
for the one who tends the ewes
and over the Arali House for the shepherd
your prince   radiant one of the Holy Woman
a lion pacing the steppe   back and forth
the wonder-causing, pure-breasted one
the Lord   spouse of pure Inanna
Dumuzi   master of the Emush

    O Badtibira   (fortress of the coppersmith)
has built this house on your radiant site
and placed his seat upon your dais

    10 lines for the house of Dumuzi in Badtibira

THE TEMPLE OF DUMUZI AT BADTIBIRA

Hardly do we disengage from the "lapis lazuli desire" of the sensuous Inanna, when we are led to the "jeweled" lapis-bedecked bed of Dumuzi, the "heart-soothing place of the Lady of the Steppe." In Dumuzi's Temple Hymn, as in Dumuzi himself, the god's prominence is linked to his revered spouse, "pure Inanna." Line after line consigns Dumuzi to the role of fulfilling that desire. He soothes her heart on his shining bed. He is her "radiant one." Then, he is praised as the shepherd "who tends the ewes," in whose guise he courted and won Inanna. Although Dumuzi gained prominence as Inanna's spouse, he has a rich history of his own.

DUMUZI — KING, SHEPHERD, YOUNG DYING GOD

Dumuzi is the subject of laments, myths, and hymns as well as the Sumerian love songs of sacred marriage texts. Temple Hymn 17 describes him as he was worshiped in Badtibira, that is, as a shepherd god. His name, Jacobsen says, means "'Quickener of the Young [in the Mother's Womb]' . . . the divine power to produce lambs and milk in the ewes in springtime."[68] While he owes to Inanna his elevation to divine status, he became the object of ritual mourning upon his early death, a ritual that was observed over three millennia, last commemorated in the eighth century CE.

Dumuzi is named in the Sumerian King List as a king of Uruk who reigned before the mythological flood. His name on that list actually precedes that of the legendary Gilgamesh.[69] In fourth-millennium Uruk he became, in the ritual of the sacred marriage, the spouse of the ruling goddess, Inanna. By this elevation the mortal king attained semidivine status in the Sumerian pantheon.

Dumuzi's many aspects make him one of the most complex gods of the pantheon. As Dumuzi-Amaushumgalanna he was god of the date palm. He is called Wild Bull, particularly in the love poems in relation to Inanna. As Damu, he is the sap rising in trees in the spring. He becomes an underworld god in the myth "Inanna's Descent to the Netherworld," sent there by Inanna as ransom for her freedom. In another myth he is cast into the underworld after his early death. In this Temple Hymn from Badtibira, he is the shepherd. His temple in Badtibira is known from late Early Dynastic times (2450–2350). Temple Hymn 17 is the only evidence we have of the existence of his temple in Badtibira in the Sargonic period.[70]

The ritual of the sacred marriage was performed in the spring to celebrate the emergence of new life in plant growth and animal birth. Spring was the time of the New Year in Mesopotamia, and in some cities the sacred marriage ritual and New Year's celebrations coincided. Texts related to the ritual involved the courtship between Inanna and Dumuzi and the consummation of their marriage. In Ur the reigning king evidently took the part of Dumuzi in the ritual, while a priestess or possibly the queen took the part of Inanna. Jerrold Cooper describes the Sumerian love songs related to the sacred marriage as recounting "the couples' tender love and its consummation." Cooper concludes that in the ritual, "most probably, sexual intercourse was involved."[71]

There is strong evidence of the rite being performed in the periods of Ur III and Early Old Babylonian, 2100–1800 BCE, but others think it may have existed long before. Songs recorded in the reign of the ruler Gudea, 2120–2100 BCE, after the fall of the Sargonic empire, contain elements similar to those in this earlier Temple Hymn of Dumuzi. Yitschack Sefati cites a song from a sacred marriage text involving Gudea's personal god Ningirsu (Temple Hymn 20) and his spouse, the goddess Baba (also called Bau, TH 21). In this song, the bed is "cushioned with flowering herbs in the temple's bedchamber, upon which Ningirsu would sleep."[72] Our Dumuzi hymn, from several hundred years earlier, says, "jeweled lapis herbs fleck the shining bed." The similarity of a bed strewn with herbs appears more than coincidental, as if a familiar tradition were being repeated in the hymn Gudea recorded. Nevertheless, there is disagreement among specialists as to the content of the sacred marriage ritual, its nature—sacred or secular—and even the probability of its existence.

Cooper characterizes the tone of the love songs as "lyric bliss" and says they "never lose the innocence of adolescent passion."[73] He makes a strong case that the love songs were written by women and express women's sensibilities. He raises the intriguing question whether the gender of the authors of these ancient texts can be discerned by their content. He says, "The tender, sensuous sexuality of the Inanna-Dumuzi poetry does not lead to conception, and privileges the female organ over the male."[74] The Sumerian love songs sing to the beauty and pleasure of the vulva, for example, "moor my slender boat of heaven / my new moon crescent beauty."[75] They never mention the phallus. The sensuous, erotic tone and "the preoccupation with love in general," as Leick says, are elements of a female voice in the poems, so unlike the aggressive, even violent, quick, goal-directed sexuality that characterizes descriptions of male sexuality.[76] The uniqueness of the emphasis on the woman's pleasure in sexuality offers a view of an aspect of the lives of women in Mesopotamia that stands in contrast to other societies in the ancient world, not to mention the bias in modern patriarchal cultures in the East as well as in the West against women's active role in seeking and delighting in sexual pleasure.

LOVE AND DEATH

The Inanna-Dumuzi mythology is built around two very different poles: love and marriage, on the one hand, and death and mourning on the other. The mourning of Dumuzi is precipitated by two apparently separate events. At the culmination of the myth of Inanna's Descent to the Underworld, Inanna is freed on the condition that she send someone to that unsavory domain in her place. Because in her absence he failed to mourn her terrible plight, Inanna chose to send her husband, Dumuzi. She finds him in Kullab, basking in *her* original glory, sitting on a splendid throne, wearing a magnificent robe. Underworld demons grab him and dispatch him to the Great Below.

In what was probably a later tradition, Dumuzi dies an early death, killed by robbers or bandits. His young widow, Inanna, laments his death, as does his mother, Turtur, and his sister Geshtinanna. Dumuzi had a premonition of his death, recorded in the text "Dumuzi's Dream," in which his sister Geshtinanna interprets a dire forecast. In a later event, his wife, mother, and sister find him dead in the desert and sing the mournful lament:

A reed pipe of dirges —
my heart wants to play
a reed pipe of dirges
in the desert![77]

The cult of mourning for Dumuzi grew from these myths. Cultic events were held in the summer after the barley harvest, when the fields were bare stubble. Dumuzi's death is compared to the barren fields, which revive in the spring, when hope is expressed in the fruitfulness of the Sacred Marriage ritual.

Reference to this tradition of Dumuzi's death occurs in the biblical book of the prophet Ezekiel (8:14–15). Living in Babylon in the sixth century BCE, Ezekiel had a vision of the women of Jerusalem mourning Tammuz, or Dumuzi: "Then he brought me to the entrance of the north gate of the house of the Lord; and behold, there sat women weeping for Tammuz. Then he said to me, 'Have you seen this, O son of man? You will see still greater abominations than these.'"[78] The last evidence of cultic mourning for Dumuzi appears in an Arabic manuscript of the eighth century CE, in which the Sabaean women at Harran in Syria reportedly continued to observe the loss of the shepherd.[79]

The question of whether the songs were written by women or men arises again with the lamentations to Dumuzi. Cooper says, "The ethnographic evidence shows that the one area in which women's music figures even more prominently than in love and wedding songs is funeral lamentation."[80] Raphael Kutcher joins the argument, saying, "The fact that the Dumuzi texts of the first millennium are written mostly in the Emesal dialect, may indicate that the mourning of Dumuzi was performed largely by women and probably also by gala cantors."[81] Emesal is a Sumerian dialect used in texts to record the voices of goddesses and women. The gala were among Inanna's temple personnel.

While this Temple Hymn presents Dumuzi as the radiant one of Inanna, it makes reference to his dark future in the netherworld. The Arali, é-arali, mentioned in the hymn was originally the name of the plain between Badtibira and Uruk, where Dumuzi pastured his sheep. The designation é-arali, as with é-mùš, is an epithet of the temple itself, the Sumerian é, meaning "house," specifying the temple in all the hymns. There in the Arali, in his own sheepfold, he met his death. Thus, Arali became identified with the netherworld, to which Dumuzi was consigned. His unexpected and unwilling committal to the dark below warrants his inclusion in this group of hymns of gods and goddesses known for their travel or domicile in the underworld.

TEMPLE HYMN 18

THE AKKIL TEMPLE OF NINSHUBUR
O house
> your face towers over all
> bounty pours from inside
house
> your storehouse—a mountain of abundance
> your fragrance—a mountain of grapevines
> your true minister—a leader in heaven

house   your princess
stellar among the gods   trusted steward of the Eanna
holds the holy scepter in her hand
Ninshubur
> true vizier of the Eanna
> house of Akkil
has built this house on your radiant site
and placed her seat upon your dais

> 8 lines for the house of Ninshubur at Akkil

THE TEMPLE OF NINSHUBUR AT AKKIL

Anyone familiar with Inanna's mythic "Descent to the Netherworld" remembers faithful Ninshubur, her minister. Ninshubur is the trusted assistant to whom Inanna imparts knowledge of her dangerous mission. Acting under Inanna's instructions, she plays the vital role of alerting the gods to Inanna's captivity and successfully persuades Enki to come to her goddess's rescue. Inanna's centrality in the pantheon asserts itself again, as in the preceding hymn to Dumuzi. Here Ninshubur's identity, twice stated, declares her to be the "true steward of the Eanna," Inanna's large temple complex in Uruk.

TRUSTED CONFIDANTE OF INANNA

The Temple Hymn contains no hint of Ninshubur's underworld connection. She is Inanna's faithful, trusted minister in the Eanna. Her temple exudes abundance and the fragrant scent of grapevines. She is hailed as a leader among the deities of heaven. Her authority is represented by the holy scepter she holds in her hand, a scepter no doubt awarded to her by the powerful Inanna of Uruk.

Tradition tells us that Ninshubur loyally served Inanna in more predicaments than just the goddess's underworld captivity. In another text, Inanna, having discovered that Dumuzi was sleeping with one of her slave girls, calls upon Ninshubur to help carry out her revenge. This text specifically mentions Ninshubur's temple in Akkil:

> [Holy Inanna
>   said to Ninshubur
> "My ever loyal one,]
> my handmaiden,
>   of pleasing words,
> my despatch rider,
>   of true words,
> [knowledgeable, of good j]udgment,
>   mistress of the Akkil temple:
>
> .   .   .   .
> "Come, let us go there,
>   Let us go there!
> Us, let us go there,
>   to the city![82]

Ninshubur, preparing to carry out Inanna's dreadful deed against the young woman, gathers a large group of people from Kullab, Uruk, Zabalam. They meet below the walls of Babylon. Ninshubur instructs the group to kill the slave by whatever means they have at hand. Inanna throws the young woman off the high wall into the crowd below. Her revenge accomplished, the goddess bathes herself, rubs sweet oil on her skin, wraps herself in "the queenly robe," and goes to meet the shepherd, her husband Dumuzi.[83]

Ninshubur serves Inanna in another capacity in the sacred marriage rite. In a text from the reign of Iddin-Dagan in the Isin period (1953–1935 BCE), Ninshubur "leads the king, wearing his hi-li wig, to the 'loins of Inanna'" and says, according to Leick's translation, "The lord whom you have called to (your) heart . . . enjoy long days. / In your delicious, holy lap, grant him a pleasant reign to come."[84] Leick describes the hi-li as "the embodiment of sex-appeal."[85]

NINSHUBUR AND THE NETHERWORLD

Although this Temple Hymn does not mention the underworld, its inclusion in the hymns of this group of gods and goddesses who in some fashion touch the Great Below implies Ninshubur's acquaintance with that dreaded realm. Before the reign of the prominent Old Babylonian king Hammurabi, (1792–1750), Ninshubur had clear underworld connections. She is sometimes listed as the wife of the underworld god Meslamtea, or even of the primary underworld god Nergal (Temple Hymn 36). Nergal was usually known as the husband of Ereshkigal, the Queen of the Netherworld and the so-called sister Inanna visits in the Descent myth. Gebhard Selz even equates Ninshubur with Ereshkigal because she seems to be interchanged with Ereshkigal on one list of deities. He cites the evidence that the šubur portion of Ninshubur's name means "earth," whose mention always insinuates the underworld.[86]

Ninshubur's temple at Akkil is thought to be located near Uruk, in the geographic neighborhood of Inanna's well-known city. The name Akkil means 'House of Lamentation,' ritual lamentation being the traditional observance on the occasion of tragic loss. Women carried out the important office of lamentation and wrote the poignant mourning hymns. The name House of Lamentation would identify Ninshubur's temple as having a major focus on death and the dreaded underworld. In an early Old Babylonian hymn she is even a minister in the netherworld: sukkal-ki-gal-la-kur-ra-ke$_4$, "vizier of the big place of the netherworld."[87] Dina Katz says, "The tradition that attributed the office of vizier to Ninšubur is firmly established, though not so much in whose service she held it."[88] In one building inscription she is called vizier to the god of heaven, An, while in the Descent myth she is minister to Inanna.

In Inanna's Descent, Ninshubur is specifically charged to carry out an act of mourning. Inanna directs her:

> I am going down below
> when I reach that place
> wail for me
> cry in lamentation by the ruins
> play a drum song
> drum for me in the throne court
> wander for me
> wander through the houses of the gods
>
> tear at your eyes
> tear at your mouth
> tear at the place you show no one
> wear rags for me
> only rags[89]

Ninshubur carefully carries out Inanna's instructions and cries in lamentation before the gods. Frymer-Kensky suggests that these laments were "intense performances which entailed dramatic and painful acts, . . . almost certainly a reflection of mourning behavior on the human scene."[90] Such lamentation was a part of the world of goddesses and women. Here Ninshubur illustrates her multiple and contradictory roles. Although she is said to be an underworld deity, in this instance she mourns the terrible fate of Inanna, trapped there in the Great Below.

NINSHUBUR — MALE OR FEMALE

Ninshubur is one of many deities whose identity shifted as societies changed over the millennia. Even her gender changed. In this Temple Hymn she is clearly the female aid to Inanna. Following the Sargonic period there were two parallel traditions. In some instances she is female and in some male. Likewise, she is sometimes related to the heavenly gods and sometimes to the netherworld.

By the time of Hammurabi (1792–1750) and after, Ninshubur had become a male steward, unrelated to the netherworld. Wolfgang Heimpel explains Ninshubur's gender variability, arguing that as a vizier figure the deity followed "the custom for a master to have a vizier of the same gender."[91] As mistress to Inanna, she was female. Later, as minister to the Old Babylonian king Rim-Sin 8 in Larsa, she occupied "a room in the sanctuary of an Inana figure" and therefore, like her goddess, she was female.[92] As a minister to Rim-Sin 12 and Rim-Sin 13, she resided in temples in Ur called "House-providing-Instruction" and "House-raising-the-Head-in-total-Power," temples decidedly masculine, and therefore Ninshubur was male.[93]

As occurred in many Sumerian deities, Ninshubur's character evolved over the four millennia that the pantheon dominated the ancient Near East. In this Temple Hymn, Enheduanna adheres to the third-millennium tradition of a female Ninshubur, right hand, minister, and trusted confidante of Inanna. Temple Hymns 16, 17, and 18, to Inanna, Dumuzi, and Ninshubur, respectively, group the principal characters in the myth of Inanna's Descent to the Netherworld. The focus on Inanna is again evidence of her prominence as the principal female deity of this era as well as of her being the adored personal deity of Enheduanna herself.

TEMPLE HYMN 19

THE MURUM TEMPLE OF NINGIRIN

O city
set fast upon its dais by abzu's magic powers
built for exorcism   a priestly craft
to chant in your house incantations of heaven and earth
and sprinkle flour heaps and barley
your princess Ningirin   your strong spouse
under holy heaven and earth
cools herself with pure water from Agubba vessels

Ningirin   Lady of the bright Agubba
O house of Murum
has built this house on your radiant site
and established her seat upon your throne

9 lines for the house of Ningirin in Murum

THE TEMPLE OF NINGIRIN AT MURUM

Ningirin's illustrious history is the subject of this Temple Hymn. In the pre-Sargonic era, around 2500 BCE, she was called upon for healing and purification rites. Her name was typically recited in an incantation's closing formula, where it invoked the auspicious power of the deity to seal the prayerful act that was the purpose of the ritual. Such incantations were performed in settings to heal the sick, to purify a sacred space, or to rectify any situation discordant with the divine order. The incantation ritual served to restore harmony in the cosmos.

ISHIB PRIESTS AND DIVINATION DEITIES

The city of Murum on a magical dais was created for the ishib priest, the important cultic figure whose elaborate training prepared him to officiate in rites of incantation to restore order in heaven, on earth, and even in the underworld. The Temple Hymn specifically connects Ningirin's city, Murum, with the god Enki and his sweet-water domain in the abzu. The abzu, thought to be the source of all life and the origin of Sumerian culture and civilization, also contained a passage to the netherworld. Ningirin's city, the hymn says, was placed on the solid foundation of a dais in Enki's abzu.

Enki is the god of ishib craft. In the myth "Inanna and the God of Wisdom," ishib craft is among the **me**, the divine essences of civilization, that the drunken Enki gives to Inanna, and that Inanna, to Enki's dismay, takes by boat to her city of Uruk. In the pre-Sargonic era Ningirin, in her role as incantation priestess, was particularly associated with Uruk. Although Ningirin is closely related to Uruk and to Enki's city of Eridu, she established her temple in Murum, a city thought to be south of Badtibira.[94]

Ningirin's prominence as an incantation deity had already begun to decline in the time of the collection of the Temple Hymns. Graham Cunningham surmises that Enheduanna included her as a significant goddess "possibly respecting a then-changing tradition."[95] Tikva Frymer-Kensky supports the thesis that "the marginalization of the goddess" was in process even at the time of the earliest written records. She writes,

> In the earliest historical period, that of the Abu Salabikh and Fara texts (ca. 2500), there was a very important goddess, Ningirin, who appears prominently in the incantation literature as the exorcist of the gods, the goddess of magical formulae and of water purification.

In later Sumerian times, exorcism and incantation are in the hands
of Enki and his son, Asarluhi. . . . Ningirin never disappears entirely
from the magical literature of later Mesopotamia, but she becomes
a very minor figure whose role in exorcism and incantation is over-
shadowed by Enki and Asarluhi and is only a faint echo of her earlier
prominence.[96]

FLOUR AND WATER

Enheduanna's inclusion of Ningirin in the Temple Hymns derives from the
goddess's history. Cunningham cites three pre-Sargonic incantations in which
Ningirin is given the epithet of *mašmaššu* priestess, a title equated with the
ishib priest.[97] The *mašmaššu* is said to create "magic circles made with flour,"
according to Richard Henshaw; this is probably the ritual action referred to
in the hymn, "and sprinkle flour heaps and barley."[98] The sprinkling of flour
as food for the dead in the underworld was an act repeated throughout the
cultic year.

Ningirin's association with the abzu is related to the "pure water" in the
hymn. She claims the bright agubba vessel, the container of the purifying
water used to cleanse in order to wash away the evil situation.

Ningirin was also known as agrig-mah-dinger-re-ne, great steward to
all the gods. Frymer-Kensky says this epithet means steward, manager, or
housekeeper and established certain goddesses in managerial roles.[99] In a
pre-Sargonic riddle, Ningirin is called "the great true-eyed one of heaven,"
an epithet that associates her with the astral deities.[100] Nevertheless, in the
Temple Hymn her domain includes both heaven and earth. The mention of
earth always involves mortality, a foreboding of the realm of the netherworld,
and thus situates Ningirin among the goddesses and gods of this group, all of
whom, in one capacity or other, have visited the Great Below.

chapter 8

HYMNS TO TEMPLES IN THE LAGASH TERRITORY

Temple Hymns to the shrines in the territory of Lagash address a family affair of the gods, led by Lord Ningirsu and his wife, Bau; his sister Nanshe and Nanshe's daughter Ninmar; and finally Dumuzi-abzu, who we assume was a relative, although the scant evidence does not reveal her connection. While the hymns depict Ningirsu and Bau as bearing the weight of the formidable political power of Lagash, Nanshe, Ninmar, and Dumuzi-abzu have other concerns: playing in the waves, inspecting the bountiful fish harvest, and singing their hearts out in joy.

Ningirsu and Bau exert their prestige to maintain the rule of law, tradition, and the autonomy of Lagash over insurgents. Their concerns lie in the external political world, while the three remaining goddesses draw us into the inner realm of dreams and divination, contemplative introspection, and exuberant worship of the gods in the temples. The predominance of goddesses in the Lagash group, with its one god named Nin-girsu, "Lady of Girsu," suggestively transports the remnants of antiquity into these late-third-millennium hymns, with the possibility that the original city god of Girsu, the capital of Lagash, was female.

From earliest evidence, each Sumerian city and town was organized around a predominant deity. The patron deity gave a sense of community and religious identity to the inhabitants. The early temple with its personnel, its holdings of land, and its control over agriculture as well as goods for the economy ruled the life of all its citizens. As populations grew, so did conflicts between cities, over land, water, the essential irrigation canals, and trade. For several

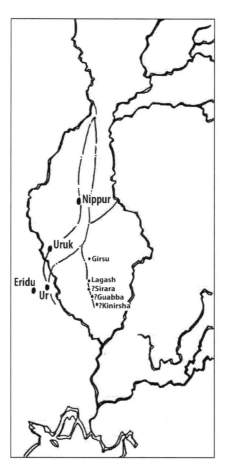

8.1.   Sketch map of Mesopotamia with
Lagash and neighboring cities. After
Postgate 1994. Reproduced by permission
of Taylor and Francis Books U.K.

centuries before the writing of the Temple Hymns, kings and military leaders
had intruded their authority into the domain of the economic and social dominance of the temples. Having to cope with increasing conflicts, the secular
rulers took charge, negotiating new rules and boundaries, usurping authority
that once was held by the priests of the temples. Thus, the last king of the
powerful First Dynasty of Lagash, Urukagina, took control of all the property
of the temples, claiming his prerogative came from Ningirsu himself, the deity
who had chosen the king to rule.

During much of the third millennium, Ningirsu, Inanna, and Enki were the
three most prominent gods of the pantheon. Enlil was not mentioned in the
early texts from Fara as the primary god he was to become, nor was Nippur

the holy city. Probably just before the Sargonic era, by means of challenges during much of the third millennium that we do not fully understand, the priests of Enlil in Nippur claimed Enlil's son Ninurta to be equal to the powerful Ningirsu of Lagash. They proceeded to elevate Enlil to the rank of highest god in the pantheon, he who alone could select and crown the secular ruler of the state.[1] In this process, Ningirsu's parentage was altered from being the son of Enki and Ninhursag to being a son of Enlil and Ninlil of Nippur. Several cities on the plain acquiesced to this transfer of power to Enlil.

The name Lagash means 'raven,' the territory thus adopting the large, intelligent black bird as its emblem. 'Raven' may have designated a particular clan that settled Lagash, as bird clans are known to have lent their names to other cities. In 1877 a French expedition led by Ernest de Sarzec carried out in Lagash the first significant archeological excavation of a Sumerian site. Sarzec led eleven campaigns, and his French colleagues dug for another nine seasons, until 1933. Because of the French archeologists' choice of this excavation site, the earliest and the most numerous readable cuneiform tablets come from Lagash. Thousands of tablets were discovered. Many are inventories of various commodities, but Lagash yielded the longest and most abundant inscriptions as well. Some sixteen hundred administrative texts and ration lists alone were found in an archive room of the Bau temple, unfortunately already looted by thieves.

The territory of Lagash, cut by a long north-south irrigation canal, extended south, apparently to what was then the northern tip of the Persian Gulf. Harriet Crawford says that the many third-millennium texts that locate Lagash on the coast may be accurate.[2] Waters of the gulf have now receded and have left a sizable fertile plain between ancient Lagash and the coast. If, therefore, Ninmar's temple once fronted on the seashore, this would explain the poet's placing it "at the sea's edge," while at the same time her mother, Nanshe, "born on the shore of the sea" was "laughing in the sea foam / playing, playing in the waves."

TEMPLE HYMN 20

THE LAGASH TEMPLE OF NINGIRSU
Eninnu

Eninnu
right arm of thick-necked Lagash in Sumer
with heavy-cloud bird Anzu's eyes
that scan insurgent mountains
Ningirsu's crowd-flattener blade a menace in all lands

8.2. Plow symbol of Ningirsu. Courtesy of the
University of Texas Press, Jeremy Black and Anthony
Green, *Gods, Demons and Symbols of Ancient
Mesopotamia,* Tessa Richards, illustrator, 1995.

battle arm   blasting storm drenching everyone
battle arm   the Annuna   all the great gods
     grant again and again

so from your skin of bricks
on the rim of the holy hill   green as mountains
you determine fates
a holy whirlpool spins in your river
blowing whirlwinds spawn from your glance

at the gate facing the Holy City
they pour wine into fine stone vessels of An
     out under the sky
what comes in cannot be equaled
what goes out never ceases
at the fiery face of the Shugalam gate
     its radiant brilliance   the fate-cutting site
Lord Ningirsu besieges with hair-raising fear
all the Annuna appear at your great wine festival

your prince   furious storm-wind
destroyer of rebel cities
your king   angry bull flaunting his brawn
savage lion that makes heads shake
warrior   the lord of lords who plots schemes
king of kings who mounts victories
mighty one, great hero, in battle has no rival
son of Enlil   lord Ningirsu
O Eninnu,
has built this house on your radiant site
and established his seat upon your throne

     22 lines for the house of Ningirsu in Lagash

THE TEMPLE OF NINGIRSU IN LAGASH

Temple Hymn 20 is one of the longest in the collection, testimony to the significance of Lagash and its ruling deity, Ningirsu. The territory of Lagash covered some three thousand square kilometers. Ningirsu's temple, the Eninnu, stood in its capital city, Girsu. The cultural distinction of Lagash is preserved in the number of cuneiform tablets that meticulously record inventories over hundreds of years, as J. N. Postgate reports, "by far the longest and most numerous historical inscriptions" yet discovered.[3]

This trove of information convinced archeologists that Lagash was a thriving Early Dynastic city-state in southern Mesopotamia. The information from the tablets, by extrapolation, describes as well the structure of other contemporary city-states. Each city-state had a capital that held the temple of its principal deity. The entire population of the area upheld the centrality of the patron deity, not only the residents of the capital, but also those in the surrounding smaller agricultural communities. The single male ruler, although secular, served under the will of the deity in the main temple. In Lagash, Ningirsu was the deity who granted "rule of the state to a human ruler."[4]

In spite of its size and political importance, Lagash is not mentioned as a principality in the Sumerian King List. Even though Ningirsu and the other Lagash deities are not included in the list, they appear throughout the large corpus of early tablets, providing ample evidence of their presence and influence. A "theology of Lagash" developed around Ningirsu. It became one of the three influential theologies along with those of Nippur and Eridu.[5]

NINGIRSU'S PARADOXICAL NATURE

The Temple Hymn to Ningirsu portrays the god's complex character, which modulates between his warrior fierceness and his gentle farmer nature. On the one hand, his temple, situated in "thick-necked Lagash," blasts with storms and swings Ningirsu's "crowd-flattener blade." Yet, the "holy hill" where the temple stands is "green as mountains," while all the great gods, the Annuna, gather "out under the sky" for a "great wine festival," as they drink from An's "fine stone vessels." War and refinement, savage destruction and divine revelry were present under one roof.

Who is Ningirsu that he attracts such contradiction? The hymn describes him as a ferocious warrior. In other contexts he is known as a gentle god of the plow. His symbolic plow appears on ancient *kudurru,* large carved stelae that were placed in the temples to record transfers of royal land. Symbols on the *kudurru* ensured the divine legitimacy of the transaction. As a fertility god, Ningirsu's powerful rainstorms filled the Tigris each spring to overflowing, allowing for the cultivation of crops along its tributaries and canals. The post-Sargonic Lagash ruler Gudea prayed to Ningirsu, praising his "seminal waters reddened in the deflowering," as though Ningirsu's sexual act awakened the flooding river.[6] Like Ninurta, his counterpart in Nippur (Temple Hymn 5), Ningirsu was both a fierce warrior and docile farmer.

TWO GODS OR ONE: MALE OR FEMALE?

Ningirsu and Ninurta may always have been identical, two names for the same god, although Ningirsu is named in the Early Dynastic period at Lagash with no comparable early mention of Ninurta. Whether one of the two gods came before the other is a point of controversy.[7] As noted in the hymns to the Nippur gods, Temple Hymns 2–7, in the Sargonic era Nippur was the religious center of the country. Nevertheless, Lagash to the south claimed an illustrious pantheon.

In Nippur, Ninurta's temple joined that of his father, Enlil, in defending the position of the city's elite priesthood. William Hallo offers a hypothesis with political overtones. Citing "the well-attested resistance of the Nippur priesthood to the claims of Lagash," he suggests that Ninurta, an "obscure local deity of Nippur," gained recognition by equating himself with the well-known Ningirsu, "the price exacted from a Lagashite deity for admission to the Nippur pantheon"; in this case, Hallo says, the well-known myth of the "Return of Ninurta to Nippur" would celebrate "the introduction of his cult there," not Ninurta's return.[8] At whatever time the equation of the two gods occurred, it was in place from the Sargonic era onward.

Although Ningirsu and Ninurta may have been identical gods in the Sargonic era, they maintained separate mythologies in their principal cities. In Girsu, Ningirsu's mother was Ninhursag, whereas, as we have seen in Temple Hymn 5, Ninurta's mother in Nippur was Ninlil. The two hymns in this collection treat the gods as different deities, each bearing influence in the religious pantheon of his geographical area. However, at some point a syncretism between the two took place, and in later god lists they became interchangeable.

In still another intriguing controversy, Wolfgang Heimpel asks why this god Ningirsu, "the image of testosterone-laden maleness," is called "Lady of Girsu"—the nin element in his name being the Sumerian word for 'lady' or 'queen.'[9] The cuneiform sign for nin clearly refers to a female, containing as it does the ancient image of the pubic triangle.

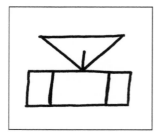

8.3.   Jemdet-Nasr 3200–3000 BCE sign for nin. After Labat, 1995. Courtesy Editions GEUTHNER, Paris.

Heimpel disputes the various philological arguments that attempt to explain the element nin in the names of numerous male deities. He suspects that sometime in prehistory city gods were primarily female and that over time male gods took their places, retaining the goddesses' names.[10] He offers that hypothetical case that in Girsu a male god could have taken over the function formerly held by the goddess Bau (Temple Hymn 21, wife of Ningirsu), who may have been the original "Lady of Girsu," that is, "divine overseer of the affairs of the city," and this god gained stature and simply retained the title Nin-Girsu.[11] He bolsters his argument by noting that by the end of the third millennium Bau did indeed lose all of the considerable property she held in the Early Dynastic III era. This scenario supports the thesis of Frymer-Kensky that over time the status of the goddesses diminished. She says that from the first written records there is evidence of "the ongoing eclipse and the marginalization of the goddesses."[12]

EARLY DYNASTIC LAGASH

While the rivalry between Nippur and Lagash may have resulted in the repression of the Lagash traditions, Lagash nevertheless, Hallo asserts, "played . . . a major role in Sumerian history."[13] Some thirty city-states developed in southern Sumer in the Early Dynastic period, each with its own principal deity and secular ruler. Early Lagash is well documented in the numerous tablets found in its ruins.

As populations grew in the cities, so did an escalation of conflicts over boundaries, water, irrigation, plunder, and trade routes, disputes common to rival hegemonies. One conflict that was to last for centuries was that between the two city-states Lagash and Umma, a dispute that spurred the erection of city walls and the creation of new rules of conduct, neither of which secured an enduring peace. On one outstanding monument, the Stele of the Vultures, commemorating a victory of the king Eanatum of Lagash over Umma (2450

BCE), Ningirsu is said to have "implanted the semen for Eanatum in the womb . . . Ninhursag offered him her beneficial breast. . . . With great joy Ningirsu gave him the Kingship of Lagash."[14] This magnificent stele would have stood in a place of honor in Ningirsu's temple. Eanatum, being progeny of the god, justified his military exploits as fulfilling divine will.

The last of the Early Dynastic Old Sumerian rulers of Lagash, Urukagina (2350), also claimed to have been appointed by Ningirsu, as he fought the wars with Umma. Urukagina was noted for his attempts at social and ethical reforms. Hallo says, "His intervention on behalf of widows, orphans and impoverished citizenry generally became a tradition repeatedly emulated in Old Babylonian times in the form of royal edicts proclaiming liberty (from debt-slavery) throughout the land."[15] Unfortunately, Urukagina also watched over the final destruction of Lagash by the Umma ruler Lugalzagesi. Lugalzagesi's tenure was short-lived, for Sargon's armies soon conquered Umma and Lagash and marched to the sea, ushering in a new dynasty named for its Semitic king, Enheduanna's father, Sargon.

THE TEMPLE OF NINGIRSU — THE ENINNU

The temple of Ningirsu in Girsu was built and rebuilt by the rulers of Lagash. Throughout the centuries it was called Eninnu, meaning 'house fifty.' Ningirsu's sacred number was fifty. As in many of the Temple Hymns, the temple Eninnu comes alive, assuming properties and powers that normally belong only to the anthropomorphic gods. Its eyes scan the mountains; its fearsome battle arm swings Ningirsu's holy weapon, menacing with deadly power and natural catastrophe. With dread and "hair-raising fear" the supplicants wait at the gate while the god dispenses to every individual his or her destiny. The temple's eyes are "Anzu's eyes," eyes of the gigantic lion-headed eagle killed by Ninurta/Ningirsu for stealing the tablets of destiny from Enki and depicted as a heraldic animal of Ningirsu on the Stele of the Vultures.[16] Its "battle arm" swings the šár-úr, Ningirsu's "crowd-flattener blade," his divine weapon that took on the personification of a divinity and, as a secondary god, may itself have received offerings.[17] The gate "facing the Holy City" must have been one of the six gates in the wall surrounding the compound of the principal temples. Here the gods drink wine from the vessels of An. The Shugalam gate, mentioned later in the hymn, may be the same gate as the first, although its "fiery face" at the "fate-cutting site" suggests quite a different ambience. The word Shugalam means 'gate of the artful hand.'

The hymn describes the sight viewers standing before the Eninnu would have seen. The Eninnu is power driven. It holds the sword of fate over each individual's head. Its description in the hymn creates a social and cultural context for the viewer, who would rightfully be awestruck and fearful of its unique gathering of power. Irene Winter describes the contrast between the reaction of the gods to their temples ("joy, pleasure, delight") and that of the spectators, who experience the temple "in terms of its awesome impact on themselves and on their lives."[18] She cites the inscription the Lagash ruler Gudea wrote for his rebuilding of the Eninnu of Ningirsu: "The temple, its awesome radiance was cast over the land; its praise reached the mountains. The Eninnu, its dread covered all the lands like a garment."[19]

As the most important temple inside the Lagash territory, the Eninnu was a haven for major festivals throughout the year. These annual festivals were marked by the names of months in the calendar. Prior to Sargon's conquest of the Sumerian cities in the south, there were several calendars in use in the Lagash cities, at least three in the cities of Girsu, Ninâ, Sirara, and in other, smaller villages. These various calendars record some thirty month names.[20] After his conquest Sargon developed a unified calendar for the area.

Given Sargon's policy of placating the conquered Sumerian population, we can assume he encouraged a continuation of the traditional festival observances. The primary festivals of Ningirsu in Girsu were the Barley Consumption festival and the Malt Consumption festival. Both lasted for two days, during which time offerings were made to Ningirsu and to his family. Participants from all the Lagash cities joined in the celebration. At least in the pre-Sargonic observances, Mark Cohen says,

> The wife of the governor was responsible for organizing the offerings and leading the procession of pilgrims from town to town, from shrine to shrine. . . . [T]he offerings remained surprisingly constant in quantity and content, consisting of meal, emmer and black beer, oil, dates, a food mixture and bundles of fish, accompanied by sheep and lambs for the more important deities and goats for the lesser gods. . . . Assuredly there were elaborate ceremonies conducted by the temple priests, with prayers, songs and other ritual acts.[21]

Festivals to deceased ancestors focused on offerings directed toward the netherworld. The temple of Ningirsu as well as that of his wife, Bau (or Baba), received these offerings. Past rulers were also honored in the annual festivals. The first day's activities, called the Courtyard Festival, focused on Baba/Bau and "was marked by offerings to deities whose statues presumably were assembled in the courtyard."[22] The second day's offerings included Ningirsu and Bau. The festival continued for two more days, during which the participants traveled to the area of Badtibira and again offered food and drink for the dead ancestors as well as for the gods. Evidence for these festivals comes from pre-Sargonic Lagash and may well have been continued into the Sargonic era.

LAGASH AFTER THE SARGONIC EMPIRE

The end of the Sargonic empire is attributed to the excesses and irreverence of the last powerful king, Naram-Sin, against the god Enlil and his city, Nippur. S. N. Kramer, citing the poem "The Curse of Agade," describes the king's iniquities: "[Naram-Sin] had acted contrary to Enlil's word: he had permitted his soldiers to attack and ravage the Ekur and its groves; he had demolished the buildings of the Ekur with copper axes and hatchets, so that 'the house lay prostrate like a dead youth'—indeed, 'all the lands lay prostrate.'"[23] Enlil in his anger called down a mountain people, the Gutians, who "covered the earth like the locust."[24]

Naram-Sin's son, Sharkalisharri, attempted to restore order in the Akkadian empire, but his territory was eventually reduced merely to the city of Akkad itself. The Gutian political control was limited and lasted only about fifty years. Lagash managed to survive as an independent state, apparently favored by the Gutians. In its prosperity, the Lagash ruler Ur-Bau rebuilt the temples and even appointed his daughter as high priestess to Nanna in Ur, the post long held by Enheduanna and subsequently by her grandniece, the daughter of Naram-Sin. The son-in-law of Ur-Bau, Gudea, succeeded him and secured Lagash as a prosperous state, establishing trade with many of the states in the civilized world.

Gudea, like rulers before him, claimed to have been chosen by Ningirsu and selected him as his personal deity. In a dream the god appeared to Gudea as the Anzu bird, the lion-headed eagle mentioned in the Temple Hymn. In the dream Gudea was told to restore Ningirsu's temple, the Eninnu. An elegant statue of the ruler Gudea shows him seated with an architectural drawing of the temple resting on his lap along with an architect's ruler. On Gudea's skirt is carved a hymn portraying the god entering his new house, the rebuilt Eninnu, described in hymnal fashion:

> The house lifted in great offices
>   the head
> was the perfection of awe and glory[25]

Thus, the god Ningirsu retained his position of power long after the demise of the Sargonic empire. As Girsu faded in importance, however, so did Ningirsu. More and more his renown and his myths were attributed to the Nippur god Ninurta.

TEMPLE HYMN 21

THE URUKU TEMPLE OF BAU
Etarsirsir

> Uruku   holy city
> seed-sprouting shrine of holy An
> called by a good name
> from your interior   the river ordeal
> washes the decent man clean
>
> house of widespread council   pure storehouse
> makes its silver and lapis endure
> Etarsirsir
> divine decision and **me** devising
> where the steadfast man worships
>
> your princess, merciful princess of the homeland
> mother of all lands
> Lady great healer of the black-haired
> who decides the fate of her city
> firstborn child of holy An
> maiden and mother
> Bau
> has   O Uruku house
> built this house on your radiant site
> and established her seat upon your dais
>
>   8 lines for the house of Bau in Uruku

THE TEMPLE OF BAU IN GIRSU

Bau's Temple Hymn follows that of her spouse, Ningirsu. The first word, "Uruku," refers to the Holy City, a sacred walled area in Girsu that enclosed the city's principal temples. Ningirsu's temple was inside the Holy City, as was that of Bau. Given Ningirsu's prominence in the pantheon and the lead position of his Temple Hymn among the hymns to temples in the territory of Lagash, one would expect that he was the principal god of the Holy City. However, as Heimpel points out, "Bau is called 'Lady of the Holy City,' while Ningirsu is never referred to in the Holy City as its king or Lord."[26] Bau's temple, Etarsirsir, even had a second name, é-uru-kù-ga, House of the Holy City.[27]

The first line tells us that from Bau's shrine the god of heaven An generated seed, implying that human seed emerged from Bau's temple according to the creative purpose of her father, An. An, then, is god the creator. In another text he is called "An who makes (made) the seed come forth, the father of all existing things."[28] The Oxford electronic text translation of this line of the Temple Hymn specifically calls the seed human: "O . . . (Holy city), shrine of holy An, which caused the human seed to come forth."[29] His daughter Bau, "first-born child of holy An," resides in the temple that houses the origin of humankind. Was she the original "Lady of Girsu?"

As the Sumerian city-states grew and consolidated, various dominating pantheons in the principal localities established themselves. Some developed their own mythologies, and consequently an assortment of origin stories emerged. The pantheon in Lagash is known from the Early Dynastic III period, prior to the Sargonic era. Undoubtedly it existed in the obscure eras before this final Early Dynastic phase when written records began. Remnants of mythological stories from the ancient past may appear in these later hymns of Enheduanna that still give authority to Bau in the Holy City and to an origin myth arising out of her temple in Girsu.

BAU — MAIDEN AND MOTHER

In literary tradition Bau is alternately a revered maiden and an all-encompassing mother. The Temple Hymn follows suit. The hymn includes her birth as child of An and refers to her as both maiden and mother. Another text relates her biography:

> your father (. . .), highest of the gods, who clothed you in divine
>   raiment,
> Gave you the hero of Enlil, Ningirsu, [to be your] husband,
> Gave you the Eninnu, the 'Holy City', the sanctuary, which 'lets the
>   seed emerge out.'[30]

Decoding this text from the following Isin period, in the light of the Temple Hymn, it says Bau is given four gifts: Ningirsu, his temple the Eninnu, the Holy City, and finally the sanctuary where the seed are engendered, her temple the Etarsirsir.

In another text, in what Gwendolyn Leick says may be "a traditional wedding song," Bau delights in her maidenhood. In this song she is called Baba, another name for Bau and possibly a pet name for Inanna:

> Now my breasts stand up,
> Now hair has grown on my vulva,
> Going to the bridegroom's loins, let us rejoice!
> O Baba, let us rejoice over my vulva!
> Dance! Dance!
> Afterwards they will please him, will please him![31]

This wedding song belonged to ritual texts of the sacred marriage celebrating the union of a divine couple, a ritual that dates back to prehistoric times. There is evidence that the ritual was observed in Lagash during the Sargonic era. In Lagash the divine couple was Bau and Ningirsu, while the most celebrated Sumerian couple was Inanna and Dumuzi of Uruk. The ritual union of Bau and Ningirsu was recorded by the subsequent Lagash ruler Gudea:

> Its bed, when it had been set up in the bedroom,
> Was (like) a young cow kneeling down in the place where it slept,
> On its pure back, spread with fresh hay,
> Mother Bau was lying down with lord Ningirsu.[32]

The timing of the festival coincided with the New Year, when the Tigris was overflowing with spring rains and snowmelt from the mountains. As the red-brown waters of the Tigris were metaphorically identified as Ningirsu's deflowering of a maiden river, so the central event of the sacred marriage ritual was the deflowering of the maiden Bau. The purpose of the sacred marriage ritual was to assure a bountiful harvest and the fertility of the land. Both Bau and Ningirsu were associated with agriculture. Bau was known as a rain goddess, and her emblem inscribed on *kudurru* is a winnowing fan.

As a mother, Bau had two sons by Ningirsu and seven daughters whose paternity is not claimed and who became minor goddesses in Lagash. In the Temple Hymn Bau is called by the epithet ama-kur-kur-ra, 'mother of all the lands.' Åke Sjöberg says this epithet is striking and reports that Aruru-Nintu (see Ninhursag, Temple Hymns 7, 29, and 39) is also called ama-mah-kur-kur-a, 'resplendent mother of all lands,' while Enki and Enlil (Temple Hymns 1 and 2) share the epithet 'father of all the lands.'[33] These epithets seem to be reserved for only the most prominent and revered parents.

SUPPLICATION TO BAU

Worshipers carried their prayers to Bau even before the Sargonic era. An inscription on a statue placed in the courtyard of Bau's temple prays, "To Bau, gracious lady, daughter of An, queen of the holy city," for the life of the ruler of Lagash, and "for the mother who bore him," begging Bau to "turn her ear, speak my prayers."[34] From the same Early Dynastic period a hymn to Bau included prayers for the king Eanatum of Lagash. She must have been thought of as kind and approachable, for supplications intended for Ningirsu were taken to her in hopes she would transmit them to Ningirsu when he was in a generous humor.

Bau's compassion as the "merciful princess" is expressed in her role as a healer. As the hymn says, she is "great healer of the black-haired," an epithet of the dark-haired Sumerians. And like other goddesses, Bau weeps in lament when her city is destroyed. Frymer-Kensky tells us that lamenting "was not only a matter of tears and songs. It was an intense performance which entailed dramatic and painful acts."[35]

Bau's involvement in determining an accused person's guilt or innocence receives brief mention in the hymn. She is said to make judgments from the interior of her temple, the traditional dark heart of the sacred cella, the place where the deity lives. There she "washes the decent man clean" by means of the river ordeal. The just man is thus exonerated. No mention is made of the deadly possibility of drowning accorded to those judged guilty.

THE ETARSIRSIR

The meaning of the name of Bau's temple in Girsu, Etarsirsir, is unclear; Sjöberg cites a variant name for the same temple, house that makes "the mes come forth."[36] Bau's worship almost without exception took place in Lagash, and her temple in Girsu was its center. Lagash was a prosperous territory, and from the Early Dynastic period through the Sargonic era its temples "did undoubtedly constitute a major component of the economy and society."[37] Postgate describes the three categories of overseers of the lands of the Bau temple. The first unit was cultivated by the temple staff "for the benefit of the temple" and was designated "property of the en," that is, of the high priest and consequently of the temple itself. The second unit, "ration fields," was comprised of lands cultivated by the temple staff for their own use. The third unit, "tenant fields," lands that were sharecropped or rented, was made up of lands not needed by the temple.[38]

This complex system was managed by temple personnel, giving its leaders power over the prosperous economy. With its location near both fresh- and saltwater, Girsu's access to boat and barge transportation was the principal means of travel and trade. George Bass estimates that there were 125 boatmen from the temple of Bau: "These boatmen, including rowers and helmsmen, were freemen, but male and female slaves were assigned to crews and even belonged, at times, to the individual sailors, among whom were foreigners."[39]

Some sixteen hundred tablets found in the Bau temple, according to Postgate, recorded its economic activities: "cultivation of cereals, vegetables and fruit trees, including the control of irrigation waters; management of flocks of sheep and goats and herds of cows and equids; fishing in fresh and salt water; manufacture of textiles, leather and wooden items, metalwork and stone; promotion of trading links with foreign lands."[40] The discovery of that number of tablets indicates the extent of managerial and scribal activities taking place in the temple. Among the finds was the earliest envelope, which Postgate describes as "simply a thin layer of clay formed round the tablet so that it looks like a fatter version of itself."[41] The purpose of the envelope can be surmised as a way to conceal the contents and assure the recipient that the tablet inside had not been tampered with or changed in any way.

While Bau is not typically placed among the most prominent goddesses and gods, she held a central position in the pantheon of the important territory of Lagash. That she was not worshiped in other cities does not diminish the significance she is given in the Temple Hymn as first child of An, as goddess of a temple that watches over his seed-generating power, as guardian of the power of divine decisions, and as a merciful goddess, the epitome of compassion.

Postgate includes his translation of Temple Hymn 21 in his book *Early Mesopotamia*. He prefaces the translation with his introduction to Enheduanna:

> The literary compilation called the Sumerian Temple Hymns is known to us from the output of scribes working in schools of the Old Babylonian period, around 1800 BC, but the text itself states that its author is Enheduanna, daughter of Sargon of Akkad and priestess of Nanna, the moon-god at Ur. Although there are some obvious later additions, like the hymn to the deified Ur III King Šulgi, this is generally accepted as

an original composition of the Akkad period. The poem is a collection
of short individual addresses to all the major sanctuaries of the southern plain. Each one describes the temple and then its deity in figurative
language which must be full of allusions now mostly lost to us.

Text 2:1 Temple Hymn No. 21 to the Temple of Bau in Urukug
    (=Lagaš)
Urukug, shrine which causes the seed to come forth, belonging to the
    holy An, called by a good name,
Within you is the river of ordeal which vindicates the just man,
House of widespread counsel, storehouse which eternally possesses
    silver and lapis lazuli,
Your princess, the merciful princess of the land, the mother of all lands,
The lady, the great healer of the dark-headed, who determines the
    destiny of her city,
The first-born daughter of the holy An, the maid, mother Bau,
Has, O house Urukug, placed the house upon your . . . , has taken her
    place upon your dais.

    8 (lines). The house of Bau in Urukug.[42]

TEMPLE HYMN 22

THE SIRARA TEMPLE OF NANSHE
Shilam

O house   you wild cow
there to conjure signs from divination
you arise   splendid to behold
bedecked for your princess
Sirara   great and princely place
you   dream-opener
highly prized in the shrine

your lady Nanshe
    a great storm   strong dark water
born on the shore of the sea
    laughing in the sea foam
    playing, playing in the waves
divine Nanshe   mighty Lady

O house of Sirara
has built this house on your radiant site
and placed her seat upon your dais

10 lines for the house of Nanshe in Sirara

THE TEMPLE OF NANSHE IN SIRARA

Nanshe, like the other goddesses in the Lagash group, is the chief deity of her city, Sirara. She is goddess of the sea and is notable for symbolically spanning the unreachable distance between the conscious civilized society and the dark and demonic waters of the unknown sea. Her paradoxical character comes across in this simultaneously ominous and charming verse of the hymn:

a great storm
strong dark water
born on the shore of the sea
laughing in the sea foam
playing, playing in the waves

As the verse implies, Nanshe is at home in the sea.

SUMERIAN COSMOLOGY

In the older Sumerian worldview of the third millennium, the defining edge of the cosmos is the sea, which harbors a brood of demons. The underworld does not yet exist in this mythology. Even when the underworld comes to be in later mythology, the sea encircles the known world and continues to provide a haven for dark, uncivilized demons.

In one account of the worldview, an ocean encircles the earth and its inhabitants. This vista from the Etana legend is seen from far above the earth. An early "map of the world" from Fara in the Early Dynastic III period (2600–2350 BCE) pictures the archaic cuneiform sign for "field," $ašag_x$, four times, each facing in a different direction. In the center of this implicit quadrangle is the sign for "mountain." Completing the outer edge of the square are four rivers. F. A. M. Wiggermann describes the drawing as "the community of mankind, effectively ordered," with the "Mountain House" of Enlil at Nippur in the center.[43] This view, with its four sides surrounding the center, is a graphic representation of the world as seen from the Akkad period forward. It was "called . . . 'the four-corners-and-sides.'"[44]

At the edge of the civilized world, thus ordered into "four corners and sides," lies the peripheral, the dangerous unknown, the sea. Evil demons and monsters emerge from the imagined edge, and kings and leaders are careful to dissociate themselves from this unsavory contact. The prominent king Naram-Sin, Enheduanna's nephew, who expanded the Sargonic empire and ruled over its demise, was the first ruler to call himself a god and was known by the epithet "Lord of the Four Quarters," lord of the civilized, safely contained world.

The god Enki, entrusted to build world order, proceeded to "ascribe sections of the culture to the tutelage of a series of divine experts" as H. L. J. Vanstiphout describes them.[45] He gave dominion over the sea to Nanshe, but before handing it over, he built a shrine in the sea:

> Then the Lord made a shrine, a holy shrine, whose interior is an artful maze (?)
> In the sea he built this shrine, a holy shrine, whose interior is an artful maze (?)
> The shrine, whose interior is a [knot of?] threads; a thing unknown to man[46]

Nanshe became mistress of the sea, now with its shrine that Enki can visit. The myth "Enki and the World Order" does not mention the dark, ominous dangers of the sea, although the shrine's "knot of threads" implies an unknown danger. Primarily, the verse emphasizes the sea's fertility:

> Nanše, the noble lady, at whose feet the holy bird is sitting
> Is now the provider of the (produce of the) sea;
> Exquisite and succulent fish
> She presents to her father Enlil in Nippur.[47]

Nevertheless, the "other side" of the bountiful sea is its unknown, potentially dangerous haven for demons. The sea, as well as the distant mountains, remains in Mesopotamian mythology a territory of strange creatures dangerous to civilization.

NANSHE DREAM-OPENER

In the hymn Nanshe is "dream-opener," the dream interpreter of the gods, "highly prized" for her skill with messages from the night. Nanshe was also adept at divination. In both capacities she used her ability to cross over the boundaries between the conscious, civilized mind and the unconscious, mysterious world of dreams and the mantic arts. Her capacity to cross between the known and unknown worlds may explain her immunity from the evil beings lurking in the sea.

In Mesopotamia dreams were thought to bear messages from the supernatural.[48] Gudea calls upon Nanshe to interpret his important dream of a new temple for Ningirsu:

> and yet, the heart (of the matter)
>   of what the nightly vision brought me
> I do not grasp!
> Let me take my dream to my mother,
> and may my dream-interpretress,
>   an expert at her specialty,
> my Nanshe, the sister in Siratr,
> reveal the heart of it to me.[49]

In another literary piece, "The Song of the Plowing Oxen," Nanshe is called upon to "induce" a dream for the supplicant, a farmer. In this poem, translated by Miguel Civil, "the Farmer goes to Nanše's house or temple to have a dream with Nanše's help."[50] The song probably was part of an agricultural festival, Civil says, "in which the king performed activities related to the plow, its oxen, and first opening of the furrows."[51] While the text comes from between 1953 and 1869 BCE, Civil gives evidence that it may have predecessors in older material.[52] Again, the song describes Nanshe in her helpful role inducing and interpreting dreams:

> (The Farmer) went to dream with Nanše in the House.
> He said good night (?) to Nanše,
> He had his leather bag filled with bread,
> He had water poured into his waterskin,
> He had her [stand]ing by (as a "dreamer")[53]

Leo Oppenheim, in his work on the interpretation of dreams, speaks to the problem of "bad" or "evil" dreams, saying, "the dream is dangerous only as long as it remains enigmatic, and therefore interpretation is necessary."[54] However, there were certain rituals to be performed to rid the dreamer of the effects of an evil dream. We know from a later document, "The Assyrian

Dream Book," a systematic and scholarly collection of dream portents and remedies, that certain rituals developed over time to protect the dreamer from the negative content of a dream. An interesting series of remedies involved projecting the evil of the dream into a lump of clay, then dissolving it in water. Ritual prayers accompanied the act. One of many examples begins with a prayer to Shamash, the Akkadian sun god:

> I bring you a lump [of clay], the product of the netherworld!
> "Oh lump, product of the netherworld, in my substance has been
>   fused
>   your substance, . . ."
> As I am throwing you, lump, (now) into water and
>   (There) you will crumble, disintegrate
> (and) dissolve, may the evil of the dream which I
>   had during the night
> . . . fall into the water and crumble, disintegrate and dissolve![55]

While the systematic collection of omen-texts such as this one occurred many hundreds of years after the hymn to Nanshe was written, the texts represent the logical intellectual development of the Sumerian's focus on dreams as messages from the gods and contain the Sumerian spirit of calling upon the gods for help in understanding dreams and their portent.

Enheduanna herself was a dream interpreter. In a poem written to her personal goddess Inanna, known as "The Exaltation of Inanna," she describes the terrible aftermath of being expelled from her temple by a usurping general. One consequence, she says, is that she can no longer interpret dreams:

> I no longer lift my hands
> from the pure sacred bed
> I no longer unravel
> Ningal's gifts of dreams
> to anyone[56]

Dream interpreters sought out by the gods and by rulers and other important persons are most often female. J. M. Asher-Greve identifies a woman lying on a bed pictured on a seal from the Akkadian period as an ensi-priestess interpreting a dream, much as Enheduanna describes in her poem to Inanna.[57]

8.4.   Dream interpreter, Early Dynastic/Early Akkadian cylinder seal. Courtesy of the
Oriental Institute of the University of Chicago.

COMPASSIONATE NANSHE

While Nanshe had powers to cross into the world of dreams and divination
and to fathom the mystery of the sea, she also had a family and cared for the
socially disadvantaged. Her husband was Nindara. Her daughter was Ninmar
(Temple Hymn 23). She was the sister of Ningirsu (Temple Hymn 20) and of
Nisaba (Temple Hymn 42). In another hymn, called "The Nanshe Hymn," she
expresses her concerns for social justice and order:

> She knows the orphan, she knows the widow.
> She knows that man oppresses man, (is) a mother for the orphan.
> Nanshe, watching over the widow,
> finding a way for houses in debt,
> the lady, she shelters the fugitive in her lap.
> She seeks out a place for the weak.[58]

Heimpel describes this unusual hymn as a celebration of the return of Nanshe
from an annual pilgrimage to the home of her father, Enki, in Eridu.[59]

Nanshe's compassion is expressed in the wailing and lamentation typical
of many goddesses. In the long narrative poem known as "In the Desert by the
Early Grass" she is among the mother deities lamenting the death of Dumuzi,
the prototype of the young dying god:

> The lady, Mother Nanshe,
>   [seeks] the sp[ot]

[where her son is lying,]
where her son is lying[60]

Of Nanshe's many diverse characteristics, the Temple Hymn concentrates on her mantic powers of divination and dream interpretation and implicitly relates them to her birth near the sea and to her connection to the "strong dark water" of the sea. Given that the sea in Mesopotamian mythological geography is beyond the inhabited world, at the very edge of the earthly cosmos, it is an unknown body with dangerous inhabitants, far from civilized society. Nanshe appears to be a benevolent conduit between her watery realm and the world of human beings, and that important capacity gave her prominence in the Sumerian pantheon.

TEMPLE HYMN 23

THE GUABBA TEMPLE OF NINMAR
O house
    stretched to the sea's midst
    built in a pure place
Guabba   at the sea's edge
inside your heart gives everything birth
and safeguards the well-built storehouse

pure shrine
    you wild cow
    you   everlasting abundance of things
your princess Ningagia
    mighty guardian   strong one of father Enlil
    ponders deep meanings with lord Nunamnir

born at [ ]
she stands on raging dark waters
like her father she is fish inspector of the pure pure sea

O house Guabba holy Ninmar
has built this house on your radiant site
and placed her seat upon your dais

        10 lines for the house of Ninmar in Guabba

THE TEMPLE OF NINMAR IN GUABBA

The Temple Hymn to Ninmar repeats several of the elements from the hymn that precedes it, written to Nanshe in Sirara. Both goddesses are called "you wild cow." Both stand at the sea's edge and ride "strong" or "raging dark waters." The similarity is no coincidence, for Nanshe is Ninmar's mother. Daughter Ninmar inherited her mother's powerful attributes as goddess of the sea, but, unlike her mother, she has no apparent connection to the mantic arts of divination or dream interpretation. Rather, the hymn emphasizes the abundance in her "well-built storehouse" inside her temple, where Ninmar "gives everything birth."

NINMAR'S FAMILY TIES

Ninmar's heritage is somewhat confusing. In the hymn she is called "strong one of father Enlil," even though her family connection is not to the lineage of Enlil, but to her grandfather Enki, Nanshe's father. It was Enki who appointed Ninmar's mother, Nanshe, to be the goddess of the sea. Nevertheless, according to the hymn Ninmar is deeply thoughtful with Enlil, here called by his byname Nunamnir. She "ponders deep meanings with lord Nunamnir," says the poet. The phrase evokes an image of a goddess of intense contemplation, sitting with mighty Enlil, almost as if from his great height he has taken Ninmar under his wing as her mentor. Whatever their relationship, the scene suggests an aspect of Ninmar's character, her intent inwardness.

Ninmar's father was Nindara, spouse of Nanshe. He is not mentioned by name, but the hymn reports that she and her father hold the same position, "fish inspector of the pure pure sea." Sjöberg cites a verse from another cuneiform tablet that also calls Nindara the munku of the sea, translated officially as 'fish inspector.' In the verse cited by Sjöberg, Ninmar's mother Nanshe is speaking:

> my husband,
> the munku of the sea,
> Umundara [Nindara], the munku of the sea.[61]

Plentiful fish in the rivers and seas of southern Mesopotamia were an important source of food, and we know from the many fish bones found in the temple excavations at Eridu that they were used in ritual worship as well. The town name, Guabba, means literally 'neck of the sea,' or seashore. What is meant by "fish inspector" is not known. However, the title acknowledges that Ninmar's powers over fish are included in her domain, along with the sea and its reeds and birds in the marshes bordering the shore.

Ninmar's consort was Ninmushbar. Records from the Fara period at Lagash (2600–2550) indicate that he and his entourage received gifts: "1 bronze-vessel (in shape of) a Dilmun boat, 1 crown, covering the head, 1 necklace (for) Nin-mar-ki."[62] The gifts were probably presented to a statue at the temple. The boat would signify good wishes for a harvest of fish in the waters of the gulf near Dilmun, present-day Bahrain.

TEMPLE AND CITY

In the hymn Ninmar is called "princess Ningagia," meaning 'Lady of the GÁ-GI$_4$.' Once again, as in Temple Hymn 6 to Shuzianna, we have reference to a section of the temple reserved for priestesses. It is sometimes written gá-gi-mah—the wondrous gá-gi. The term may also mean 'locked-house.' In later eras, as discussed in the hymn to Shuzianna, the Akkadian term gagû designated the buildings in which women called nadītu chose to live without marrying, devoting their lives to the sun god. Here in the Sargonic era, Ninmar may have presided over a group of women or priestesses also devoted to a deity. This intriguing possibility is intimated in another example from Enheduanna's hymns to her personal goddess Inanna, in which she speaks of "women's rooms" in the Inanna temple and calls on "warrior women" who live apart in devotion to Inanna.[63] The mention in the Temple Hymns of women living apart in special quarters suggests that the better-known nadītu had predecessors several hundred years before they established their tradition in Sippar.[64]

Ninmar's city of Guabba, before the writing of the Temple Hymns, was long known to have had an active textile industry. Archives that mention textiles from the pre-Sargonic period precede the "massive textile enterprise" that developed in the Ur III period after the fall of the Akkadian empire.[65] Presumably, this industry thrived in the Sargonic era as well. Fifty years after the collapse of the Sargonic empire, the rulers of the Ur III dynasty greatly expanded textile production in Guabba. Postgate writes,

> A factory of over 6000 workers, the great majority women and children, is located in Guabba alone. . . . Types and grades of cloth are specified with great precision, and the quantities produced are recorded along with the work-days required. . . . (In) the Pre-Sargonic archives . . . institutional textile production was divided into a "wool

place" (ki siki) and a "flax place" (ki gu), reflecting the different processes needed.[66]

Ninmar was one of the lesser-known local goddesses and became identified with a specific locale, her city of Guabba. She presided over her temple and her city for many hundreds of years. An annual fecundity festival took place in Guabba, in which, one text says, "the governor's wife offered a sheep to Ninmar and a sheep (at) the é-tùr," the cattle pen that may have been part of Ninmar's temple.[67] Records of her worship in the existing archives indicate her importance as the mistress of the fishing and the textile industries, and one to whom worshipers appealed to ensure bounty in their production and well-being in their pursuits.

TEMPLE HYMN 24

THE KINIRSHA TEMPLE OF DUMUZI-ABZU

O house Kinirsha   created for its Lady
rising from the platform   a verdant mountain
O house   joyful cries erupt deep in your interior

house
    your princess
    a storm wind astride a lion
lifting holy song and countersong
loud voices constantly singing

child   true wild cow
tended with care at the pure breast
    of the mother who bore her

O shrine Kinirsha

Dumuzi-abzu has built this house on your radiant site
and placed her seat upon your dais

    7 lines for the house of Dumu-zi of Kinirsha

THE TEMPLE OF DUMUZI-ABZU AT KINIRSHA

The goddess Dumuzi-abzu resided in her temple in the village of Kinirsha, or Kinunir. The few extant references to her give us little information. Minor

goddess though she was, the poet thought her worthy of inclusion and portrays her with vivid imagery.

Dumuzi-abzu was easily confused with the god Dumuzi (Temple Hymn
17), who also had an important temple in the territory of Lagash. She was
sometimes called merely Dumu-zi, as in the ending line-count of this hymn.
However, several texts refer to her as Dumuzi-abzu of Kinunir, differentiating
her from the well-known Dumuzi, the consort of Inanna. Dumuzi-abzu was
female, not male. This hymn in the first line identifies her as "Lady," clearly
portraying her as a goddess.

DUMUZI-ABZU'S TEMPLE

Dumuzi-abzu's "house" is said to rise from the temple platform. This house
refers to the small temple on the very top of the stepped pyramid, the sacred
sanctuary of the goddess. From this height our attention is seized by "joyful
cries" from the inner sanctum, the holy of holies inside the sacred building. The
cries actually are loud voices singing in antiphonal chorus. Their exuberance
is matched only by the entrance of Dumuzi-abzu herself, who appears like
"a storm wind astride a lion." The hymn builds an unusual momentum with
its description of the singing. The hymn to Dumuzi-abzu is the only Temple
Hymn that describes a performance of music in the worship of the deity.

In another era, the Isin-Larsa period that followed the downfall of Sargon's
empire, poets composed sorrowful laments bewailing the destruction of the
great city of Ur. Little known as she was, Dumuzi-abzu is one of the goddesses in this composition who deserts the fallen city, leaving her temple "to
the winds." Women and priestesses in a typical role in the temple must have
sung the Lamentation over the "Destruction of Ur":

> Kinirsha's mistress was abandoning it,
>   and her sheepfold, to the winds,
> at its dwelling house Dumuzi-apsû was abandoning Kinirsha,
>   and her sheepfold, to the winds.[68]

LINEAGE OF THE GODDESS

Dumuzi-abzu's name, meaning 'good child of the deep sweet waters,' emphasizes her role as a child. In contrast to riding astride a lion and leading the
joyful loud voices in song, she next appears in the Temple Hymn as a child ten-
derly cared for at the breast of her mother. The verse implies that her mother

was a significant goddess, but none of the existent texts reveal her mother's identity. Her relation to the abzu places her in the lineage of the god Enki (Temple Hymn 1). Her home in Kinirsha in southeastern Lagash includes her in the Lagash group along with Ningirsu, Bau, Nanshe, and Ninmar. She was a goddess of the sea, just as Nanshe and Ninmar were.

Dumuzi-abzu never rose to prominence in the Sumerian pantheon. Raphael Kutscher reports that by the Ur III period (c. 2150 BCE), she was already losing her identity and becoming identified with the god Dumuzi. He suggests that by the Old Babylonian period (1800–1600 BCE), she had disappeared completely.[69] Other evidence suggests she kept her identity into the Old Babylonian period. Her name appears in an Old Babylonian god list as a goddess in the family of Marduk. In another Old Babylonian list of gods, she is included in Enki's family of Eridu.[70] Thus do the gods and goddesses rise and fall and transfigure over the ages. At the moment of the writing of this Temple Hymn, however, Dumuzi-abzu had an independent identity and character intriguingly expressed by the poet.

chapter 9

HYMNS TO TEMPLES IN THE UMMA REGION

The city of Umma leads a group of neighboring cities located in the area of the central grasslands of ancient Iraq. Late in the fourth millennium Umma was the only city in the southern alluvium to rival Uruk. Its population and prosperity had expanded significantly. The two large cities interacted and dominated other settlements. By the end of the millennium, Uruk and Umma and as many as twenty or thirty other communities had successfully created a viable new social structure, the city. Evidence from seals at this time suggests the cities cooperated in some way, may even have formed a league of cities, and had a common pantheon.

In the first half of the third millennium, populations increased across the board, in villages, towns, and cities. With the spread in settlement size, the amount of irrigable land decreased. Conflict between neighbors was an inevitable consequence, as the demand for land and water stretched the available resources.

One of the most persistent conflicts, lasting several hundred years, was that between the territories of Lagash and Umma. Kings of the two regions fought each other, one periodically triumphing over the other. Outside rulers occasionally tried to arbitrate, but peace was short-lived. Their efforts, however, precipitated experiments in conflict management based on early rules of law.

The last king of Umma to conquer Lagash, Lugalzagesi, even proceeded to subdue Uruk and other major southern cities. His rule was cut short by the armies of Sargon, whose conquest of all of southern Mesopotamia put a final end to the Umma-Lagash conflict.

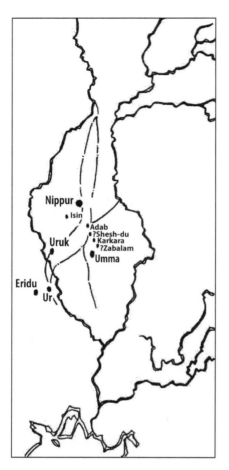

9.1.   Sketch map of Mesopotamia with Umma and neighboring cities. After Postgate 1994. Reproduced by permission of Taylor and Francis Books U.K.

This group of Temple Hymns is not lacking in notable deities—Inanna, Ishkur, Ninhursag—in prominent cities—Umma, Zabalam, Adab, Isin. All six of the cities in this group occupied the eastern side of the alluvium, and all except Umma and Isin were located on the banks of an ancient course of the Tigris or one of its tributaries.

The city of Umma bore an illustrious history, by now one thousand years old. During all of that time, its patron deity, Shara (TH 25), presided over Umma, but as the Temple Hymn makes clear his status depends largely on his mother, Inanna. A hymn to Inanna from her city Zabalam (TH 26) follows that of Shara. Inanna's city was the mythical location of the cosmic mountain out of which the sun rose each morning. Inanna at Zabalam was the most ancient of the astral deities. The oldest archaic text containing her symbol was found in the city's ruins. Ishkur (TH 27) was patron deity of the neighboring city of Karkara, where, as the essential storm god, he brought the rain without which the land would perish. The name of the city of Temple Hymn 28 is unknown, as is that of its deity; no trace of the names remains on the tablets that contain the hymn. It must have been situated on the Tigris between Karkara and Adab, home of the celebrated mother goddess Ninhursag (TH 29). Her Adab temple was secondary to her main temple in Kesh (TH 8), northwest of Adab, but her son Ashgi may have presided at Adab with her, as he is mentioned in the hymn. Isin, the city of the final hymn of this group (TH 30), lay inland, west of Adab and southwest of Nippur. Its patron was Ninisina, a goddess of healing and another of the deities with a strong connection to Inanna.

TEMPLE HYMN 25

THE UMMA TEMPLE OF SHARA
Emah

O house   graceful stone jars stand in the open air
lofty cella   holy speech resounds
abundance from the sea's midst held in the smaller basin

the pure shepherd delivers prayers   spreads acclaim
O Emah   majestic house of Shara
the faithful man makes it thrive in plenty for you

your house   splendid house Emah
your prince   the holy woman's princely son
keeps expanding its good fortune
its site of bounty and well-being

the unfailing hair dresser
keeps his eye on the wild cow
Shara   who offers sweet bread to eat
son who gives powers to his mother
O house in Umma   has built this house on your radiant site

and placed his seat upon your dais

   10 lines for the house of Shara in Umma

THE TEMPLE OF SHARA AT UMMA

Shara, a god who seldom plays a part in the best-known Sumerian myths, is nevertheless forever imprinted on the reader's mind. In the myth of "Inanna's Descent to the Netherworld," it is he who tends the goddess's long hair and paints her nails. Dutifully performing this office, Shara endears himself to Inanna, like a son. The hymn opens with images of beauty and abundance. "Graceful stone jars" evoke a sense of elegance and calm. Ritual chanting from the holy cella causes the listener to pause in reverence to the deity.

SHARA AND INANNA

Enheduanna, who in a devotional poem to Inanna calls herself "child of yours," writes the Temple Hymn to Shara in his role as child of Inanna, saying he is "the holy woman's princely son."[1] Shara offers Inanna sweets, and more. "He gives powers to his mother," powers that are a portion of the divine **me** allotted at the beginning of time to Shara by great An, god of heaven.

Inanna is not known as a mother goddess and rarely demonstrates the trusted caring of a mother. In spite of Inanna's dearth of mothering characteristics, in this and several other texts Shara is said to be her son. In "Lugalbanda and the Thunderbird" Shara is called "beloved son of Inanna."[2] Mythological texts do not include tales of Inanna giving birth; neither do they suggest who Shara's father was. Was Shara, like Enheduanna, "child of Inanna," revering Inanna as he would a mother?

In the myth "Inanna's Descent to the Netherworld" Shara is not specifically called her son, but as in the Temple Hymn he is her beautician, a beloved figure who mourned her captivity in the underworld, wearing rags for her and rolling in the dust. Inanna refused to surrender him to the underworld demons who demanded a hostage substitute before freeing her completely:

Shara
sings my praises
Shara
cuts my nails
combs my hair
I will never give him to you[3]

More in keeping with Inanna's character is this Temple Hymn's designation of her as "the wild cow" on whom Shara must "keep his eye." In one of the devotional poems to Inanna, Enheduanna also calls her "wild cow." "O my divine ecstatic wild cow," she exclaims, entreating Inanna to rescue her from captivity, "drive this man out / hunt him down / catch him."[4]

In this hymn Shara is "princely son" of the nu-gig, a term often used to identify Inanna. A difficult word to translate, nu-gig can simply mean 'holy woman,' gig meaning one who is unapproachable, taboo, set aside, and dark. The term has been thought by some to refer to sacred prostitution, translated 'hierodule,' a Greek word, *hieros,* meaning 'holy' or 'sacred,' and *doulos,* 'slave,' thus rendering sacred slave or servant. Richard Henshaw reports that the term *hierodule* applied to a class of temple personnel in the Greek temples of Aphrodite, some two thousand years after the writing of the Temple Hymns. While the Greek hierodules were both female and male, the female hierodules engaged in acts of prostitution for money that was then donated to the temple. However, he says, this practice did not occur in Mesopotamia: "This Greek practice is what was read back onto a Mesopotamian practice by many commentators," and the repetition of this belief became accepted lore.[5] Henshaw concludes that "in Mesopotamia sacred prostitution simply is not supported by the available evidence."[6]

Nu-gig is a term known from the Early Dynastic period through the Neo-Assyrian, almost three thousand years later. It was used in many contexts and evolved in its meaning.[7] Nu-gig signifies the goddess as separate, untouchable, unapproachable, imbued as she is with the numinosity of her divinity as well as the dark of her unpredictable fury and her link to the underworld of primal nature and death. Nu-gig is a common epithet of Inanna. It designates a title of office, a sacred position that Inanna exemplified. In Temple Hymn 30, the goddess Ninisina binds the crown of the high priestess on the nu-gig, a priestess in her temple. Placing this auspicious crown "indicates," Sjöberg says, "that the nugig originally had a very high rank."[8] While the term may include Inanna's domain of sexuality, it does not refer to "sacred sexuality" as an institution in the temple, for no evidence has been found that such an institutionalized practice existed.

SHARA IN UMMA

Shara, known primarily from his association to Inanna, was never a prominent Sumerian god. The first mention of the temple of Shara appears on an exquisite gold plaque, inscribed as a tribute, "For [the god] Shara, lord of the E-mah" from Bara'irnun, the wife of the Early Dynastic king Gishakidu.[9] In the Emah, Shara was city god of the important territory of Umma. Its disputes with Lagash had precipitated the creation of laws to manage such conflicts. The establishment of a centralized state under Sargon brought about "the formation of an institutionalized level of decision making higher than that of the city," according to Hans Nissen; this new authority was able "to regulate conflicts [in a manner] that had not existed previously in this form and with which the old rules therefore could not cope."[10]

Shara, "the pure shepherd," presided over his temple in Umma, a city on the edge of the central grasslands in ancient Sumer. While he is called shepherd in the hymn, he was also connected to the cultic plow, ^{giš}apin-^{d}Šará-da-sù-a, "the plow [called] 'Marching with Šara.'"[11] Such godly implements were imbued with the essence of the divinity, were worshiped and given offerings and tribute. The cultic calendar of Umma was built on seasonal farming events that included various offerings to Shara in his temple. As "plow," he presided over the seasonal year from planting to harvest. The shepherding of livestock may have been an important occupation in Umma, but the use of the term in the hymn may simply refer to Shara as the shepherd-caretaker of his people. Unlike other southern cities whose year began at the spring equinox, the New Year in Umma began with the summer solstice. Sargon apparently changed the civil calendar in Umma to conform with that of other cities, but the local cultic calendar preserved its New Year at the beginning of summer.

Shara is mentioned in numerous offering lists related to the monthly ritual observations at his temple. The first month at the New Year solstice celebrated the barley harvest. In the second month a ritual was enacted at the laying of brick clay in the brick mold. By the third month the barley was already piled high along the quays for shipment. Each month tended to have its special significance. The fourth month, called nisag, or 'first,' celebrated the first fruits and the making of the first malt of the season. In this month Shara's statue was carried in a ritual barge to the nearby village of Kian, where he was also worshiped. The barge carried bundles of rope, hides, oil, and grain. The oil and various aromatics were used for a ritual washing of the statue of Shara. The barge and the chariot that transported Shara's statue to it were decorated for the trip to and from Kian. The eighth month was called House-of-the-Moon and involved astrological beliefs related to the phases of the moon. Again in this month, the statue of Shara was ritually washed and cleansed with fragrances and oil poured from an ibex horn.[12]

SHARA OUTSIDE UMMA

Our knowledge of Shara, indeed of ancient Mesopotamia itself, depends upon the discoveries of archeologists. One such excavation uncovered a temple to Shara far north of Umma, a site called Tell Agrab, near the confluence of the

9.2.   Kneeling man holding a vessel.
Tell Agrab, Shara Temple 2900–2650
BCE. Courtesy of the Oriental Institute of
the University of Chicago.

Tigris and the Diyala rivers. This important crossroads marked the junction of two major communication routes, one north and south along the Tigris and another east along the Diyala into the Zagros foothills and on to the Iranian plateau. Southern Mesopotamians, in their search for scarce resources in the alluvium, had colonized the area of the Diyala basin throughout the fourth millennium, the Uruk period, prior to the beginning of the Early Dynastic era. Still an important center a thousand years later, the city of Akkad may have been located somewhere in the area (see TH 40). The plain south of the Diyala/Tigris junction supported two major cities, Der and Eshnunna, to each of whose primary temples a Temple Hymn was written (see TH 33, 34).

   In the ruins of the temple to Shara at Tell Agrab lay one of the most unusual pieces of art yet discovered, a statue of a man kneeling in devotion to his deity. The figure in the gypsum statue balances a vessel on his head, an offering to the god. The piece dates from the beginning of the Early Dynastic period, 2900–2650 BCE. The figure is poised in the act of rising to his feet, "an indication of both moment and movement that is extraordinarily rare in Mesopotamian art."[13] The figure could be half a millennium older than the Temple Hymn to Shara. This statue and the above-mentioned gold plaque, along with the intricate and evocative rituals dedicated to Shara, point to intense acts of devotion by the Sumerian people, even to a minor god. Furthermore, the beauty and realism of the statue are visual evidence of the development of an artistic sensibility and sophistication that would have to reach back well into the fourth millennium for its origin. The longevity of the Mesopotamian culture forces us to stretch our imagination of the beginnings of complex urban civilization back at least another thousand years before the Early Dynastic period.

TEMPLE HYMN 26

THE ZABALAM TEMPLE OF INANNA

O house   wrapped in beams of light
wearing shining stone jewels   wakening great awe
sanctuary of pure Inanna
(where) divine powers, the true **me,** spread wide

Zabalam
    shrine of the shining mountain
    shrine that welcomes the morning light
she makes resound with desire
the Holy Woman grounds your hallowed chamber with desire

your queen   Inanna of the sheepfold
that singular woman   the unique one
who speaks hateful words to the wicked
who moves among the bright shining things
who goes against rebel lands
and at twilight makes the firmament beautiful
    all on her own
great daughter of Suen
pure Inanna
O house of Zabalam
has built this house on your radiant site
and placed her seat upon your dais

    12 lines for the house of Inanna in Zabalam

THE TEMPLE OF INANNA AT ZABALAM

From its height on the jeweled mountain, the Zabalam temple of Inanna looks out over the alluvium. There, on the eastern edge of the Sumerian heartland, the rising sun, the moon, and all the bright planets seem to emerge from its holy sanctuary, wrapping the temple "in beams of light." The shrine at Zabalam, "wakening great awe" with its shining Šuba-stone jewels, sits on top of the kur-šuba, the mythical mountain at the center of the cosmos.

From her temple in Zabalam, Inanna's splendor casts its light back another thousand years before the writing of this Temple Hymn. Zabalam's relationship to Uruk, Inanna's principal city, began around 3100 BCE, at the time of its first occupation. Inanna reigned in Zabalam from the start, and her dominance there was "especially profitable to [Zabalam's] mutual relationship" with Uruk, already the established economic and political force in the southern alluvium.[14]

EARLY ASTRAL DEITIES

The Temple Hymn describes Inanna's temple as "shrine of the shining mountain." With these words the poet recalls a very ancient myth, one that by 3300 BCE was inscribed on the oldest archaic tablets and seals from Uruk. From these texts we learn that the first deities of the Sumerians were all astral beings, whose ever-recurrent paths across the sky began with their emergence from a sacred mountain.[15] The first three of the cosmic lights were the moon, Nanna; the morning star, Inanna; and the sun, Utu.[16] The sacred mountain from which they emerged was the shining mountain kur-šuba, at Zabalam. This shining mountain was the *Axis Mundi*, the cosmic intersection that connected the heavens, the earth, and the underworld.[17] The Temple Hymn confirms the heavenly procession at Zabalam, when it heralds the arrival of Utu the sun, describing the temple as "shrine that welcomes the morning light." Through the gate at Zabalam, the procession of celestial bodies enters the sky, the sun itself flooding the temple at Zabalam each morning with its light.

The earliest recorded hymns to the temples of the gods, the zà-mì (praise) hymns from 2600 BCE, found at ancient Abu Salabikh, were, as Bendt Alster says, "from the beginning more concerned with celestial archetypes of the temples than the concrete temples on earth[,] which really are no more than secondary representations of the celestial houses."[18] He asserts that the myth of eternal return was "the central concern of the Mesopotamian religion, . . . its astral aspects are as old as literature itself."[19] Krystyna Szarzynska imagines the origin of the worship of the astral deities: "The beginning of the cult of astral deities reaches probably the proto-Sumerian, and even more ancient times; perhaps it was adopted—at least partly—by Sumerians from primal people of south Mesopotamia."[20] So far, little is known about the inhabitants of the southern alluvium who preceded the Sumerians. The deepest layer of archeological discovery beneath Enki's temple at Eridu dates to 4900 BCE and was occupied by the earliest inhabitants of the Ubaid culture. Seton Lloyd, one of the archeologists who participated in the excavation, argues that the "continuity of religious beliefs and practices" at Eridu and other sites "seem[s] particularly convincing that the original inhabitants were the Sumerians."[21]

As the cosmic *Axis Mundi*, the sacred mountain in Zabalam houses the opening through which the celestial procession emerges. The opening is called "the gate of battle," "viewed," Alster says, "as the place of eternal cosmic battle."[22] Upon her rising Inanna as the morning star opens the gate of battle. Indeed, Inanna is rarely spoken of without allusion to her warrior character, as in this hymn: she "speaks hateful words to the wicked" and "goes against rebel lands." Inanna-kur, Inanna of the mountain, is an auspicious epithet of the goddess's birthplace and abode on the sacred mountain at the center of the cosmos.

Inanna's cult symbol appears at the beginning of writing, "the high pole made of reed stalks bound together, tapering upwards, and rolled into a ring/volute in its upper part, with an additional reed bunch plaited into the ring with ends standing on the outside."[23] Its many appearances designate the goddess, both in the written texts and in scenes carved on plaques and seals, the same image in both writing and art. This symbol appears in the earliest pictographic texts that list offerings to the temples, occurring far more frequently than that of any other deity.[24] Later, in cuneiform texts, Inanna's name was transliterated as mùs, sometimes written $muš_3$.

At Zabalam, the kur-šuba is the place of Inanna's birth, a location mentioned in two other mythological descriptions of her birth, "Enmerkar and the Lord of Aratta" and a poem attributed to Enheduanna, "Inanna and Ebeh." One of the ancient zà-mì hymns uses the term "ki-sikil" to describe Inanna's birthplace, a term employed three hundred years later in "Inanna and Ebeh." Both call the mountain of Inanna's birth ki-sikil, 'a pure place.' In the zà-mì hymns she is ^{d}Inanna-kur, 'divine Inanna of the mountain,' as well as ^{d}Inanna-húd, 'morning-Inanna.'[25] A text from Uruk from around 3000 BCE designates an important priest, EN-AN-$MUŠ_3$-KUR-DUG_3, 'lord of the sweet goddess Inanna from the mountain.'[26] Szarzynska concludes that the designation "Inanna-kur," repeated in texts over a thousand-year period, is

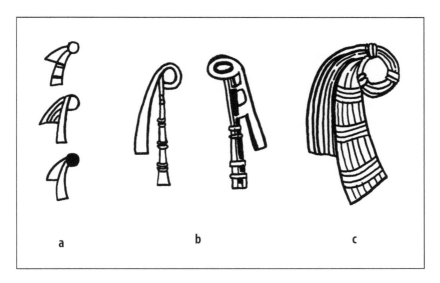

9.3.   Archaic symbol of Inanna (a) archaic Sumerian script, (b) on seals, (c) wall frieze relief from Uruk. After Szarzyńska, 1997. Courtesy of Academic Publishing House DIALOG.

a constant mythologem referring to the auspicious birth and appearance on the sacred mountain of the astral Inanna.[27] The use of identical epithets in the long history of the goddess is evidence of the conservation and continuity of the Sumerian religious tradition.

We know from texts from the Jemdet-Nasr period, 3200–3000 BCE, that record offerings to Inanna that she was worshiped in her astral aspects as ᵈInanna-húd, 'morning-Inanna,' and ᵈInanna-sig, 'evening-Inanna,' that is, the morning and evening star.[28] Other texts record separate festivals to morning-Inanna and evening-Inanna. The worship and festivals of the two Inannas had their own locations and specific offerings, emphasizing the separate character of the two aspects of the goddess. This Temple Hymn at Zabalam may speak to both morning- and evening-Inanna. When she "goes against rebel lands," she may be morning-Inanna, who specifically is said to open the gate of battle at daybreak. Evening-Inanna, the hymn says, appears at night, moving "among the bright shining things," the stars, "and at twilight makes the firmament beautiful all on her own."

Texts from Uruk IV, older than those mentioned above, record Inanna's most ancient epithet, ᵈInanna-nun, 'regal-Inanna.' As in the case of the astral Inanna, offerings to Inanna-nun were specific and different from those to

Inanna-húd and Inanna-sig; some thirty commodities were offered to regal-Inanna. Inanna-nun is not mentioned in texts from the later period at Uruk, Uruk III. Nor is there any record of offerings to Inanna-kur. These four aspects of Inanna, kur, húd, sig, and nun, so prominent in the earliest records, do not occur in later Sumerian religious texts of the Early Dynastic or the Akkadian periods. However, as in this Temple Hymn from 2300 BCE, her characteristics in all four guises continue to describe aspects of her identity in later texts, myths, and other literature.

CULTIC ELEMENTS IN THE HYMN

Images of Inanna as the radiant morning and evening star emerging from her auspicious birthplace on the sacred mountain and opening the gate of battle at Zabalam dominate this Temple Hymn and secure Inanna in the minds of the worshipers as one of the Sumerian deities, if not the most magnificent one. She seems to control the very movement of the deified celestial bodies. Another tradition answers the question posed in Temple Hymn 13 to Utu the sun god: where does the sun, and indeed all the planets, go when they exit through the locked western gate? They proceed, it is said, down through the abzu and into the underworld, where, resting from their long journey, Enki regenerates them, allowing their procession to continue the next morning through the eastern gate of the shining mountain at Zabalam.[29]

The hymn moves in succession from the celestial to the mundane, overlapping levels of the goddess's realm. Inanna, the hymn says, is guardian of the sheepfold, a reed birthing hut pictured on ancient cylinder seals and sacred objects, her stately reed-post symbol emerging from the roof, protectively bending over the new lambs.

On the other hand, Inanna is the deity who opens the gate for the celestial procession at this nodal point of the cosmos. The energetic force with which she enlivens this celestial entrance is the energy of desire. The shrine "resounds with desire." The holy of holies, the sacred inner chamber, is firmly grounded in desire. Desire is the generative force of the universe. Inanna, the epitome of desire, embodies the energizing force that animates creation. As in the preceding hymn to Shara, she is the nu-gig, the Holy Woman, who firmly fixes the temple's foundation in desire.

Inanna's father is Suen, the hymn says, using the Akkadian name for the moon god. She is his "great daughter." Daughter of the moon and twin sister to the sun, Inanna opens the gate of battle for these three heavenly lights, whose ancient procession stirred the original Sumerians to revere them as their first

9.4.   Limestone sculptured trough, 3200–3000 BCE. Courtesy of the Trustees of the British Museum.

divine beings. The moon, the morning star, and the sun, all three appear in this Temple Hymn to Inanna, in praise of the astral origin of the Sumerian religion.

TEMPLE HYMN 27

THE KARKARA TEMPLE OF ISHKUR

O house
terrifying   where you rise like a great lion
divine decisions rendered skillfully
each day   over the high plain

house of Ishkur
   your front side spreads abundance
   your back flourishes in pleasure
your foundation is a horned bull, a lion
a pure shen-vessel   the breasts of heaven
moist wind for late barley

the gate-house of your temple—a fierce-horned wild bull
from your true bulwark the brick wall rises in wonder
[you spawn] the billowing cloud   the rainbow
[you are] the poison-spitting snake
Ishkur's whole estate [shines] in the moonlight

the ravager Ishkur spills over cities a devastating flood
sends strong storms flying
the seven north winds   raging south winds

9.5.   Lion-dragon symbol of Ishkur. Courtesy of the University of Texas Press, Jeremy Black and Anthony Green, *Gods, Demons and Symbols of Ancient Mesopotamia*, Tessa Richards, illustrator, 1995.

running from . . .
[his loud] resounding [voice]
splits open the bright stone of the diorite mountain

seed of the land
prince, canal inspector of heaven and earth
life-bringer of the many
Ishkur
O house of Karkara
has built this house on your radiant site
and placed his seat upon your throne

(the tablets were broken where the line count customarily appeared)

THE TEMPLE OF ISHKUR AT KARKARA

No deity in the Sumerian pantheon needed to be praised and cajoled more than Ishkur, the rain god. The prosperity of Sumer depended entirely on water. The first inhabitants began life there with nothing but their ingenuity, fertile soil, and two rivers, whose fickle meandering, flooding, and drying up left them at the mercy of natural forces. Ingenuity indeed created their unprecedented prosperity. A complex web of irrigation canals crisscrossed the alluvium, making dependable agriculture possible. But if Ishkur failed to send his timely rain or ravaged the land with devastating floods, he could cause catastrophic damage.

The exaggerated fierceness the hymn ascribes to Ishkur—terrifying lion, horned bull, poison-spitting snake, ravaging wind—describes both the devastating storm winds, rain, and floods that plagued ancient Mesopotamia and the desperate need of the citizens to beseech this god for mercy. Humility, not hubris, was the appropriate attitude in the face of Ishkur's threats.

ISHKUR IN SUMERIAN MYTHOLOGY

Ishkur gained his power over rain from the wily god Enki, god of sweet waters. In the myth "Enki and the World Order," Enki organized the world, assigning elements of nature and civilization to chosen deities. The power of Enki called the rain down to earth, the life-giving rain, and gave it to Ishkur to command.[30]

As in this hymn, Ishkur can be the epitome of nature's fury. In the pre-Sargonic "Lugalbanda and the Thunderbird" the hero Lugalbanda asks for the strength of Ishkur from the magical Thunderbird:

> like the sevenfold storm
>   of Ishkur
> let me rise up like fire,
>   flash like lightning[31]

The Temple Hymn repeats similar imagery when it describes Ishkur as a "ravager" who "sends strong storms flying / the seven north winds / raging south winds." The sacred number seven reappears in the hymn as the number of totality, the number which leaves out nothing that should be included, a divine number that pertains only to the perfection of the gods.

The myth "Enmerkar and the Lord of Aratta," also a pre-Sargonic myth, portrays Ishkur as "the crowned lord" who brings the miracle of rain to the starving citizens of Aratta:

> Ishkur,
>   the thunderer
>   of heaven and earth,
> the whirling storm,
>   the great lion
>   saw fit to come by.
> The mountains were shaking
> the mountain ranges
>   roaring with him
>   in laughter.
> As they met his awe and glory
> the mountain ranges
>   lifted their heads
>   in delightful verdure . . .[32]

In this myth, written several hundred years before the Temple Hymn, the description of Ishkur expresses similar themes, here emphasizing his loud thunder, his devastating storm, his lionlike fierceness. The character of this god, like that of most gods, seems to have remained fixed in place over time in the memory of the worshipers and the stories they told.

ISHKUR IN THE TEMPLE HYMN

Ishkur's Temple Hymn describes the god as fierce and aggressive, but also as a gentle blessing of beauty and abundance. His fundamental nature is "a moist wind for late barley" and a pure vessel, the shen, an amphora-type jar shaped like a large breast. He is the source of "billowing clouds" and "the rainbow." His rain-washed landscape glistens in the moonlight. And, practically speaking, he is the "canal inspector of heaven and earth," the overseer of the essential annual cleaning of the buildup of sediment and debris in the irrigation canals.

In the Sargonic era the "ravager Ishkur" of the hymn had his dramatic image carved on cylinder seals. He is shown riding in a chariot pulled by a wild, composite animal, who has the head, body, and forelegs of a lion but brandishes the huge wings and rear-legged talons of a bird. Out of his mouth he spits fire or lightning. Ishkur guides the chariot, holding the reins on the wild creature, while his free hand wields a long, menacing whip, later called "the holy whip." A nude goddess stands between the wings of the creature and holds bundles of lightning or rain in her hands. The goddess may be Ishkur's wife, Medimsha or Shala.[33] The lion-dragon, as the "great lion" of the Temple Hymn, is the symbolic animal of Ishkur.

Ishkur, like many of the deities of the Temple Hymns, claims the great god of heaven, An, as his father. He is also called brother of Inanna, although Inanna's father was the moon god Nanna and her brother was the sun god Utu. Such filial claims that go against tradition are not unusual. Often they are metaphorical, the proposal made to add prestige to the claimant. In spite of his power, Ishkur never gained the status of being one of the major Sumerian deities.

TEMPLE HYMN 28

THE TEMPLE AT ŠEŠ-DÙ

[O house. . . . .], bolt founded by An
(line missing)
[the . . . .], which [has grown up] with heaven and earth
[the. . . . .], which Enki [. . . . .]

gap of undetermined length

[. . . . ., deity x],
[house y, has built his house on your radiant site
and placed his/her seat upon your dais]

(no line count)

THE TEMPLE OF X DEITY AT [ŠEŠ-DÙ]

Even though there are thirty-eight separate cuneiform tablets that contain portions of the forty-two Temple Hymns, not one of them has more than a few
tantalizing signs for Temple Hymn 28. Although many of the thirty-eight tablets are broken, chipped, or incomplete, those we have have enabled specialists
to piece together most of the text of every hymn except this one. Nowhere in
all the tablets do we find the name of the deity of this temple or the name of
the city where the temple was situated.

A tablet designated 'Q' has the few words that make up the hymn printed
here. The colophon in the final lines is the assumed text that all the hymns
(except the last one) contain. A second badly broken tablet, designated 'A re-
verse I,' contains a word or two of six consecutive lines that belong somewhere
in this hymn. The readable words are "your throne / your wall / your **me** /
your prince/princess / radiant / bright daylight." These are familiar phrases
from the previous hymns. Even having these, however, we do not know if the
deity of the temple was female or male, for the Sumerian word nun can mean
'prince' or 'princess.'

The name of the city in the hymn is unknown. ŠEŠ-DÙ is an educated
guess. Given the geographical progression of the hymns from south to north,
the city for this hymn would lie between Karkara (Temple Hymn 27) and
Adab (Temple Hymn 29). Both of these cities were situated on a branch of the
Tigris that became part of the Iturungal canal. Between them, another ancient

canal connected the Iturungal westward to the Euphrates, the ancient Amar-Suena canal. Douglas Frayne identified the city at the intersection of the two canals, saying, "The intersection of this canal with the Iturungal in the east falls just south of Adams' site 1459 . . . which should be identified with ancient ŠEŠ-DÙ-a."[34] The excavations at this city discovered that its occupation lasted from the Jemdet-Nasr period, 3100 BCE, to the Larsa period, 2025–1763 BCE. It was a thriving village or town during the Sargonic empire, when the Temple Hymns were written.

Frayne determined that this town lay halfway between the important cities of Umma in the south upstream to Sarrākum in the north, "a distance boat-towers could cover in four days" on the Iturungal canal.[35] The town of ŠEŠ-DÙ, the halfway mark, would have provided food and shelter for boatmen on this heavily used trade route.

The details that the text of the hymn might provide must remain unknown until further discoveries offer more information.

TEMPLE HYMN 29

THE ADAB TEMPLE OF NINHURSAG
Esharra

[house. . . . . . .]   (epithets)
[. . . . .]   (epithets)
your [. . . . .] which Enlil. . . . .
here on your site An gave you dominion
majestic house   envisioned for the Lady
Esharra   house for the multitude
your face stirs great fear
your depth shimmers in fiery splendor
Mother Nintu determines fates with Enlil and Enki
leads all feet running toward Esuga

breath of life for the black-haired
An gave you matchless powers from the heart of heaven
exalted house   Adab house
house where dawn breaks
your holy fattening shed keeps replenishing the shrine
as in Kesh   Ninhursag built a propitious shrine
house of the great cosmic forces

where hand washing on the holy altar is shining pure
   Ashgi   deity of Adab
O Adab   house stretched along the canal
has built this house on your radiant site
and placed her seat upon your dais

   15 lines for the Ninhursag house in Adab

THE TEMPLE OF NINHURSAG AT ADAB

Ninhursag, whom we met at her formidable temple in Kesh (Temple Hymn 7), appears again as the patron goddess of Adab. To reach Adab from Zabalam and presumably from the unknown temple at ŠEŠ DÙ, the traveler heads north on the dependable Iturungal canal. Kesh has never been found, but we know it lay on a canal near Adab, probably on an offshoot canal from the Iturungal. The cities of Kesh and Adab were in close proximity and shared a similar pantheon and cultic observance. As William Moran notes, "The clergy of Kesh had their counterparts at Adab."[36] In an unusual bow to Kesh, this hymn links the two temples, mentioning Kesh as the model for Ninhursag in Adab:

as in Kesh, Ninhursag built a propitious shrine

The bow to Kesh suggests that it was the more important city. Moran confirms that at least by Old Babylonian times "Kesh completely overshadows Adab."[37]

Ninhursag is the indispensable Sumerian mother goddess, goddess of conception, gestation, and all the stages of labor and delivery. In Temple Hymn 7, she is described in metaphors true to her name, goddess of the hursag, the rocky slopes of the mountains that make up the borderlands between civilization and the wilds of raw nature. The rhythm of birth is situated deep within the body, in the silent processes of natural forces. Ninhursag is the fierce and fearsome presence who, like a stalking lioness, guards the essential and inevitable stages of human and animal birth. She is an earth goddess of great significance as she watches over that function crucial to ongoing civilization, the birth of both animal and human young.

In contrast, this Temple Hymn captures Ninhursag's civil and political stature, saying nothing explicit about her connection to gestation and birth. Instead, she is anointed with "matchless powers" by the great god of heaven, An, twice in the hymn. As "Mother Nintu" she sits with the gods Enlil and Enki to determine fates, no doubt for "the black-haired" citizens of Sumer, the "multitude" whose "feet" are "running toward" her awesome house. For centuries before this hymn was written, Ninhursag, together with An and Enlil, was one of the three great gods. This hymn from the Akkadian period is an example of the intrusion of the god Enki into the triumvirate, making it a foursome. Eventually, several hundred years after the fall of the Sargonic empire, Enki replaced Ninhursag altogether.

An additional snag in the placement of Ninhursag in the seat of power is, as the hymn states, "Mother Nintu," who sits with Enlil and Enki to determine fates. Nintu, at times a separate birth goddess and at times the aspect of Ninhursag that propels gestation, appears here to be a distinct individual. Or is she? Jacobsen says that in the naming of the three ruling gods, An, Enlil, and Ninhursag, Nintu's name hardly ever appears as a substitute for Ninhursag.[38] Still, he notes that originally Nintur and Ninhursag were separate deities.[39] On the other hand, Frymer-Kensky asserts that the two were identified as one goddess in prehistory.[40] Sjöberg enumerates examples from other texts, some of which conflate the two while others clearly separate them.[41] Gene Gragg, who translated the Early Dynastic "Hymn to Kesh" from Fara (2600 BCE), says, "This interchange of Ninhursag, Nintu, Ninmah, and other 'mother-goddess' figures in the Adab-Kèš pantheon becomes increasingly common as time passes."[42] Gragg goes on to say, "We will continually encounter" the association of the two cities Kesh and Adab "right down to the end of the Mesopotamian cuneiform tradition."[43]

The hymn presents a puzzle regarding the name of the temple. In one line it is called é-šár-ra, 'house for the multitude' or 'house of the universe,' and in the colophon at the end of the hymn, é-UD-NUN[ki], 'house at Adab.' Sjöberg surmises that Eshara is an epithet chosen for the Ninhursag temple because of the similarity in sound to another notable temple in Adab, the é-sar-ra (pronounced E-sar-ra, not E-shar-a) temple of Inanna. In one text the Esarra in Adab is listed as number ten in a series of the taverns or brothels of Inanna. Inanna says in another text, "In Adab, the Esarra belongs to me."[44] The conflation of the names E-shar-ra and E-sar-ra may indicate a borrowing from one to the other in order to lend prestige and numinous power to the site. In a limestone statue a tufted-skirted king, Lugaldalu, stands reverently over the inscription, "For the E-sar. Lugaldalu, king of Adab," testifying to the prominence of the Esarra Temple in pre-Sargonic Adab. Atypically, no name of the deity there is given, but the king's prayerful gesture in the statue bears witness to his adulation of Inanna and confers royal prestige on the temple.[45]

NINHURSAG'S FAMILY

Ashgi, Ninhursag's son, is named "god of Adab" at the end of the hymn. Typically, at this point the Temple Hymn names the deity of the temple, in this case Ninhursag. The unusual appearance here is similar to the unusual mention of Kesh in the hymn and accentuates the interchangeable similarity of the pantheons of Adab and Kesh. An archaic copy of the more ancient Kesh hymn from Fara repeats a line about Ashgi several times, for example, "One as great as its hero, Ašgi—has any mother ever borne such a one?"[46] This earlier hymn from Kesh, discussed in the chapter on Temple Hymn 7, is not connected to the Sumerian Temple Hymns. Its antiquity testifies to the long tradition of the heroic Ashgi and his mother, Ninhursag, at Kesh. Both Ashgi and Nintur/ Ninhursag are also well attested in the Adab pantheon.

Ninhursag's husband was the god Shulpae, suitable for her because he was a god of the wildlands, just as she was goddess of the border between civilization and wild nature. Another child is mentioned, a daughter or son, Lisin or Lulil. Neither Ninhursag's husband nor her children achieved the stature of the mother goddess.[47]

THE CITY OF ADAB

The city of Adab during the flourishing of the first cities was among the thirty or so city-states in Early Dynastic southern Mesopotamia. This six-hundred-year period was one of striking developments in the culture and solidification of the identity of Sumer as "the Land." In this period true cities with strong separate identities evolved. Adab was one of them. City seals have been found dating from Early Dynastic I, 2900–2750 BCE, and one such seal contains thirteen separate ideograms, each possibly denoting a separate city, the seal indicating the thirteen cities aligned in some manner.[48] Evidence suggests that the early Sumerian cities interacted with one another, traded, and exchanged cultural inventions but seemed not to interfere with each other's local affairs. They were held together by a common language and common religion that centered in Nippur with its chief god, Enlil. Each city had its own primary and secondary gods, but all Sumerian deities belonged to an interwoven pantheon. As noted above, Adab was located on what was at the time one of the principal irrigation canals, the Iturungal. Following the geographical sequential order of the Temple Hymns, we deduce that Adab was north of Zabalam and Karkara, cities also on the Iturungal.

Adab, being located on a major waterway, benefited from trading activity. It developed trade connections both south to the centers on the Persian Gulf, where it seems to have had special relationships, and north and east into Elam and the Iranian plateau. During Sargon's reign there was a great expansion of foreign trade, and, being on a north-south waterway, Adab at that time undoubtedly expanded its trading ventures. Its importance as a city seems to have diminished during the Isin-Larsa/Old Babylonian period (2000–1600 BCE), although tablets found in its ruins date from the Early Dynastic all the way through to the Neo-Babylonian periods and the end of the Mesopotamian tradition (3000–539 BCE). During this long period, the import of various Sumerian cities rose and declined, but at the time of the writing of the Temple Hymns, Adab was flourishing and duly honored its principal goddess, Ninhursag.

TEMPLE HYMN 30

THE ISIN TEMPLE OF NINISINA
È-gal-mah[49]

Isin   city
built from the ground up by An
a nest in a low-lying plain
your outside is strong and firm
your inside artfully tied and woven

divine powers fated by An
the low altar that Enlil loves
An and Enlil's fate-forging ground
bread-eating place for all the great gods
filled with terror and hair-raising fear
all the Anunna surely stand at your great wine feast

your princess   the sacred mother
purifies the glistening jeweled cella
[and] prepares the dark inner chamber   in that holy place
where she binds the crown for the sacred woman

seven teats overflow for the priestess
seven desires resound
your lady   great physician of the country

Ninisina   child of An
O house Isin
has built this house on your radiant site
and placed her seat upon your dais

   16 lines for the house of Ninisina in Isin

THE TEMPLE OF NINISINA AT ISIN

At the time of the writing of this Temple Hymn, Ninisina was a minor goddess
in a small, relatively insignificant town a few miles south of the holy city of
Nippur, situated inland, west of Adab and Karkara. Still, the characteristics of
Ninisina that the hymn extols became magnified when, a few hundred years
later, she became the patron goddess of a powerful new kingdom, the Isin-
Larsa Dynasty.

The hymn calls her "great physician of the country," clearly one of her major
attributes. Likewise, she is closely associated with the great god of heaven An;
three times in the hymn An is mentioned as investing her with powers. Significantly, her similarity to or identity with Inanna—more apparent in the later
Isin-Larsa period (2000–1800 BCE)—is well in place at the writing of this
hymn several hundred years earlier. During that later period, Ninisina became
prominent as the "Lady" of Isin, the capital of the dynasty. There she was
the bride of kings in the sacred marriage ritual, testimony to her importance,
further extending her identification with Inanna, the prototype of the bride in
that ritual.

PHYSICIAN, DAUGHTER OF AN, RIVAL OF INANNA

Ninisina, a goddess of medical healing, was called "the great physician of the
black-haired"—a familiar epithet for the Sumerian people.[50] She was identified with Gula, a noted goddess of healing. Her healing skills were medical,
not magical, and doctors called on her to assist in their work. However, both
types of healing, medical and magical, were used side by side, and neither was
more legitimate than the other.

Ninisina was one of the daughters of An who assisted in the birth process.
Her mother was Nintur, the goddess of birth frequently identified with Ninhursag of the preceding hymn. These daughters of An served as midwives or
assisted in birth, as Frymer-Kensky describes: "holding the pail to catch the
placenta and the knife for cutting the umbilical cord."[51] She is also known as

a dream interpreter,[52] and it is said of her that she "revives the (near-) dead."[53] A hymn to Gula describes the activities of the physician:

> I am a physician, I can heal,
> I carry around all (healing) herbs, I drive away disease,
> I gird myself with the leather bag
> containing health-giving incantations.
>
> I carry around texts which bring recovery,
> I give cures to mankind.
> My pure dressing alleviates the wound,
> My soft bandage relieves the sick.[54]

Ninisina, like Bau in Temple Hymn 21, is called dumu-sag-an-kù-ga, 'first-born daughter of holy An.' Ninisina's position as daughter of An is complicated by her designation as An's lover in the myth "Enki and the World Order." Because of An's eminent position as the greatest of the great gods, he occupied many roles in relation to the other deities. He was father to all the assistant birth goddesses, including Ninisina. Rather than paternity, as we think of it, this designation may have meant simply that the great god was the author and protector of the birth process. Likewise, to have been chosen by An as a lover does not necessarily imply incest in the world of the deities. Such a designation would elevate Ninisina to the highest rank.

In "Enki and the World Order," Inanna complains that Enki has given other goddesses selected areas of authority and has given nothing to her. She is incensed. She summarily lists the powers he gave, one by one, saying of Ninisina,

> My noble sister, holy Ninisina
> Received the šuba-stone, and is now An's lover;
> She stands ready for him, and shouts loud [her?] desire.[55]

Inanna has reason to complain, for it appears that Ninisina is taking over aspects and properties that she claims as her own. Is she not sometimes designated as lover or bride to An? These lines from Enheduanna's devotional poem to Inanna seem to indicate so:

> you lie with great An
> on an unblemished bed[56]

And does Inanna not claim the precious šuba-stones? In Temple Hymn 26 she is described as wearing these very stones as jewels. And is Inanna not the one and only nugig? Yet Ninisina's hymn calls her nun-zu ama nu-gig, 'your princess, the sacred [woman] mother.' In Hymn 26 Inanna is the quintessential source of desire. In that hymn she makes her shrine at Zabalam "resound with desire" and grounds the "hallowed inner chamber / with desire." Here again Ninisina claims desire as she, too, fills the sacred chamber with desire: "in that holy place / . . . / seven desires resound."

The similarities in the two hymns are striking and uphold the claim that Ninisina became identified with Inanna. Another possibility is that she was a separate and lesser goddess who took on the powerful sensual qualities of Inanna as a way to absorb some of the prominence of the inimitable Inanna. Both goddesses have access to the shining, gemlike šuba stones, a stone that Joan Westenholz says is connected to women's sexuality.[57] The term nugig, as Sjöberg says, is "a title of a woman of special status." In other texts it is frequently translated by the Greek term "hierodule," or as "tabooed woman" or "sacred woman" or even by words that imply "concubine."[58] In this hymn Ninisina wraps a crown on the "nugig," who, Sjöberg maintains, refers in this case to a special priestess in the temple. This wrapped headgear, the mùš, is the one worn only by the high priestess and implies that the nugig was a person of "a very high rank."[59] In most instances of the use of this term, nugig, designates Inanna.

DESIRE IN THE SANCTUARY

Both Hymn 30 of Ninisina and Hymn 26 of Inanna describe the goddesses as they fill with desire the innermost sanctuaries of the temples, the holy of holies. For the Mesopotamians, desire seems to have been the energetic force that moves all creatures, all life in the universe. The sacred marriage ritual, a wedding of the goddess and the god, who may have been portrayed by persons of high rank, perhaps a high priestess and a king, is described as an act that ensures fertility for the coming year. One sacred marriage poem makes this explicit:

> my man enters the noble house my house
> I am his lady   He is my husband
> the shoots rise back of the door
> the cedar bough rises in the lap of the king

then the vine rises
then the grain rises
Eden's garden fills in jeweled light
. . . .
bounty spreads from the great house
cream & beer & cheese & oil
Holy Inanna stands at the door
gives her gifts of life
gives life from the house Dumuzi fills

the Lady his queen
the beloved pair
it is strong it is strong
source: tablet Ni 9602 (my translation)

The potency of the sexual image made its way into later religions: for example, Catholic nuns call themselves brides of Christ, and among the Gnostics
the union of the soul with the deity takes place in the bridal chamber. However, the later versions seem pale in comparison with the full range of desire
that Inanna and her counterpart Ninisina embody: Inanna shouts, "I want
YOU, Dumuzi," and Ninisina "stands ready for him [An] and shouts loud her
desire."[60]

THIRD-MILLENNIUM ISIN

Ninisina's prominence greatly increased with the rise of the Isin-Larsa Dynasty (c. 2000), in which she became the goddess most adored and claimed
by the kings. Nevertheless, she was present in the third millennium before Isin
grew in power. The Sargonic king Manishtushu, son of Sargon, dedicated a
mace to her,[61] and in the late third millennium a clay tablet inscribed with a
petition from a worshiper was laid at her feet.[62]

Isin was located in the northern farming regions, where cereals and grains
were grown. Ninisina was connected to its prosperous storehouse and celebrated its agricultural festivals. Herds of cattle enabled an important leather
industry to flourish.[63] In an Ur III festival Ninisina traveled by boat to Umma,
no doubt carrying shares of Isin's bounty to the patron god Shara, but her
main purpose was to participate in a festival for Dumuzi, with whom the Ur
III kings identified. Once again Ninisina claims Inanna's prerogative as she
brings offerings to Inanna's husband, Dumuzi.[64]

A final puzzling element in this hymn is a line that is repeated in Temple Hymn 20 to Ningirsu. In both hymns, following the phrase "hair-raising fear," the line "all the Anunna surely stand at your great wine feast" appears. In both hymns the formidable temple, from its great height, imposes itself upon the terrified worshipers, then introduces a wine feast attended by the council of deities, the Anunna. Ninisina's stature is thus bolstered by the presence of the Anunna at her feast. The poet may reveal her purpose, to elevate Ninisina's status in the obscure village of Isin, when she repeatedly invokes An and even claims for Ninisina the support of mighty Enlil from neighboring Nippur. No one would ignore this goddess, who has the attention and support of the status-pronouncing deities An and Enlil. Implicit in their appearance in the hymn is their embrace of Ninisina, welcoming her into the presence of the two most eminent gods of the pantheon.

chapter 10

HYMNS TO TEMPLES IN KAZALLU AND MARDA

Kazallu and Marda are connected by their geographical location on a north-south stretch of linked irrigation canals west of an ancient course of the Euphrates. The exact location of Kazallu is uncertain, but it is known to have been situated on a canal that bore its name, possibly near the town of Borsippa. The bow-shaped canal spanned the western edge of northern Sumer, beginning just above Sippar and reaching south almost to the midsection of the alluvium. At the city of Dilbat, the Kazallu joined the Arahtum canal, which also ran north-south, west of the Kazallu, through Babylon, south to Dilbat, continuing south and ending at the city of Marda, where it converged with the Me-Enlila canal. Marda gave its name to an encompassing province that included the holy city of Nippur, almost due east, situated on the Euphrates itself.[1] The complexity of the canal system is a testament to the ingenuity of the Sumerians, who invented, constructed, and maintained their waterworks, the lifeblood of their survival and prosperity.

Numushda, the patron deity of the city of Kazallu, was a son of the moon god, Nanna. His temple was far north of the Ur temple of Nanna. Nevertheless, Numushda is known to have participated in the cleansing rites at the Ekishnugal of Nanna and to have been connected to its powerful **me**. Numushda figures prominently in a myth, "The Marriage of Martu," described below, a myth that pits the virtues of settled civilization against those of nomadic "barbarians." While this conflict must have been an issue the early settlers of the cities encountered, it is not apparent in any of the Temple Hymns and only arises in this hymn because of Numushda's appearance in the myth.

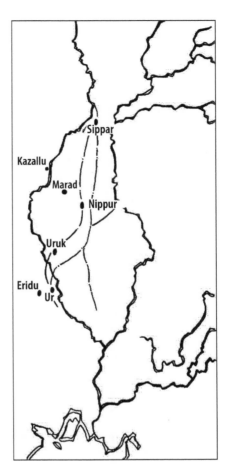

10.1.   Sketch map of Mesopotamia with Kazallu and Marda (Marad). After Postgate 1994. Reproduced by permission of Taylor and Francis Books U.K.

The hymn to Lugalmarda's temple in Marda (Marad) is one of two hymns whose text on the tablets is almost completely destroyed. His name means 'Head Man of Marda,' lugal being one of the original words for the ruler of a city. Apparently, he was a powerful deity, often identified with the fearsome god Ninurta.

Both Kazallu and Marda may have been somewhat isolated by their locations. Nevertheless, they were chosen to join the cities of the Temple Hymns. Enheduanna could have visited both temples and presented these hymns to their illustrious deities.

TEMPLE HYMN 31

THE KAZALLU TEMPLE OF NUMUSHDA
Kunsatu

O Kazallu
   your glow spreads to the midst of the sky
   a widening shine rising in awe
your prince   seed of the stud bull
born to the wild ox in the pure mountains

towering speckled-eyed bison
a lion-fanged lord   snatches a calf with his claws
catches a man in his nets

strong one who grabs the weanling bull
strength-giver against the evil
Kunsatu   ladder of the mountain
great lord Numushda
O Kazallu has built this house on your radiant site
and placed his seat upon your dais

    10 lines for Numushda of Kazallu

THE TEMPLE OF NUMUSHDA AT KAZALLU

Numushda is a minor god from the important city of Kazallu, a city that figures in a number of historical documents. Using clues from ancient texts, specialists locate Kazallu close to and variously north or south of Babylon, but all place the city in the general area northwest of the key city of Nippur.[2] The city lay on the Kazallu canal, a waterway that ran east of an ancient course of the Euphrates. The oldest reference to Numushda comes from Early Dynastic III (2600–2350 BCE), and his name is included in texts from Ur III (2112–2004 BCE) and from the Isin-Larsa Dynasty (2000–1800 BCE). Only this hymn and a later hymn from the time of the Larsa king Siniqisham describe the god in any detail.

    The descriptions of Numushda in the two hymns agree on his character almost completely. In the Temple Hymn Numushda is an aggressive god, lion-fanged, exceptionally virile and strong. Lion-clawed as well, he snatches a calf, he nets a man, and grabs a weanling calf. In the Larsa hymn he is similarly described as "a great wild bull," "raging lion," "poisonous snake," "furious dragon," and "terrifying flood."[3] Both hymns extol his beauty, like that of the shapely bison. "Lofty, speckled-eyed bison," says the Temple Hymn, while the Larsa hymn addresses him as "God with the limbs of a bison, fitting to behold."[4]

Numushda is the son of the moon god, Nanna. The Temple Hymn calls him "seed of the stud bull / born of the wild ox in the pure mountains." The stud bull may refer to Enlil, Numushda's grandfather, who has the epithet of a great bull. The wild ox may refer to Nanna, particularly a "wild ox in the pure mountains," since Nanna has a connection to the "high mountain," which Sjöberg calls a "mythological locality."[5] Gods are frequently said to be born in the mountains. Numushda's temple is called 'Ladder of the Mountain,' kun₄-sa-tu, a term that may refer to Nanna's high mountain or may describe the stepped platform structure of the temple. This temple in Kazallu, the Larsa hymn says, was built by Enlil as the cult place of Numushda.

In the Larsa hymn Ningal, wife of Nanna, is said to have "formed him [in her holy womb]," while he is "carefully tended by the great Lady Ninlil," his grandmother and the wife of Enlil. In that hymn, as in the Temple Hymn, his powerful lineage is connected both to his father, Nanna, and to his grandfather Enlil, but his propitious birth and early care are under the protection of his mother, Ningal, and grandmother Ninlil. These details appear to be an elaboration included in the Larsa hymn in order to invoke the power of the great god Enlil and to enhance the stature of King Siniqisham. The similarity of the images of Numushda in the two hymns, written some five hundred years apart, is an example of the conservative nature of the religious traditions in Mesopotamia.

Numushda figures prominently in an interesting myth, "The Marriage of Martu."[6] The story takes place in the town of Ninab, near Kazallu, where Numushda was the tutelary deity. Numushda and his wife, Namrat (Fairy), and their daughter Adnigkidu have arrived in Ninab to attend a festival. The divine hero Martu is scheduled to wrestle the strongest opponents. He wrestles vigorously and leaves his opponents wounded, some even dead. A joyous Numushda offers Martu precious stones and silver, but Martu wants only to marry Numushda's daughter Adnigkidu. Numushda agrees to the marriage, but Adnigkidu's girlfriend objects, saying,

> He eats uncooked meat,
> In his lifetime has no house,
> When he dies, he will not be buried:
> My girlfriend—why would you marry Martu?!

Adnigkidu answers, "I will indeed marry Martu."[7]

The admonitions of Adnigkidu's friend describe Martu as a rather uncouth, uncivilized barbarian. Indeed, Martu was the god of the nomadic people, the Martu, who "were roaming the hill-country on the verges of Mesopotamia."[8] The myth relates a fateful encounter between the Martu people and the inhabitants of the city-state of Ninab. If anything, the myth describes the attempted integration of the nomadic Martu into the established urban culture of the Sumerians in Ninab. For the Martu, this transition represented a new beginning. Indeed, the first lines of the myth have the familiar ring of a creation story: "(When) Ninab was existing, (but) Kiritab was not existing, / The holy priestly cap was existing, (but) the holy crown was not existing, / . . . Holy salt was existing, (but) holy soap was not existing."[9] The next lines contrast high civilization with the habits of nomads or uncivilized wanderers, "who live by the side of the city."[10]

There is some implication that by marrying Adnigkidu, Martu will be brought into the fold of the strong and explicit Sumerian culture, a highly civilized and well-defined norm. By contrasting these two ways of living, the Sumerian authors of the myth kept in their consciousness not only the preciousness of being civilized, but also the thin line between civilization and barbarism. This contrast occurs in other myths, specifically in the myth "Inanna's Descent to the Underworld," in which the highly civilized queen of heaven chooses to go to the underworld. There she is beaten, killed, hung on a peg to rot, and ultimately transformed and returned to the land above. The wisdom she brings back is an expanded awareness of the everlasting power of the dark, barbaric layer just beneath the highly prized and hard-won order in the civilized world.

The Sumerians — and the author of the Temple Hymn — seem to be aware of the paradoxical contrasts in human nature. The contrast is not only between urban and nomadic ways of life, but between the orderly norms and rules of civilization that human beings attempt to follow and the aggressive barbarism individuals contain beneath the surface. Numushda himself exemplifies both sides. His fierce aggression resides within his radiant temple, which seems to have stair steps to the heavens. Even his name, "Snake Person," combines the elemental earthly creature with the divinity of a god. The Sumerians seem to have had the wisdom to uphold the paradoxical in human nature as an antidote to the perilous delusions of hubris that threaten civilized urbanites who forget their roots in the natural world.

TEMPLE HYMN 32

THE MARDA TEMPLE OF LUGALMARDA
Igikalamma

O house   eye of the Land
[your] foundation hard-set
hill grown high   standing on the wide earth
[you] crush the evil-necked rebels
the [xxxx] of heaven place of Ninsunanna

[three lines fragmentary]

O house of Marda
has built this house on your radiant site
and placed his seat upon your dais

    8 lines for the house of Lugalmarda in Marda

THE TEMPLE OF LUGALMARDA AT MARDA

Temple Hymn 32 is one of only two hymns (Temple Hymn 28 is the other) in which little or nothing can be read on the remains of the tablets. Only fragments of five lines out of eight are decipherable. These lines include the name of the god, Lugalmarda, and the name of his temple and his city, "Eye of the Land Temple" in Marda (or Marad).

Lugalmarda, Head Man of Marda, is identified with the god Ninurta of Temple Hymn 5, the powerful son of Enlil who occupied an important place in Enlil's Nippur pantheon. Temple Hymn 5 depicts Ninurta as a fierce, heroic warrior god whose temple, the Eshumesha, was an eternal center of strength and dreaded violence. As "power-gatherer of heaven," Ninurta's temple was a magnet for divine forces that served to refine cosmic order.

Little of this vigor and potency remains in the description of Lugalmarda in his Temple Hymn. One line is a near duplicate of a line in Temple Hymn 5 to Ninurta. Lugalmarda is said to "crush the evil-necked rebels," while Ninurta "destroys evil-necked rebels." Only the verb differs in the two versions. It is impossible to know whether the missing lines of Temple Hymn 32 extolled Lugalmarda's powers as Temple Hymn 5 does Ninurta.

A goddess is mentioned in the hymn, and the fragments of her name suggest she may be Ninsuanna, the wife of Lugalmarda. Her name, meaning 'Lady—

flesh of heaven,' insinuates her sensuous nature. Nevertheless, the fragmentary cuneiform signs cannot be read with certainty.

During his reign the Sargonic king Naram Sin dedicated an inscription to Lugalmarda of Marda, adding further substance to the record of his significance during the Sargonic period.[11] In addition, Numushda of Temple Hymn 31 had a temple in Marda.[12] Other than that, very little is known about this god or his city or his temple.

chapter 11

HYMNS TO TEMPLES IN DER AND ESHNUNNA

Temple Hymns 33 and 34 are written to the temples of Ishtaran in Der and Ninazu in Eshnunna. The two cities, Der and Eshnunna, were far to the north of the alluvium and east of the Tigris in the territory of present-day Iran. The two cities are the only ones among the Temple Hymns that are located outside the traditional Sumerian homeland. This Iranian territory bordering today's Iraq stretches from the southern Susiana plateau, north across the Hamur plain to the Diyala River. By the time of the writing of the Temple Hymns, the land had been settled by Sumerians for over a thousand years.

The area was of strategic importance. Major trade routes ran north and south, from Der to Eshnunna and beyond. The main road east from the confluence of the Diyala and the Tigris rivers followed the Diyala into the Zagros Mountains. This east-west corridor still remains the major route between Baghdad and the Iranian plateau. In the Sargonic period, trading activity enabled the two cities to prosper. Sargon's forces gained control of the territory, and the king himself accepted tribute from the local citizens.

Der and Eshnunna were virtually Sumerian cities, so thoroughly had the Sumerian immigrants established their complex culture over that of the indigenous inhabitants. Temple Hymn 34 is the second hymn to Ninazu. The first, Temple Hymn 14, is written to his temple in Enegi in the heart of southern Sumer. In this northeastern outpost, both Ninazu and Ishtaran were in foreign territory. Although both were thoroughly Sumerian deities, they absorbed characteristics from the ancient Semitic population who first occupied

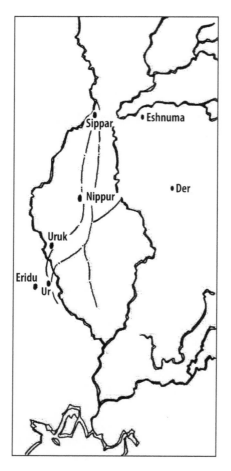

11.1.   Sketch map of Mesopotamia, the Diyala region with cities of Der and Eshnunna. After Postgate 1994. Reproduced by permission of Taylor and Francis Books U.K.

the land. Each of their hymns reveals the cross-cultural complexity the two deities had acquired.

TEMPLE HYMN 33

THE DER TEMPLE OF ISHTARAN
Edimgalkalamma

O Der
divine decisions   made with great care
protect the multitude

in the dread and splendor of your gate
the horned snake and dragon lie snared in your trap

your prince   leader of all the gods
fit to give counsel   rendered augustly

child of Urash
expert in true **me** of princeship
Ishtaran   evil-thwarting sovereign of heaven
house   great mast pole of the country
has built this house on your radiant site
and placed his seat upon your dais

    8 lines for Ishtaran of Der

THE TEMPLE OF ISHTARAN AT DER

In order to journey to Der from the cities of Kazallu and Marda, the third-millennium traveler would catch a boat traveling north, either on an ancient course of the Euphrates or on a north-south irrigation canal, disembark at Sippar, wait for transportation, donkey or cart, to carry him or her overland, east across the alluvium into the territory that is now modern Iran. The city of Der was situated on a major Iranian trade route between Susa in the south and Eshnunna near the Diyala River in the north.

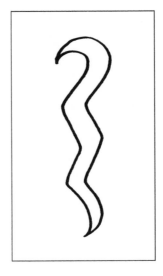

11.2.   Horned snake symbol of Ishtaran. Courtesy of the University of Texas Press, Jeremy Black and Anthony Green, *Gods, Demons and Symbols of Ancient Mesopotamia*, Tessa Richards, illustrator, 1995.

Early in the fourth millennium, the Uruk period, large numbers of settlers from southern Mesopotamia began to relocate eastward, to the Susiana plain in the Elamite territory of neighboring Iran, south of the city of Der. The colonists came for the rich resources, water, timber, and minerals, all of which were scarce in their homeland. They built cities whose administration, religion, and building structures were essentially identical to those of southern Sumer. The archeologist Guillermo Algaze describes the emigration as "a process of wholesale colonization."[1]

Farther north, the area around the confluence of the Tigris and Diyala rivers was of critical strategic importance. Sumerian traders established outposts in the area. Not only did the plain beyond the river crossing provide easy access south to Elam, but the road east along the Diyala crossed the Zagros Mountains and entered the Iranian plateau. Algaze describes the route:

> The most important of these routes [across the Zagros] was the Khorasan Road, which remains to this day the main route linking Baghdad and Kermanshah. . . . This route follows the Diyala River into the highlands and snakes its way upward across the central Zagros through a number of intermontane valleys before emerging onto the Iranian plateau in the vicinity of Hamadan.[2]

The ancient route led eventually to Central Asia and China.[3] Travelers, traders, and settlers intermingled in the area, and a fertile exchange of differing cultures took place along the north-south trade route from Susa to Der to Eshnunna. From the Tigris-Diyala confluence, roads led east into Iran and west on the trade route that crossed Sumer, leading to its western boundary at the Euphrates. Another critical route followed the Tigris north and south, making the area a hub of exchange and prosperity.

Der was situated in the grasslands of the Iranian Hamur Plain, on the trade route north of the Elamite lands the Sumerians first occupied. J. N. Postgate says, "During all our time span [this trade route passed] the city of Der."[4] The earliest mention of Ishtaran as the city god of Der was found on a tablet from Abu Salabikh, 2550 BCE. From the same era came a city seal of Der, picturing a crossroad or intersection drawn on a central circle. The seal simply and explicitly portrays the essence of the city of Der as the crossroads on this north-south trade artery.

11.3.   Early Dynastic I city seal of Der 2900–2750 BCE. After Postgate, 1994. Reproduced by permission of Taylor and Francis Books U.K.

SNAKE OR DYING HERO

Ishtaran, the patron deity of Der, resides in the well-anchored temple Edim-galkalamma, 'Great Mast Pole of the Country.' Firmly planted though he may be, Ishtaran has a puzzling dual identity, a complexity that may arise from his having been displaced from Sumer proper into the territory east of the traditional Sumerian boundary, the Tigris River. While the Sumerians in the fourth millennium had infiltrated, if not taken over, the civilization in the Susiana plain, they were not immune to the Semitic cultural influence of the indigenous population. Ishtaran, who may have been originally one of the young dying gods of Sumer, migrated to the Iranian territory and the city of Der and became a snake god of the underworld. F. A. M. Wiggerman explains:

> Religious interest in snakes in these regions goes back deep into prehistory and through the ages remains quite visible in the iconography of Elam and the Iranian mountains. The influence of an Iranian substrate helps to explain the histories of two gods that are hardly chthonic snake-gods in origin, Ištaran and Inšušinak. . . . Both gods settled down in Iranian territory, and apparently became chthonic snake-gods in their foreign homes.[5]

Ishtaran's mythology and iconography bear the marks of his conflicting identities. His acquired snake iconography appears in the horned snake and dragon that are carved on the impressive gate to the temple in this hymn:

> in the dread and splendor of your gate
> the horned snake and dragon lie snared in your trap

11.4. Akkadian cylinder seal showing Ishtaran before a fire altar. Courtesy of the Trustees of the British Museum.

Ishtaran, whose decisions "protect the multitude," sets the trap that captures the horned snake and the dragon pictured on the gate. Caught in the trap they are, but Ishtaran might release them at any moment were his divine decisions to be disobeyed. Punishment for such an offense is explicit: "may the lady of the earth let a snake from out of the earth bite him in his foot."[6]

The mythological snake serves to dispense justice. Its appearance "on a large variety of objects, among them boundary stones" is a reminder of the punishment that will be meted out to anyone who dares to disobey limits or rules of order.[7] Akkadian cylinder seals combine Ishtaran's role as judge with his snake attributes. Having a human head and torso, he sits on a throne of judgment while his winding snake legs and feet dangle below. Frequently, a fire altar stands before him, which may serve to warm the cold-blooded snake or may depict his "bright visage" named in the dying god laments.[8]

Like the underworld queen Ereshkigal and like Ningishzida in Temple Hymn 15, Ishtaran is associated with the constellation Hydra, carved on cylinder seals as a horned dragon with lion paws and a long snakelike tail. Occasionally, a star and moon appear on Ishtaran's seals, or he may have rays on his shoulders. Wiggerman tells us that Ishtaran was a snake god who eventually became totally anthropomorphic.[9] His ophidian traits were then carried by his sons, Nirah, a deified snake and vizier to Ishtaran, and Irhan, the deified river Euphrates.[10]

Unlike the deities consigned entirely to the netherworld, Ishtaran is associated with the growth, flourishing, and death of vegetation. Thus he was celebrated in death and rebirth rituals, and his attributes were connected to the cycles of nature. He is mentioned in two laments to the young dying gods:

Woe the lad, Ishtaran of shining visage![11]

and

In the desert, by the early grass,
   she [holds not back
   the flood of tears

    for her husband,]
. . .
Alas the lad, Ishtaran of bright visage![12]

Adding to this mix, the Temple Hymn says that Ishtaran is "child of Urash," the original creatrix, wife of the god of heaven, An. Even though born of the heavenly father deity, Ishtaran's sky god attributes do not fit his chthonic nature. Those attributes must reflect the tenacious remnants of his Sumerian origin. Because of his name, he may have a sky deity connection to the Semitic Inanna/Ishtar, the morning and evening star, as well as to his sky father, An. His wife, according to a late text, is Manzât, 'the rainbow.'[13]

The prominence of the dragon and snake deities wanes in the second millennium as the god Marduk overcomes them. "Marduk [is] a god that is in no way chthonic," says Wiggerman,[14] and with Marduk's elevation, the Mesopotamian deities lose their unusual capacity to carry opposite attributes so prevalent in life's forces: both the "bright visage" of the sky and the dark underworld realities of cyclical nature and death.

TEMPLE HYMN 34

THE ESHNUNNA TEMPLE OF NINAZU
Esikil

O Esikil   pure house
divine powers unsurpassed in all the land
exalted residence of the warrior   its name is proud and lofty
holy house of Ninazu   house of purest dominion
house   your powers are holy powers
your cleansing rites are shining lustrations

in your dwelling the hero refreshes
Ninazu dines on your cella platform

your sovereign   the great lord son of Enlil
is a rampant lion spitting poison on enemy land
a ferocious sandstorm rising on evil-necked lands
a dragon, baring his fangs at the walls of the rebels
a storm smothering the disobedient   trampling the enemy
when he strides out   the wicked cannot escape
standing victorious   he destroys their cities
frowning   they crumple into the dust

O house   your prince is a great lion
hangs evil ones from his claws

your king in the rigor of battle
is a terrifying mighty storm
called into combat
shield over his mighty arm   a net over the multitude
the enemy cannot escape his reach

when the great lord comes forth in splendor
his magnificence has no equal

born of Ninlil   true seed of the great mountain
Esikil   pure house   your sovereign the warrior Ninazu
has   O Eshnunna   built this house on your radiant site
and placed his seat upon your dais.

    21 lines for the house of Ninazu at Eshnunna

THE TEMPLE OF NINAZU AT ESHNUNNA

The Temple Hymns to Ninazu, 14 and 34, attribute to him such diverse characteristics that they appear to be describing two separate gods. In Temple Hymn 14, Ninazu is a priestly god of the underworld whose shadow of death falls over prince and commoner alike. A musician, he plays his lyre sweetly and listens to prayers.

In contrast, the Ninazu of Temple Hymn 34 is a ferocious warrior, spitting poison, baring his fangs, and stomping his powerful feet on the enemy. Ninazu of the first hymn was at home in the traditional Sumerian land between the two rivers in the south, in Enegi. The home of the second hymn to Ninazu is far to the north, east of the Tigris, near the Zagros Mountains. Eshnunna was a large city located on a major trade route that crossed the Tigris at its junction with the Diyala River. The route followed the Diyala east, eventually reaching the Iranian plateau, a well-traveled road that, as noted, remains today the main route from Baghdad across the Zagros and east into Iran.

Long before Enheduanna's lifetime, the route was crucial for strategic as well as for trade and communication purposes. By the latter part of the fourth millennium, the people from Sumer had intermingled with the indigenous people of the plain south of Eshnunna, the Susiana plateau in Iran, to the point that, as Algaze says, there is "little doubt that Susiana was culturally as much a part of the Mesopotamian world as the alluvium itself."[15]

OPHIDIAN TRANS-TIGRIS INFLUENCE

After the Sumerian emigration into Susiana, religious influences from east of the Tigris so penetrated their ideologies that it is difficult to separate the original beliefs. Snake features in particular, typical in prehistoric Iranian iconography, entered into the character of certain Sumerian gods, especially apparent in Ninazu, his son Ningishzida (Temple Hymn 15), and Ishtaran of the previous hymn.[16] Nevertheless, the two gods, Ninazu north and Ninazu south, are said to have developed separately, "but without obscuring [their] basic identity."[17] Ninazu in this hymn displays the warrior characteristics similar to Ninurta (Temple Hymn 5) and, according to Wiggerman, may have identified with Ninurta and his genealogy—for example, in this hymn as he claims Ninlil and Enlil as his parents.[18] The first Ninazu hymn mentions Ereshkigal, goddess of the underworld, as his mother. In the second hymn, his claim to Ninlil as his mother is supported in the myth "Enlil and Ninlil," in which he is the third child engendered in Ninlil's pursuit of Enlil (see Temple Hymn 3).

Ninazu in the third millennium was a prominent god of the underworld, an identity apparent in Temple Hymn 14. In hymn 34, his underworld character is made known by the ušumgal, a dragon who, like the snake, lives under the ground. Wiggerman suggests that Ninazu's ophidian traits, even in Enegi (Temple Hymn 14), may have been imported from the area east of the Tigris.[19] An alabaster relief from a private home in Eshnunna shows the god—Ninazu—with a human head and scaled snake body. In this grouping a dragon behind the god has a scaled body and a snake's head. On an earlier seal from the Early Dynastic period, a lion with a long tail in the shape of a snake faces the god. The lion-snake-dragon as the animal or even the vizier of Ninazu developed over hundreds of years in the area of Eshnunna and accounts for his appearance in this hymn as lion and dragon.

THE CITY OF ESHNUNNA

Eshnunna was situated near a great river, the Diyala. It flows southwest from the Zagros Mountains and joins the Tigris in the area where the Tigris and Euphrates bend closely together, forming a boundary that enclosed Sumer proper. Irrigation from the Diyala "fingered out into the lands to the southeast, and enabled the growth of major cities such as Ešnunna," Postgate says.[20] Not only did Eshnunna become a major trading center and agricultural area, but it lay not far from the ancient passageway to the east along the Diyala, the Silk Road, over the Zagros Mountains and on into Central Asia and China. Eshnunna was the principal city in a large area; it was called uru-sag—head city—a term first attested in the Sargonic era.[21] Archeologists who explored the site of Eshnunna, Tell Asmar, determined that its occupation began in the protoliterate Uruk period and lasted a thousand years until the end of the Ur III and beginning of the Larsa period.[22]

Irrigation allowed for agricultural production that probably was watched over by Ninazu, who is credited, along with his brother Ninmada, for bringing barley to Sumer. We have evidence in this period at Eshnunna that commercial weaving was done on a large scale, no doubt connected to the herding of sheep in the grasslands of the area. His dual chthonic and earthly aspects appear on an Akkadian seal in which the deity holding a plow seems to be riding on a tier of four snakes. A human figure standing in front of him also holds the plow with his hands.[23] On this seal the god has an underworld base, the snakes, while he bestows the earthly plow to humanity. This duality of Ninazu, his connection to seasonal agriculture and his underworld role, makes him one of the young dying gods whose death is mourned with the drying up of the crops and whose resurrection is celebrated in the spring at the beginning of the New Year.

ENHEDUANNA, NINAZU, AND TISHPAK

At some point in the Akkadian period the god Tishpak replaced Ninazu in Eshnunna. Wiggerman describes Tishpak as "a god of foreign origin about whose original character nothing is known."[24] Tishpak assumed Ninazu's roles and characteristics as the god of Eshnunna, a warrior god with a chthonic substratum.

When Temple Hymn 34 was written, Ninazu was the patron god in his temple in Eshnunna. Tishpak must have taken over the temple after the writing of the hymns, later in the Akkadian period, evidence that lends weight to the assertion that Enheduanna wrote this hymn during her lifetime.

Sargon's capital city of Akkad, according to Sabina Franke, lay "somewhere at the confluence of the Diyala and Tigris rivers" (see TH 40 for further discussion of the location of Akkad).[25] Eshnunna was situated near the same river intersection, east of the Tigris and somewhat south of the Diyala. While we do not know the dates of Sargon's extensive military campaigns, we do know something about their sequence. His first objective was to subdue the southern city-states in Sumer proper. After he accomplished this goal, he began to look north and east to establish control over the major trade routes. No doubt this interest in the trade route east from the Tigris/Diyala confluence led him to conquer Eshnunna. Records make the point that the Elamites, the inhabitants of the Iranian land bordering the Tigris, paid Sargon tribute.

The bellicose nature of Ninazu in the hymn suggests that, in writing it, Enheduanna could have been supporting her father's conquest of the area. The hymn lauds the warrior Ninazu, destroyer of cities, standing victorious in the heart of battle. The combative nature of this Ninazu matched Sargon's expansive military designs. Some attribute the composition of the hymns to her desire to assure the Sumerians that her father's regime upheld the Sumerian religion. The hymn to Ninazu both praises a Sumerian deity and also provides divine sanction to Sargon's campaigns and territorial expansion, articulating both themes that support her father's regime.

chapter 12

HYMNS TO TEMPLES IN AND AROUND AKKAD

From the city of Eshnunna in hymn 34, the traveler must head west across the Tigris again to enter the heart of northern Sumer. The seven cities of these hymns cluster around Akkad, Sargon's capital, which continues to elude the search of archeologists.

The seven temples would have been familiar to the king and to his daughter Enheduanna, who spent her early life in this area. Sargon began his career at Kish (TH 35) serving the king Ur-Zababa, whose overthrow he attempted as he began his ambitious seizure of the Sumerian territory. The city of Kish was legendary. The Sumerian Kinglist came down from heaven to Kish. With the subsiding of the Great Flood, history began. The names of the first kings of Kish were recorded on the list. Acknowledging this honor, Sumerian kings claimed the esteemed title King of Kish, no matter which territory they ruled.

Zababa, the deity in the first hymn, was the patron of Kish. Zababa was a warrior sometimes equated with Ninurta (TH 5) or Ningirsu (TH 20). Nergal in the next hymn (TH 36), husband of the underworld queen Ereshkigal, lives—as his hymn says—in his "frightful house of the underworld"; his temple in Kutha is the center for the cult of the dead.[1] Nergal is the second born of the children of Ninlil and Enlil, younger brother to the moon deity, Nanna.

These two deities, Zababa and Nergal, add to the sense of this group as a grand finale to the Temple Hymn composition. The group continues with the illustrious deities Nanna, Utu, Ninhursag, and Inanna, and the important cities of Urum, Sippar and the capital, Akkad. Nanna, Utu, and Inanna are the three original celestial lights, the moon, the sun, and the morning and evening

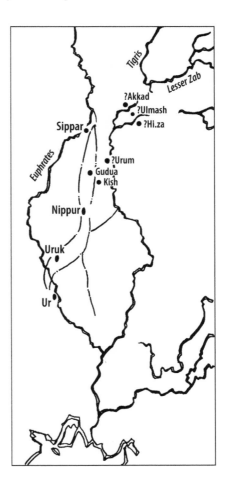

12.1. Sketch map of northern Mesopotamia with Akkad and neighboring cities. After Postgate 1994. Reproduced by permission of Taylor and Francis Books U.K.

star. Nanna's temple (TH 37) in the northern city of Urum was connected to his primary temple at Ur for almost a thousand years. Utu's city of Sippar became a thriving center of trade located at the crossroads between Sumer and the northern plains.

Utu showers abundance on his humbled worshipers (TH 38). Ninhursag assures the stability of the culture, giving birth to kings, to priestesses and priests (TH 39). Inanna, as patron deity of Akkad, takes on the role of warrior in Temple Hymn 40. Aba in Temple Hymn 41 is named, probably by Sargon himself, to be the ruling deity of the whole empire. He is a god of Semitic origin from the territory north of Sumer. His presence here adds nothing to reassure the Sumerians of Sargon's intent to respect their religion; his hymn is brief and perfunctory. The six other star-studded hymns add a sense of closure to the composition, establishing these six prominent Sumerian deities far to the north, assuring the populace that Enheduanna as high priestess oversees a thoroughly Sumerian pantheon.

TEMPLE HYMN 35

THE KISH TEMPLE OF ZABABA
Ekishib

O house   built in abundance
Kish   lifting its head with princely might

well-founded settlement
your sturdy groundwork will not shatter
your heavy clay wall spread wide fills the heart of heaven

he adorned your inner chamber with a battle mace
     its right side is a mountain shaker
     its left   a wicked squeezer
your prince   strong and mighty
a great storm bound to earth vents terrifying awe

Ekishib   house of the Seal
your sovereign   the hero Zababa
has built this house on your radiant site
and placed his seat upon your throne

     8 lines for the house of Zababa in Kish

THE TEMPLE OF ZABABA AT KISH

The city of Kish is mentioned in some of the earliest records of antiquity. According to the Sumerian Kinglist, kingship descended to Kish after the mythological Flood, a pivotal event in whose aftermath recorded history began. Zababa was the patron deity of this important city. Some thirty city-states, Kish among them, evolved around 2900 BCE, in the first phase of the Early Dynastic period. Each had a principal deity, and each maintained its independence, apparent in the erection by 2700 BCE of large city walls around them.

That the deities bestowed kingship on the city of Kish separates it from the others. Its importance may derive from its geographical location. Kish lay in the northern part of the fertile land between the Tigris and the Euphrates, south of the point where the bending of the two rivers toward each other created a narrowing plain. Hans Nissen speculates that the low-lying course of the Euphrates at Kish could easily have changed during a flood. He says, "From the time of the consolidation of the irrigation system on, it was of decisive importance for the south of the country for the river to be kept under control at this danger point."[2] Cities downstream depended for their survival on the careful tending of the Euphrates at Kish.

Zababa's temple was known both as the E-mete-ursağ, 'befitting house of the warrior/hero,' and, as in this hymn, the Ekishib, meaning 'house/temple of the seal.' Various seals are known from the Ubaid period in Sumer, 5000–4000 BCE, long before cuneiform writing or even numerical notation began. Stamp seals were used in this early period to authenticate documents and proceedings. The stamps did convey information, and thus they are clearly in the line of progression that ultimately produced a readable script. Apparently, each of the thirty southern cities had its own stamp seal, the distribution of the seals being another indication of the cooperation among the cities and the development of common social forms. Postgate attributes the unusually sophisticated development of these first cities to the "strength of communal ethos" among them.[3] The name of Zababa's temple, Ekishib, conveys its importance as House of the Seal, the temple whose seal verified the legality and standing of the city and its god.

SECULAR RULE AT KISH

By 2500 BCE, a new form of ruler assumed leadership at Kish, the lugal, meaning 'big man,' creating an office later translators designated "King of Kish." The institution of kingship marked the beginning of bold secular authority. A new large building was constructed, a palace or administrative structure, the first one appearing at Kish in the Early Dynastic III period, 2600–2350 BCE. Postgate describes it as a "visible expression of the formation of a permanent secular authority separate from the temple."[4] The palace at Kish was surrounded by a large wall that further separated it from the rest of the city. Its form was different from the traditional temple. Harriet Crawford describes it as being divided into sections, its main entrance "a flight of steps flanked by monumental towers with buttressed and recessed walls."[5] Some of the walls were elaborately decorated with ivory inlay and mosaic friezes.

These buildings, found not only at Kish but also in excavations at Eridu, Uruk, and Eshnunna, among others, make evident the growing importance of secular rule. The prestige of the title King of Kish became the symbolic des-ignation of supremacy and authority. It was successively claimed by rulers of other cities as far from Kish as Lagash and Adab in the south. A new form of secular rulership had come into being.

While the kings of Kish were traditionally men, one was a woman, Ku-Bau or Ku-Baba. She is reported to be the founder of the Third Dynasty of Kish. The uniqueness of her elevation led to legendary tales. She is said to have been a tavern keeper. She was the grandmother of Ur-Zababa, the King of Kish who was eventually challenged by Enheduanna's father, Sargon.

The young Sargon, cupbearer to Ur-Zababa, began to consolidate his power in Kish, eventually confronting his own king. Legend portrays Sargon as a usurper who killed Ur-Zababa and took over the throne of Kish. This story conflicts with the Kinglist, which names several succeeding kings of Kish who followed Ur-Zababa. Sargon may have attempted a coup that led to his being "driven out of Kish."[6]

Another impediment to Sargon's ambitions was Lugalzagesi of Umma, who had successfully established his rule over Lagash, Uruk, Ur, and eventu-ally all the southern cities. Lugalzagesi received the coveted blessing of the god Enlil, through his powerful priests in Nippur. Sargon may have established his fledgling kingdom out of reach of Lugalzagesi's army, in Akkad somewhere on the Tigris, possibly near the river's confluence with the Diyala. Eventually, Sargon built a large military force and defeated Lugalzagesi, "along with his 'fifty governors'—i.e., the petty kings of all the separate city states."[7] These events led to the establishment of a new dynasty that was to rule for two hun-dred years. Sargon took the name Sharrukin, 'true king,' a name corrupted to Sargon. He and his descendants each called himself King of Kish.

HOLY ZABABA AND HIS DIVINE WEAPONS

Zababa was a warrior god, and in the later Old Babylonian period, 1800–1600 BCE, he was frequently identified with the quintessential warrior/heroes Ninurta or Ningirsu. In his city of Kish, he claimed Inanna as his wife, en-hancing his standing with this nationally recognized goddess at his side. Kings called upon them to bless their reigns, the Old Babylonian king Samsu-iluna declaring himself to be "their twin brother," thus assuring that the two deities, Zababa and Inanna, would bless his success and long life.[8]

The Temple Hymn to Zababa begins with typical admiration of the house, its abundance, the solidity of its foundation, and its imposing place among the authoritative princes. The portrayal of the sacred inner chamber, šà-zu, 'the dwelling place of the god,' departs from the poet's typical description of a darkened, holy room, picturing it instead as the source of Zababa's invincible power. Its right side is a weapon, kur dúb-ba, 'mountain-shaker,' and its left is the weapon erím sal-e, 'wicked-squeezer.'

In other texts Zababa is said to have two scimitars, one a lion and one an eagle. These two weapons, named Igalima and Shulshagana, were personified and deified as properties of the god, belonging to his right and his left hands.[9] The tradition of giving life to weapons and other possessions of the gods is as ancient as the written texts. The two scimitars of Zababa may be connected to the two personified weapons mentioned in this hymn. Gebhard Selz points out that weapons of the gods had divine powers of their own, for example, ig and ig-gal in Zababa's weapon, Igalima, "are metaphors for the borderline or the threshold between this and the other world."[10] In the mind of the ancient Mesopotamians, the gods infuse even inanimate objects and bring them to life with their own innate divinity and individuality.

TEMPLE HYMN 36

THE KUTHA TEMPLE OF NERGAL
Keshda

O house   dam of the land
bull   princely arm-twister of all the gods
   terrifying the wild cows
   reigning over the bulls

Kutha   your wharf lies low   water laps at its edge
your inner chamber is artfully crafted
your udug is a heaven-sent weapon
your face   a lapis glow spreading over the meslam

your prince Girra   king of the Meslam
frightful house of the netherworld
lord of the setting sun
Nergal   who comes out of Meslam   Lord of Kutha
has built this house on your radiant site
and placed his seat upon your dais

   10 lines for Nergal of Kutha

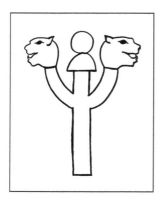

12.2.   Lion-headed staff of Nergal. Courtesy of the University of Texas Press, Jeremy Black and Anthony Green, *Gods, Demons and Symbols of Ancient Mesopotamia,* Tessa Richards, illustrator, 1995.

THE TEMPLE OF NERGAL AT KUTHA (GUDUA)

Throughout Nergal's long history as a Mesopotamian god, he had a dual character: underworld god and warrior. From time to time one of his two aspects gained dominance over the other. In Temple Hymn 36 he is praised both as a warrior, terrifying with his heaven-sent udug weapon, and as lord of the setting sun, whose descent in the west each evening marked the entrance into the netherworld. In the hymn Nergal's temple is praised as a locked gate, a dam between the world of the living and the world of the dead.

Parts of the Temple Hymn to Nergal are obscure. He is a warrior with his udug weapon, which may be his mace; but the word can also mean an evil spirit, the only evil spirit referred to in early incantations. Twice the hymn mentions "the meslam." Meslam was a type of tree, and Meslamtea was a god, assimilated with Nergal in the second millennium and perhaps identified with him even at the time of the hymn's composition. Nergal is called Girra in the hymn, another of his names. The emphasis in the hymn is on his netherworld aspects, the water at the edge of the wharf and the setting sun both being traditional entrances to the underworld. Still, Nergal kept his powers as a warrior god throughout his history.

NERGAL ABOVE AND BELOW

Nergal's dual aspects gave him access both to the world of the heavenly gods and to the Great Below. This double access went against divine custom, which decreed that underworld gods could not ascend to heaven and that gods of heaven were barred from going below. Messengers were allowed to go back and forth, keeping the two lands informed of each other's activities. Nergal's special status was explained in the myth "Nergal and Ereshkigal," written much later than the Temple Hymns. Without explanation, however, Nergal enjoyed dual citizenship as early as records exist. He was both an underworld god and a heavenly warrior. First mention of Nergal occurs in the Early Dynastic III period (2600–2350 BCE) in god lists found at Fara, Abu Salabikh, and Ebla and in an ancient zà-mì hymn from Abu Salabikh. Most of the netherworld gods in god lists on these ancient tablets are grouped together. On one list, Nergal is called Enlil of the Netherworld, further recognition of his status there.

The myth of Nergal and Ereshkigal first appeared in the Middle Babylonian period around the fifteenth century BCE. In the myth Ereshkigal, queen of the underworld, is invited to send a messenger to a great banquet for the gods of heaven in order to receive her portion of the food. The messenger mounts "the long stairway to heaven."[11] The gods stand to honor the queen of the Great Below, all except Nergal. Enraged, Ereshkigal orders Nergal to descend to the netherworld that she may kill him. Instead, she seduces him. Advised by Enki not to accept her hospitality, Nergal "could resist her cooking, but he was lost when she took her clothes off and displayed her charms."[12] After seven days of lovemaking, Nergal had had enough and managed to escape. Ereshkigal, longing for her lover, ordered him back to her abode. They were married and ever after ruled the netherworld, although Ereshkigal remained its primary deity.

AUSPICIOUS BIRTH

Perhaps his special position both above and below derived from Nergal's birth. In the myth of Enlil and Ninlil, recounted in Temple Hymn 3, the maiden Ninlil consorts with the god Enlil and becomes pregnant. Her child became the moon god, Nanna. For his offense against the maiden, Enlil is banished to the netherworld mountains by the heavenly god council, but Ninlil, hopelessly enamored, chases after her lover. Enlil disguises himself at the city gate of Nippur, the home of his temple. There, the disguised Enlil lies with her again and engenders Nergal, a son, who Ninlil thinks can take the place of her beloved firstborn, Nanna, in the netherworld. Two more sons are spawned as Ninlil continues to follow Enlil to the netherworld. The myth concludes with Enlil restored to heaven, "praised as Lord of heaven—Lord of the earth, and praise to mother Ninlil."[13]

Nergal's birth marks him as an underworld god, twin of Nanna. They were known as the two stars called in Western astronomy the Twins. In the third millennium, the period when the Temple Hymns were written, Nergal was worshiped more often as a warrior than as a god of the underworld. Enheduanna's nephew, the powerful king Naram-Sin, elevated Nergal to lead his army and praised him on an inscription as a warrior.[14] With Nergal in the lead, Naram-Sin's armies marched to "the Upper Sea," the Mediterranean. After suppressing a great revolt against him, Naram-Sin declared himself a god. He may have elevated Nergal after his victory, since Kutha, Nergal's city, took part in the revolt and was subsequently subdued. Nergal continued to be worshiped in the north more than in the south of Mesopotamia, and under Naram-Sin his cult extended into all the territories under Akkadian political rule.[15]

NERGAL AFTER THE AKKADIAN KINGS

Nergal continued to be worshiped throughout the Mesopotamian era. A mythical Assyrian prince named Kumma reported the appearance of Nergal in a dream visit to the underworld: "When I raised my eyes, there was valiant Nergal sitting on a royal throne, crowned with the royal tiara, grasping in both his hands two grim maces, each with two . . . heads. . . . The Anunnaki, great gods, knelt to [his] right and left."[16]

Other ancient images show Nergal with double or single lion-headed staffs. Cylinder seals depict him with his foot raised upon a mound or upon the body of a victim. He endured in his position as spouse of the underworld goddess Ereshkigal from the second millennium until the end of the Mesopotamian era, and he is mentioned even in obscure texts of Gnostic material from the Common Era.[17]

As home to an underworld deity, Nergal's temple in Kutha upheld the cult of the dead in the north of Sumer. In the third millennium, a separate tradition in the south centered on the deity Ninazu in Enegi (TH 14). The northern tradition contained elements influenced by the Semitic population. In the south the majority Sumerian population shaped beliefs about the underworld. Eventually in the second millennium, when the Semitic population in the south began to outnumber the Sumerians, the two streams merged.

TEMPLE HYMN 37

THE URUM TEMPLE OF NANNA
Eabulua

Urum   the mighty
Suen's judgment place
Eabulua   teeming with cows in the wide pen

Ashimbabbar   unique with his shining crescent
acts alone as your shepherd
O house   my king
you stretch your scepter into the sky
house on the earth [. . . . .] joyous moonlight
your quay [. . .. .] abundant light

your prince is a joyful prince of pure delight
who comes joyously out of the bright sky
youth greet [him] with their hearts
Suen who keeps shining over the land

O house Urum
has built this house on your radiant site
and placed his seat upon your dais

     10 lines for the house of Nanna in Urum

THE TEMPLE OF NANNA AT URUM

Nanna's temple at Urum is located in the far north of the Mesopotamian plain, near the point where the Tigris and Euphrates bend closest together just south of the present-day city of Baghdad. Urum, identified as Tell 'Uqair, lay on a bow-shaped canal, the Zubi canal, connected at both its ends to the large Irnina canal. This places the city slightly northeast of Kutha, the home of Nergal's temple on the Irnina (TH 36).[18] Among the Early Dynastic city seals Leonard Woolley found in rubbish debris during his excavations at Ur was a seal for the city of Urum. This seal placed Urum in 3100 BCE, among the cities that seem to have formed some sort of cooperative alliance. The discovery of Urum's seal indicates that this very early league of city-states included cities in the north of the plain as well as in the south.[19] Urum, whose god was Nanna, remained a significant city a thousand years later, both during and after the Sargonic era. The powerful Sargonic king Naram-Sin, Enheduanna's nephew, fought a revolt against his dominance, one of the principal battles taking place near Urum. In the later Old Babylonian period, Urum is the likely capital of the small kingdom of Mananā.[20] The longevity of Nanna's position as principal god of Urum once again attests to the continuity of the Sumerian religion and the culture that maintained it.

Perhaps Enheduanna chose to include a hymn to the god of Urum because of the city's long-standing historical importance. Another reason may have been that the god of Urum was Nanna, the moon god in Enheduanna's home city of Ur, the lord whose spouse she became when taking on the role of the goddess Ningal. The hymn includes a locution unusual in the hymns, "my king," as though Enheduanna were speaking to her heavenly spouse directly. This uncommon salutation adds weight to the possibility that Enheduanna wrote this hymn.[21]

THE TEMPLE HYMNS TO NANNA

Three hymns to the moon god, Nanna, are in the collection of Temple Hymns, numbers 8, 12, and 37. Hymn 8, to Nanna at Ur, is the longest and most complex of the three, evidence of the primacy of his temple in the south at Ur and of the prestige of the high priestess who makes her home there. Nevertheless, all three have common elements. In all of them the moon god is called by his three names, Nanna, Suen, and Ashimbabbar. Interestingly, his common Sumerian name, Nanna, is mentioned only in the line count at the end of each hymn, while he is called Suen and Ashimbabbar within the text of all three. Nanna's role as shepherd of the multitude of cows and bulls and the beauty of his shining light set the tone of each hymn. The first two hymns, 8 and 12, mention the gipar, the dwelling of the high priestess Enheduanna, and describe the sacred rites performed there.

Hymn 37, the shortest of the three, is a song of praise for the joy and delight that Nanna's bright light brings to his worshipers. He "keeps shining over the land" stretching his "scepter into the sky," as though Nanna's protective presence emanates from the passage of the moon. Only this hymn calls him "your shepherd," guardian of the animals, a metaphor for the vulnerable humans who worship him and a precursor of the biblical shepherd who appears a thousand years later in the Hebrew bible and later still in the Christian New Testament. In this poem of tender protection, love, and joy, the "youth," as in current romantic notions of the moon, "greet [him] with their hearts."

Nanna, too, has his underworld aspect, kin to his brother Nergal. Each month he travels into the Great Below, leaving the earth in darkness for three days. There, it is said he decides fates (TH 8) and renders judgments (this hymn). Miraculously, like the sun, he returns, and the appearance of his slender crescent is cause for ritual celebration every month at the sighting of the new moon.

TEMPLE HYMN 38

THE SIPPAR TEMPLE OF UTU
Enunana

Sippar   dais of Utu where he sits by day
Enunana   House of the Prince of Heaven
always shining in the heavens   crown given birth by Ningal
house of Utu   your prince
his light rising from the horizon   fills heaven and earth

when the lord lies down   the people lie down
whenever he rises the people arise

Utu the bull gathers the people
they bow in obedience
for Utu   herds stand in their pasture
for Utu   the black-haired bathe with soap
   the land humbles itself before him

your city's shrine measures its essence in abundance
he who renders judgments where the sun rises
hangs down his beard in sunbeams
and at night binds the shining crown around his head
Utu   King of Sippar
O house of Sippar has built this house on your radiant site
and established his seat upon your dais

   14 lines for Utu of Sippar

THE TEMPLE OF UTU AT SIPPAR

In Sippar, the northernmost city of the Sumerian plain, the god Utu had a second major temple, as central to his worship as his temple in Larsa in the south

(TH 13). Named here as the Enunna, the temple is sometimes referred to as the Ebabbar, a name otherwise used for Utu's temple in Larsa. The oldest object found in the temple excavations is a stone vase from the Jemdet-Nasr period, 3200–3000 BCE. The last archeological records date from the Persian kings who ruled the city until 600 BCE. Thereafter, the city was abandoned.

Utu maintained his central position in Sippar for three thousand years, from the time of the earliest development of cuneiform writing. His worship thrived in Sippar during the second millennium while the neighboring Hebrew tribes consolidated their identity. It continued in the fifth century BCE, as Plato was writing his treatises. Sippar, according to the Kinglist, was revered as one of the oldest cities, a city that existed before the Flood, along with Eridu, Badtibira, Larsa, and Shuruppak. Like Nippur in the central plain, it grew to be an important religious center in the north.

ANCIENT SIPPAR

Sippar's importance derives largely from its geography. The Tigris and the Euphrates bend toward each other at Sippar; in fact, there is evidence that there was a confluence of the two there, but the large silt deposits of the Euphrates began to separate them. The older Tigris channels were buried, pushing the river farther east. The intervening land became habitable, and Sippar was settled on the levees built up by the Euphrates. Since the rivers provided the main mode of transportation for the entire southern plain, their proximity in the north engendered Sippar's growth and importance.

North of Sippar the land opened to the east upon the Jebel Hamrin, a forbidding plateau and location of the mountain Ebeh, the subject of Enheduanna's devotional poem to Inanna.[22] To the northwest, the middle Euphrates gave access to the Syrian valleys and beyond, to the Mediterranean. As a hub of transportation, Sippar became a meeting place of cultures. It grew into a cosmopolitan city, a crucial center of trade from both north and south, and a crossroads of economic and cultural activity. One element, KIB, in its Sumerian name, UD.KIB.NUN.NA, means 'crossroads.'

THE JUSTICE AND COMPASSION OF UTU

Utu, the sun god whose light shone evenly on all people, was a god of justice and compassion. His city, Sippar, became known as a city of equality and tolerance. In this hymn the people of Sippar are the metaphoric cows in the herd of the great bull, Utu. Their bond is likened to the instinctual, protective impulse of a young stud bull guarding his herd. He leads them to rich pasture, where they stand for him and flourish. He gathers them together, and they bow in obedience. More than any of the other hymns, this one portrays a universe lovingly constructed to embrace and nourish its people, warmed and illuminated by the sun. As in Temple Hymn 13 to Utu, the people held in his "soaring light" are bathed in streams of light falling from his "lustrous lapis beard" as it "hangs down . . . in the sunbeams." When he sleeps, they sleep. When he wakes, they wake. Worshipfully, they perform ritual libations and humble themselves to his rule. He provides them with portions of the me, cosmic gifts from the divinely ordained categories of a civilized society. Each gets his or her fair measure. Utu renders justice over disputes. Some five hundred years after the writing of this hymn, the Old Babylonian king Hammurabi wrote in the prologue to his famous laws that he was "appointed to make justice appear in the land, to destroy the evil and wicked so that the strong might not oppress the weak, to rise like Shamash over the dark-haired people to give light to the land."[23]

Sippar bordered on the Semitic lands northwest of Sumer. A steady flow of Semitic traders came to the city, and many settled there. Shamash is the name of the sun god in the Akkadian language the Semites spoke. However, the two names, Utu and Shamash, belong to the one god of the sun worshiped in the ancient Near East.[24] The interplay of the god of justice with society contributed to the development of a civilized rule of law, which reached a high point with the writing of Hammurabi's code.[25]

At sunset, Utu entered the western gate to spend the night in the underworld, where, the hymn says, he "binds the shining crown around his head." The crown called mùš is worn by the high priestess, among others, and is described as a shining halo. Binding implies that he wrapped the crown around his head, perhaps dimming or containing his light as he slept. The crown assured that no one in the underworld would mistake him for a permanent occupant of that realm. The quotidian life of the sun god set the rhythm for earthly inhabitants who worshiped him and depended on the fair blessings and judgments of this very personal god.

THE SARGONIC KINGS AT SIPPAR

Sippar was a thriving city, one of the three most prestigious cities of the southern plain along with Babylon and Nippur. Sargon's conquests not only included the southern cities, but also extended north beyond Sippar along the Euphrates into the Syrian plain and east beyond the Tigris.

After Sargon's death his successors continued to honor Utu in Sippar. His son Rimush plundered Elam, the territory in Iran once settled by Sumerians, and presented a piece of his booty, an inscribed bowl, to the shrine in Sippar.[26] Inscribed mace heads belonging to Rimush, to his brother Manishtushu and to Sharkalisharri, son of Naram-Sin, were among the gifts from the Akkadian kings found in Utu's Sippar temple.[27]

Naram-Sin, Enheduanna's nephew, was, after his grandfather Sargon, the most powerful of the Akkadian kings to gain the position. At some point in his reign, he declared himself a god, claiming Shamash in Sippar had joined other of the major gods in approving his appointment as god of his city Akkad.[28] He showed his respect for and adulation of Utu in Sippar by naming one of his daughters high priestess in Utu's temple. An inscribed bowl that once belonged to this daughter was found in Mari, a city on the Euphrates northwest of Sippar. The inscription read:

Naram-Sin, king of the four quarters
Shumshani, *entu* priestess of the god Shamash in Sippar, [is] his
daughter[29]

Naram-Sin became a cultural hero, remembered two thousand years later by the Neo-Babylonian king Nabonidus. In Sippar, Nabonidus restored the temple of Utu/Shamash, uncovering in the process the foundation Naram-Sin had originally constructed. Out of respect for the great Akkadian king, Nabonidus reburied the foundation "to prevent further desecration."[30]

THE TEMPLE OF UTU/SHAMASH

While in much of the literature to the sun god in Sippar he is called Shamash, in Enheduanna's Temple Hymn he is Utu, his Sumerian name. Sippar, as noted, was a crossroads between the Semitic north and the Sumerian south. Both ethnic groups prospered in this vibrant city. While Enheduanna undoubtedly spoke Akkadian, the language of her father, she had full command of the Sumerian language, the prestigious language of sacred literature.

The temple of Utu in Sippar, as noted above, received booty and expensive gifts from the Akkadian kings, by which they sought to control this central organ of the city's power. The Utu temple was one of the richest in all the southern plain. With the lord of justice at its helm, the temple gave Sippar the reputation of being "a city of fair dealing."[31] Its personnel were overseers of a sizeable amount of land. Much of it was cultivated for the temple itself, yielding crops to be stored or distributed as wages. Some of the temple personnel farmed plots allotted to them as part of their remuneration. Still other plots were farmed by individuals who paid rent or a share of the crop to the temple.

A large contingency of scribes enriched the intellectual life of the city, preserving a library within the temple. This tradition continued throughout the city's life. Archeologists found thousands of cuneiform tablets in the Neo-Assyrian temple (870 BCE). Hormuzd Rassman, a native of Mosul, Iraq, excavated the temple in 1880. He sent fifty thousand cuneiform tablets to his employer, the British Museum. In this tablet level of the excavation he found "some 300 rooms and courtyards" as well as numerous objects of great value and historical importance.[32]

The power and influence of the temple rose and fell over the three thousand years of its existence. One of its most significant flowerings came in the Isin-Larsa/Old Babylonian period (2000–1600 BCE), five hundred years after Enheduanna's death. A cloister-like institution flourished in the temple in which women, often from wealthy, prominent families, dedicated themselves to the god Utu/Shamash and his wife, Aya. They lived in a walled compound within the temple grounds, two hundred or more women and officials in private houses. The compound included its own administration building, workshops, storage areas, and plots of cultivated land. Called nadītu, meaning 'fallow, unplanted' (land), the women joined the cloister at puberty. They were known as daughters-in-law of Shamash, entering his house as a young woman traditionally entered the house of her father-in-law before marriage. They remained childless and lived active private lives, many pursuing businesses by investing the allotted inheritance from their fathers. Some were literate and served as scribes.[33] A large number of cuneiform tablets were found in the nadītu compound. The nadītu, because of their number and the amount of wealth they controlled, were a force in the economic prosperity of Sippar.

Similar groups of women dedicated to a god are evident in the same era at Babylon and Nippur;[34] Kish; Ishchali, east of the Tigris; and Susa, east of the southern plain in Elam (Iran).[35] Evidence suggests that even before the Old Babylonian period groups of women lived apart in dedication to the gods. The Sumerian lukur, equivalent to the nadītu but attached to the court of the Ur III kingdoms (2112–2004 BCE), may have been precursors of the Sippar cloister.[36] Postgate asserts that "the Sippar cloister was a transformation of something altogether smaller and comparable to the gipar at Ur."[37] Enheduanna may have been the first high priestess resident of the gipar at Ur, although there is some evidence of high priestesses before her.[38] She held the office around 2300 BCE, prior to the Ur III period. In her devotional poem to Inanna, "Lady of Largest Heart," she mentions "women's rooms" within the gipar where Inanna performs a ritual ordination of a woman and a man, a "head overturning" in which she presents each initiate with the traditional regalia of the opposite gender.[39] Later in the poem Enheduanna describes a group of women devotees of Inanna:

> those warrior women
> like a single thread
> come forth from beyond the river
> do common work
> in devotion to you
> whose hands sear them with purifying fire
>
> your many devoted
> who will be burnt
> like sun-scorched firebricks
> pass before your eyes[40]

In another instance, the Temple Hymn to Shuzianna in Nippur (TH 6) contains a unique phrase added after the line count: "the lofty closed house for consecrated women." These examples suggest that in Enheduanna's time women lived apart in devotion to a goddess, just as the Sippar women dedicated themselves to a god. Although these institutions are for the most part hidden in obscurity, they represent intriguing illustrations of women choosing a very different kind of existence from that of marriage and childbearing, one in which they lived independent, private lives devoted to a deity. Enheduanna's "warrior women" are burned "with purifying fire," suggesting an orderly and progressive spiritual discipline. Hazardous as it is to apply modern concepts to understanding a four-thousand-year-old text, the verses suggest a correspondence to a present-day perception of psychological development in which desires of the ego are "burned away" in favor of a more holistic, mature conception of reality.

In sum, the temple of the sun god in Sippar was the center of a vibrant, thriving city. Utu's principles of equality and tolerance seem to have fostered creative growth in the arts, in civic institutions, and even in the implementation of the religion. A city at the crossroads, Sippar embraced a multitude of cultures that lived together peacefully and successfully.

TEMPLE HYMN 39

THE HIZA TEMPLE OF NINHURSAG

Ehursag

O mountain Ehursag house
lovely sweet-smelling herbs   luxuriant among the grasses
Hiza   abundance lies in your deep heart

where fates are decreed may you decide destinies
may the crown of Nintu bring joy to your site
    your hidden root is the Great Snake sleeping
may long days last for your holy foundation

mother Nintu   lady of molding
works in your dark interior
gives birth to the king   binds the true adornment on his chest
gives birth to the high priestess
crowns her safe in Nintu's hands

midwife of heaven and earth   Ninhursag
O house Hiza has built this house on your radiant site
and taken her seat upon your dais

    12 lines for Ninhursag of Hiza

THE TEMPLE OF NINHURSAG AT HIZA

Temple Hymn 39 is the third and final hymn to Ninhursag, one of the original three great Sumerian deities. In texts from the end of the Early Dynastic period, she is named in the trio along with An and Enlil. Enheduanna would have known Ninhursag as the goddess who occupied this prominent position throughout the third millennium.[41] Enki began to appear among the three around the turn of the second millennium, adding a fourth to the august trio. Early in the new era his name moved up in the list before that of Ninhursag. Eventually, he replaced her altogether. Nevertheless, in Enheduanna's lifetime Ninhursag occupied a position of unique stature among the Sumerians, known to all as one of the three great deities.

This hymn is written to the Ehursag, Ninhursag's temple in Hiza, a city whose Sumerian name and actual location are unknown but that is thought to be in the vicinity of Sippar, Utu's city in the preceding hymn. In other geographical lists of cities, Hiza's placement in the sequence suggests it lay southeast of Akkad, both cities being on the Tigris, which flowed approximately north and south between Sippar and Eshnunna.[42] In Hiza, Ninhursag's name is embedded in the name of the temple, Ehursag; she is 'Lady [nin] of the hursag,' hursag being the name given to the wild, rocky foothills of the mountains. In this inhospitable place only wildlife found refuge. The goddess's very name tells us that she is at home in the wild. Her son Ningirsu was born in these foothills and nursed by deer.[43] Some of her children are wild animals.[44] Her husband, Shulpae, is a god of wildlife. Ninhursag's character embraces wild nature. She inhabits the surging dominance of natural process. In her form as Nintur (Nintu), she is the lady of birth, not just human birth, but animal birth as well. On a harsher note, she is the unpredictable force of nature. In Temple Hymn 7 Enheduanna says of Ninhursag, "you spread fear like a great poisonous snake." She is "terrifying," a "great lion of the wildlands/ stalking the high plains." In Hymn 39, that same "Great Snake" lies sleeping. He is the hidden root of her temple, waiting to stir from his rest. Beneath the abundance and beauty of nature lies the indomitable force of natural disasters, the potency of irrepressible instinct, and the inevitability of death. While the worshipers of Ninhursag praised her generosity and bowed to her power, they were also terrorized at being held in her grip.

From the human perspective Ninhursag is the mystery of life surging through matter. She is a power to contend with, uncontrollable, awesome, inexplicable, to be handled with care. The human ingenuity of the Sumerians, whose cities seemed to be on a trajectory of progress and unimaginable invention, could be pulled up short by the vicissitudes of nature, Ninhursag's realm. Her position among the great gods may have diminished as the civilizing dominance of wealth, centralized government, agricultural progress, military might, unfettered foreign trade, and artistic and intellectual advances sheltered the populace and lulled them into an illusion that they had control over their lives. Increasingly, they relied on magic and incantation to alter the inevitable. Enki, god of wisdom, god of the sweet waters of the Abzu, an earthy, trickster god, and, significantly, god of magic, must have seemed a more reliable fellow to sit in the seat of power.

THE HYMN

Temple Hymn 39 is a hymn of adulation. Only the sleeping "Great Snake" sounds a discordant note in the poem's benevolent portrait of Ninhursag. The setting is peaceful and idyllic as the gracious temple awards worshipers her abundant treasures while "sweet-smelling herbs luxuriant among the grasses" surround and grace her beauty. The hymn has a coherent structure. The tone is calm as the poet moves from Ninhursag's appointed authority of deciding fates to her formidable power over birth, the joyous "crown" of her domain. Here she is "mother Nintu," in her role as "form-shaping lady." The "dark interior" of the temple becomes the fruitful and formidable womb that gives birth to the king, gives birth to the lord.

In this hymn Nintur is an aspect of Ninhursag, representing her dominion over human and animal birth. In other times and locales the two were separate goddesses.[45] Nintur's name—nin, meaning 'Lady,' tur$_5$, meaning 'birth-hut'—originally referred to her authority over the dome-shaped reed hut with calves leaping out of its doorways pictured on numerous cylinder seals. Over time, the cuneiform sign for "birth-hut" came to designate "womb." Jacobsen says that "a curious omega-shaped Ω emblem found on boundary stones and on Old Babylonian clay plaques is an emblem of Nintur/Ninhursaga."[46] This womb-shaped emblem is thought to represent the uterus of a cow. The "dark interior" of this Temple Hymn, as it denotes the womb of birth, corresponds to the dark cella in other Temple Hymns, the sacred dwelling place of the divine resident of the temple, and suggests that the holy of holies in the temple was a place of fecundity and creation.

The ultimate affirmation of divine assent is the claim of birth from the goddess herself. In this hymn Nintu gives birth to a king, gives birth to a priestess. These lines have parallels in two other myths. In "Enki and the World Order" Inanna says of Nintu, "To give birth to kings, to give birth to high priests is verily in her hand."[47] The myth of the creation of the hoe contains a similar line, mentioning the goddess Ninmenna, the Lady of the Crown: "The mistress of giving birth to high priests, of giving birth to kings, Ninmenna was setting birthgiving going."[48] Hands, so crucial to the midwife, are blessed with a divine Sumerian name, Shugalanzu, "the expert hand."[49] In her role as midwife, with her skillful hands Ninmenna delivers babies destined to become distinguished leaders.

Ninhursag's powerful forces are tamed in the Ehursag temple. The "Great Snake" is sleeping. Its goddess is charged with decreeing fates, gracious ones if the next line's expression of joy in Nintu's crown comes to pass. In the holy of holies, the inner sanctum, Ninhursag as Nintu molds the shape of future kings, future priests and priestesses, doing her part to fabricate civic and religious order. All takes place in the bounty of Ehursag's deep heart, whose beauty among the sweet grasses stands in an aura of calm and equanimity.

TEMPLE HYMN 40

THE AKKAD TEMPLE OF INANNA
Ulmash

O Ulmash
the one on the left side   in the highlands of the country
savage lion battering the wild bull
spreading a net over stiff-necked wicked

dazed silence falls on the rebel land
as long as they defy   tell slanderous lies
she spits her poison

O house of Inanna   silver and lapis blue
storehouse built of gold
your lady a waterbird   sacred woman of the inner chamber
fit out for battle   exuberant   beautifully adorned
prepares the seven maces
washes weapons in the blood of battle
throws open the gate of battle
great wise one of heaven   Inanna
O house of Ulmash
has built this house on your radiant site
and established her seat upon your dais

    10 lines for Inanna of Ulmash

THE TEMPLE OF INANNA AT AKKAD

In this third hymn written to Inanna as city goddess of Sargon's capital, she occupies a particularly important temple in Akkad, the new city Sargon built for his headquarters. Her temple, 'Ulmash' or 'Eulmash,' was in Akkad (Agade), not in a separate town. Wall-Romana suggests the name Ulmash may indicate "that the temple(s) of Inanna, and their lands, formed a somewhat separate area from that of the city of Agade proper, at least in the time of Enheduanna."[50] The god Aba (TH 41), a rather insignificant god, was the patron god of Sargon's empire. Inanna's hymn says she was "the one on the left side," while Aba's hymn places him in a "house on the right side."[51] We have no archeological evidence that would explain these designations; the city of Akkad has never been found. We can imagine that one temple was on the left bank of the Tigris or the Euphrates while the other was on the right, or any number of other possibilities. The designation does point out, however, that two ruling gods presided in Akkad, Inanna and Aba.

INANNA'S CHARACTER IN ENHEDUANNA'S THEOLOGY

In contrast to Inanna's hymns 16 and 26, this hymn portrays the goddess as an unabashed warrior. Her furious powers, the hymn says, have the superiority of a lion over a wild bull. Her awesome weapons are bathed in blood. The hapless victims of her fury are those who dare to rebel against her city or the state she champions—Akkad. Her enemy is wickedly stubborn with stiff necks—disobedient liars. She spits poison all over them.[52]

In an earlier hymn, Temple Hymn 16, Inanna is portrayed as "dazzling" in her "irresistible ripeness." Hymn 26 describes her as the bright star who alone, at twilight, makes the firmament beautiful. In this hymn, her joy and exuberant beauty shine only when she is adorned for battle. While we have hints of her cold fury in Temple Hymns 16 and 26, as she "throws the ever-rolling stone dice" (TH 16) or speaks "hateful words" against the wicked (TH 26), we have heard nothing to match the vicious, bloodthirsty delight she takes in leveling the evil enemy in this hymn.

Throughout Enheduanna's other major work, the devotional poems to Inanna, she elevates the deity above all others, calling her "greatest of the great gods."[53] In the poem "Lady of Largest Heart," Enheduanna describes Inanna as "foremost of the gods"; "she shrieks / and the gods start shaking / she raves / the Anunna quaver."[54] She not only terrifies the populace, but also strikes fear in the gods themselves. In raising Inanna to supreme importance, Enheduanna implies that Inanna's character, with its contradictory aspects, rules the given world. As greatest of the deities, Inanna demands that all life, all matter, be infused with her divine paradox.

The three Temple Hymns to Inanna emphasize three separate aspects of her character: she is a goddess of sensuality (TH 16), the divine astral light of the morning and evening star (TH 26), and, in this hymn, a vicious goddess of overpowering force. The Inanna of the Temple Hymns is consistent with the Inanna of Enheduanna's three devotional poems, a paradoxical goddess whose realm includes the vicissitudes of life on earth, the shining brilliance of beauty, joy, creativity, the pleasures of sensuality, and the dark brutality of human hatred, evil, and the painful sorrow of misfortune and death.

In this hymn Inanna in all her fury throws open the gate of battle, an act she repeats in Enheduanna's poem "Inanna and Ebeh":

> with screech of hinge
> she flings wide the gate
> of the house of battle
>
> her hands pull the bolt lock
> on its lapis lazuli door[55]

In the Temple Hymn her foe is "the rebel land." Her awesome weapons stun the enemy into "dazed silence." Inanna enacts the divine counterpart of her king, Sargon, thus supporting and justifying his brutal attacks against the southern cities and his army's forays into the surrounding lands. This hymn to her temple in Akkad, a city created by Sargon as the emblematic command center of his conquests and power, unequivocally grants him the authority to continue on the trajectory of an imperial conqueror by the authority of the divine imperative of Inanna. Meanwhile, Inanna as city deity is elevated to untouchable status — "sacred woman of the inner chamber" — in her storehouse of gold, her temple of silver and lapis lazuli. A paradoxically playful image pictures her as "a waterbird," a beautiful creature dipping and flying up from the river. From her perspective above, she sees all.

CITY GODDESS OF AKKAD

Inanna was a goddess who could match the ambitious driving force of all the Sargonic kings. Sargon claimed her blessing as divine sanction for his overthrow of the Uruk ruler Lugalzagesi, whom he humiliated by dragging him in neck-stock to Nippur. There he, Sargon, was crowned king, claiming the support of the great god Enlil. From the beginning he initiated nontraditional changes in the organization of his kingdom. He conquered the Sumerian southern cities, destroying their walls and installing men from his Semitic retinue, "sons of Akkad," to replace the city leaders, the ensik.[56] His ambition fueled territorial expansion north along the Euphrates, west to the Mediterranean, and east into present-day Iran. While many of these forays were only temporary raids, they alerted foreign cities to the intentions of his powerful army, and in some locations the Akkadians settled and annexed the foreign territories.

Sargon created a new city to house his expanding rule and named it Akkad. He claimed Inanna as goddess of the city, she who, as noted earlier, is called Ishtar in his Semitic language. She led him into battle, as she did all of his successors. The city soon gave its name to the entire surrounding area. The language Sargon spoke he called Akkadian. He developed "a more syllabic form of cuneiform writing more suitable for the rendering of the Semitic characters."[57]

Akkad became the center of the growing empire. It held the distinction of being the first capital city of the entire country, a lively city, the hub of activity as individuals in the newly centralized government created an ever-expanding bureaucracy, and traders from far corners brought their products and ethnic diversity, stirring up a fertile mix. The myth "Curse of Akkad" describes the cosmopolitan city's luxury and prosperity, generated by Inanna's active stewardship:

Curse on Akkad: the city in its heyday
So that the warehouses would be provisioned,
That dwellings would be founded in that city,
That its people would eat splendid food,
That its people would drink splendid beverages,
That those bathed (for holidays) would rejoice in the courtyards,
That the people would throng the places of celebration,
That acquaintances would dine together,
That foreigners would cruise about like unusual birds in the sky,
That (even) Marhaši would be reentered on the (tribute) rolls,
That monkeys, mighty elephants, water buffalo, exotic animals,
Would jostle each other in the public squares. . . .
Holy Inanna did not sleep.[58]

In this myth Inanna is the progenitor of the city's vitality. Her city prospered like no other. The organization of the evolving central government and the regional state became the prototype for future kingdoms, and though its city was abandoned and even disappeared, it remained legendary throughout Mesopotamia's long prominence in the ancient Near East.

THE BROTHERS AND THE NEPHEW

After Sargon's death, his sons, Enheduanna's brothers Rimush and Manish-tushu, followed one another as kings of Akkad. Rimush and Manishtushu continued Sargon's territorial expansion and his tightening of control over the southern cities, directed from the capital, Akkad. Military garrisons occupied these cities, and from the fertile surrounding lands the two brothers carved out large plots for themselves and their military leaders. The cities of the south were virtually occupied territories. The citizens organized repeated rebellions against their occupiers. One great rebellion against Rimush cost thousands of lives.[59]

After Manishtushu's death, his son, Enheduanna's nephew Naram-Sin, came to the throne. Naram-Sin became a legendary king and transformed the regional Akkadian state into a true empire, controlled from its central capital in Akkad. After defeating a particularly fierce rebellion, Naram-Sin declared himself "god of his city." Akkad, being a new city, had no long tradition of a city god, as did the other southern cities. Inanna remained the goddess who led the king into battle, but, with the acquiescence of the leaders of other prominent cities, Naram-Sin claimed divinity and "built his temple" in Akkad. From an inscription of Naram-Sin, we read, "Inasmuch as he established the foundations of his city under duress, his city requested him as god of their city Akkade, from Ištar in Eanna, from Enlil in Nippur, from Dagan in Tuttul, from Ninhursag in Keš, from Enki in Eridu, from Sin in Ur, from Šamaš in Sippar, [and] from Nergal in Kutha, and built his temple in Akkade."[60]

Enheduanna included in the Temple Hymns seven of the eight cities Naram-Sin named as supporters of his divine elevation. These cities range from Eridu and Ur in the extreme south, to Nippur in the central plain, to Sippar on the northern edge of the alluvium. Naram-Sin's declaration elevated the empire to a new level of authority and created an indisputable power located in the capital city of Akkad.

WHERE IS AKKAD?

Ancient documents variously place Akkad in the vicinity of the cities of Babylon on the Euphrates, Kish, some fifteen miles to the east of Babylon, Ishan Mizyad, a few miles north of Kish, and east near the junction of the Tigris and Diyala rivers. Numerous archeological surveys have sought to discover its exact location.

Texts tell us that in the Old Babylonian period (1894–1595 BCE) Hammurabi cared for the Inanna/Ishtar temple in Akkad, the E-ulmash, "in the midst of a still-thriving 'broad-marted' Agade [Akkad]."[61] In the later Neo-Assyrian (950–610 BCE) and Neo-Babylonian (626–539 BCE) periods, documents indicate that the location of Akkad was known. Kings of these periods, "Kurigalzu, Esarhaddon, Aššurbanipal, Nebuchadnezzar and Nabonidus undertook intensive excavations at Agade," searching for the site of the E-ulmash temple.[62]

Harvey Weiss deduces that Akkad would have been located in the large marshy basin that still exists in the area north of Kish. Citing texts that describe the clay soil used in the construction of the city and the watery depression where it was built, he names Ishan Mizyad because it is the only one of the three cities that lies inside the large depression and is seasonally soaked with water.[63] Weiss says, "With only brief interruptions, the area around Kish, identified in our ancient sources as 'Akkad' or 'Babylon,' has remained the political center of Mesopotamia for almost five thousand years."[64]

Others postulate that Akkad was located in the area of present-day Baghdad.[65] If so, Akkad would have been slightly north and east of Sippar, near the confluence of the Tigris and Diyala rivers. Christophe Wall-Romana challenges a claim "widely accepted among Assyriologists that Agade [Akkad] must lie somewhere along a former branch of the Euphrates."[66] He speculates that the city Sargon built was originally a small town whose name Sargon retained and that is located not far from Kish, where Sargon served King Ur-Zababa and then attempted to overthrow him.[67] Wall-Romana examines and synthesizes all the pertinent references to Akkad and finds "a definite connection between Agade and the Tigris."[68] He concludes that all the evidence considered places Akkad east of the Tigris, northwest of its confluence with the Diyala. He continues, "In sum, the evidence locating Agade in the Lower Diyala region close to the ancient Tigris is overwhelming both in terms of the amount and consistency of the data. Counter-evidence is conspicuously lacking."[69]

This location lies slightly outside the boundaries of the southern cities but central to the ambitious Sargonic expansion beyond traditional Sumer. Wall-Romana speculates that Akkad was located at Robert Adams's survey site #414, Tell Muhammad, "on the southeastern outskirts of Baghdad."[70] By 1978 excavators at the site had reached Kassite and Isin-Larsa levels but had not explored the deeper levels that would correspond to the Akkadian period. "One wonders," says Wall-Romana, "whether Baghdad was not a later development of the city of Agade itself."[71] Seldom is so historic a city as Akkad hidden from contemporary exploration.

TEMPLE HYMN 41

THE AKKAD TEMPLE OF ABA

O house on the right side
power broker of the unique one
crouching down in green meadows
. . . destroy
divine Nintur set it up there

your prince the warrior who strikes the rebel land
who defeats the multitude in battle   exalting

Aba   god of Agade
has built this house on your radiant site
O Agade
and taken his seat upon your dais

    8 lines for the house of Aba in Akkad

THE TEMPLE OF ABA AT AKKAD

The god Aba owes his notoriety to the Sargonic kings who built his temple in their capital city of Akkad and named him as patron of their empire. He was probably a Semitic god imported from the north of Mesopotamia, where his name appears among those of other Semitic gods. Some specialists believe his name should be read Ilaba.[72] He is recognized as the Akkadian patron deity on numerous cylinder seals of the era. After the two-hundred-year-long Sargonic dynasty, Aba virtually disappeared. He is unknown in Sumerian/Babylonian mythology.[73]

The tablets that contain fragments of this hymn are badly broken. They state that Aba's house is on the right side, while that of Inanna is on the left. On the other hand, the Sumerian phrase may mean that the house/temple is the right arm of "the unique one," namely, the god Aba. Aba is portrayed as a warrior god, appropriate to his role as the patron god of warrior kings. His temple is said to lie low in green meadows, a fertile image, placed there by the goddess of birth, Nintur.

Imaginative imagery in the hymn is sparse, making it poetically undistinguished. Enheduanna embellishes Inanna's temple in Akkad with silver, gold, and lapis. She vividly describes Inanna's fearsome encounters with the enemy, even washing her weapons in their blood. At this point, we have come to expect the poet's graphic, evocative descriptions of the deities and wonder why they are absent in the hymn to Aba.

The Temple Hymns served to acknowledge the claim each city made for the exceptional nature of its deity. Except for Aba, all the gods and goddesses of the Temple Hymns have an ancient history in Sumer, reaching back hundreds of years into the Early Dynastic period or even to the earlier Uruk period. Enheduanna draws on this history as she describes each temple and deity. Aba was neither a god with a well-known, illustrious history nor a Sumerian god. If part of her purpose was to reassure the Sumerians that under Sargon's rule their treasured gods and goddesses and their religion would remain intact, that purpose would not be served by writing an elaborate hymn to an unknown foreign god, now elevated to the role of patron deity of the conqueror.

If Enheduanna is the author of the Temple Hymns, we do not know when she wrote them, whether during her father's reign or later in the long reign of her nephew Naram-Sin. Probably she became high priestess at a young age, late in her father's reign. The maturity of the poetic voice suggests that Enheduanna wrote the hymns as an older woman. Possibly, the thin hymn to Aba is related to Naram-Sin's desire to be god of Akkad himself. We know that Aba's brief, undistinguished history enabled Naram-Sin either to replace or to overshadow him, to build a temple to himself, and to declare himself the "strong god of Akkad," as he inscribed a seal found at Girsu, declaring himself god of the dynasty.[74]

chapter 13

NISABA'S TEMPLE AT ERESH

This final hymn to Nisaba stands alone, as does the first Temple Hymn to Enki in Eridu. Neither belongs to a defining group of deities. Each has a purpose in its singularity. Enki's hymn presents his temple as the ancient locus of creation. Nisaba's temple holds its place as the guardian of human achievement. She is, after all, the goddess of writing, the divine inspiration that made the recording of the Temple Hymns possible. Even more, Nisaba is the power in the creative process itself.

The final hymn is the crown of Enheduanna's collection. Nisaba, of all the deities, inspires the unrivaled achievements of the human mind. Starting with the civilizing effect of grain cultivation, a gift of Nisaba, she made human habitation in settled groups necessary, leading to the development of cities. Nisaba is the divine underpinning of urban culture. From the interactions of the early cities and their deities, there evolved the necessity of record keeping and the eventual successful invention of true writing. Writing, with Nisaba as its guide, enabled the next step, the experimentation that nurtured inventiveness and the lively pleasure of the creative mind. In the area of the sciences, she spawned the art of measurement and the motivation to record and categorize the encyclopedic elements of the culture and of the natural world.

Nisaba claimed a comprehensive wisdom that led her to open her temple to a whole mix of people—offering common shelter to the diversity that was Sumer. Enheduanna ends her collection of hymns with an idealized vision of all lands coming together under the roof of Nisaba's temple to receive her strong counsel and all-embracing wisdom.

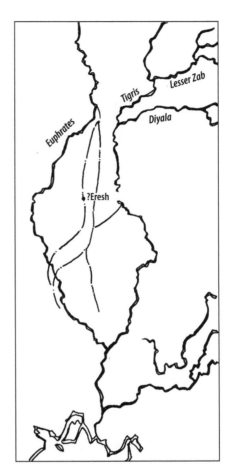

13.1.   Sketch map of Mesopotamia
with Eresh. After Postgate 1994.
Reproduced by permission of Taylor and
Francis Books U.K.

TEMPLE HYMN 42

THE ERESH TEMPLE OF NISABA
Ezagin

this shining house of stars   bright with lapis stones
has opened itself to all lands
a whole mix of people in the shrine   every month
lift heads for you   Eresh
all the primeval lords

soapwort   the very young saba on your platform
great Nanibgal   Nisaba   Lady of Saba

brought powers down from heaven
added her measure to your powers
enlarged the shrine   set it up for praising

faithful woman exceeding in wisdom
opens [her] mouth [to recite] over cooled lined tablets
always consults lapis tablets
[and] gives strong council to all lands

true woman of the pure soapwort
born of the sharpened reed
who measures the heavens by cubits
strikes the coiled measuring rod on the earth

praise be to Nisaba

13 lines for the house of Nisaba in Eresh

the person who bound this tablet together
is Enheduanna
my king   something never before created
did not this one give birth to it

the incipit: é-u$_6$-nir
the count of its lines is altogether 548

THE TEMPLE OF NISABA IN ERESH

To reach Eresh from the capital at Akkad, the passenger must travel to a dock on the ancient course of the Euphrates and follow the river past Kish, on the way to Nippur. Eresh lay south of Akkad, between Kish and Nippur. An ancient city, Eresh is mentioned in a list of geographic names from the turn of the fourth millennium, a time that marked the end of the Uruk period and the beginning of the Early Dynastic. From the same period in a zàmì hymn of praise, Eresh is called Nisaba's town.[1] The city flourished in the first years of the Early Dynastic period, and its treasure trove of early literary tablets may identify the site as ancient Abu Salabikh, the archeological site of the discovery of the earliest cuneiform tablets.[2]

Enheduanna ends her collection of Temple Hymns with this one to Nisaba at Eresh. She calls the goddess affectionately "young saba," using the women's dialect, Emesal; 'saba' is the Emesal word for naga, the Sumerian name of the soapwort plant and, like 'Nanibgal,' is a byname of Nisaba. The soapwort plant, from the genus *Saponaria*, has fragrant clusters of pink and white flowers and leaves that yield a soapy substance when rubbed. In the Emesal dialect, Ni-saba, [i.e., Ni(n)-saba] means 'Lady of Saba.'[3] Emesal, 'tongue of woman,' was a dialect of Sumerian used in literary texts to record the speech of women and, as in this instance, to distinguish the names of female deities. Nisaba was the goddess of writing, but also the goddess who presided over intellectual pursuits.

In the hymn Enheduanna calls upon "all the primeval lords," alluding to the thousand-year history that preceded her father's empire. Nisaba, the hymn implies, is the exemplary goddess who, during the entire past millennium from the beginning of writing in the mid to late Uruk period into the Early Dynastic, watched over the Sumerians' remarkable achievements in the arts, sciences, and literature.

The Sumerian cultural tradition evolved even before the invention of writing, as far back as the Ubaid period, 5000 to 4000 BCE, whose first small temple at Eridu became the foundation upon which replacements were built, one on top of the other, in the same, but larger, configuration.[4] Enheduanna would have been aware of the continuity of this tradition that reached back into hoary antiquity. She addresses the primeval lords in the hymn, the "en-ul," who gather at Nisaba's temple in Eresh, suggesting that under Nisaba's gaze, in monthly rituals, Sumer's ancient traditions were celebrated. Nisaba, the hymn tells us, brought powers from heaven to enhance the temple. Her powers, emanating from her exceeding wisdom, include the recitation of wise council, recorded with her sharpened reed on treasured lapis tablets, as well as the application of measurement by which she counts the stars and scans the earth.

THE ORIGIN OF WRITING

Before there was writing that represented the spoken word, there was record keeping and counting. In the second half of the fourth millennium in Uruk, "the mother of all cities," the enterprising Sumerians began to trade their excess foodstuffs and products over an expanding territory that eventually ranged beyond present Iraq into southwestern Iran, northern Syria, and southern Turkey. While on these excursions, the resource-poor Sumerians bartered for essential raw materials such as timber, metal ores, and bitumen, in exchange for their manufactured textiles, leather products, and agricultural surplus, grains, dates, and dried fish.[5] Gradually, the Sumerians established trading centers, primarily along established routes that crisscrossed the northern plains east and west from Syria into Iran. Population centers grew, particularly at the junctions of the major rivers and fords. Guillermo Algaze describes the importance of this expansion:

> By the second half of the fourth millennium, societies of the Mesopotamian alluvium were already in the midst of an intense process of expansion that took diverse forms and affected a number of areas differently. This process may be considered to represent the earliest well-attested example of the cyclical "momentum toward empire" that was to become a recurrent phenomenon throughout millennia of Mesopotamia history.[6]

On their trading ventures, the Urukeans carried diagrams of their monumental buildings and plot-plans for town layouts to be built in the north, just as they had at home. The southern Uruk urban way of life spread throughout the region, and their culture dominated most of the fourth millennium. No other culture in antiquity extended its influence over so large an area.[7] They had inherited from the Ubaidians, their predecessors in the preceding millennium, tools in the form of stamp seals and a variety of uniformly shaped clay tokens used for counting and record keeping. Scholars believe that the differently shaped tokens denoted different weights or numbers.[8] Still, the growing marketplace of Uruk needed even more complex methods of recording transactions. Bureaucracies organized and evolved. Cylinder seals, tiny carved stone cylinders, enabled the sender to roll his mark across damp clay and thus secure the packaged goods and name its contents, its sender, and its receiver more effectively than he was able to do with a stamp seal. Most significantly, to keep accounts of daily transactions, the Urukeans began to draw symbols with sharpened reeds onto pads of damp clay. Certain uniform symbols signified numbers, and simple pictographic signs denoted the goods in the transaction or payment for services. This accounting system, clever as it was, in no way recorded the spoken language. The system was understood, but could not be "read."

Even the prosperous Uruk culture eventually met its demise. Just at the end of the Uruk period, enterprising scribes began to adapt the pictographic signs into syllabic, spoken sounds. Gwendolyn Leick gives a simple example. The word for water in Sumerian is transcribed "a," pronounced "ah." The pictographic sign is drawn with two parallel wavy lines depicting a river. The clever scribes found that they could substitute the sign for water wherever the sound "ah" appeared in a word and transfer a clue to the speech sound on the clay tablet, thus creating the written vowel.[9] The full development of true writing evolved in the following six hundred years of the Early Dynastic period. The language the scribes transposed into written texts was Sumerian. By the Early Dynastic IIIa period (2600–2350 BCE), texts found at Fara, ancient Shuruppak, included administrative documents, sale contracts, and "a hundred lexical and literary texts."[10] Harriet Martin says of the find, "What does seem beyond question is that Fara, ancient Šuruppak, was dotted with establishments (including many that had no pretensions to a high status) that made use of basic literacy to record simple economic transactions. Literacy appears to have been surprisingly widespread for such an early period."[11]

As the overwhelming dominance of the Uruk culture faded, the other southern cities seem to have pulled closer together, more than they had during the expansive throes of the prosperous Uruk period. Early in the third millennium, the new writing was adopted in a number of cities in the south. As we have seen, Shuruppak, the home of Nisaba's daughter Sud/Ninlil, harbored the earliest literary tablets discovered so far. Somewhat later at the Syrian city of Ebla and at the southern city of Abu Salabikh, possibly Nisaba's city of Eresh, additional literary tablets were found. Robert Biggs, one of the principal epigraphers at Abu Salabikh, says the evidence from these tablets constitutes "the first great flowering of Sumerian literature and culmination of the archaic Sumerian tradition of scholarship."[12] Nisaba was the goddess whose divine office presided over this ancient Sumerian invention.

NISABA AND THE ARTS OF CIVILIZATION

The Early Dynastic people in the southern plains prospered in their cities between the two rivers, and now enhanced their already complex and expanding culture with a major invention: the capacity to record and read the spoken word. From its inception writing was a product of the thoughtful and creative men and women, scholars, and storytellers, who used it to preserve the ideas and creative works that defined their culture. A new profession emerged to master this craft, that of the scribe. Using their skills, the members of this honored profession recorded not only encyclopedic lists, but also mythology and literature, theology of the deities, the precepts of science and medicine, astronomy, mathematics, collections of magic formulas and incantations, accounting, surveying—in short, a whole body of knowledge. Scholarly pursuits grew in kind and status, and this diverse, newly expanded class worshiped Nisaba as their protector, guide, and inspiration.

The earliest pictographic rendering of her name is a stalk of grain. From this association with grain, Nisaba became a goddess of the staple, namely,

13.2.   Pictographic sign for Nisaba. After Labat, 1995. Courtesy of Editions GEUTHNER, Paris.

cereals and grains, that enabled the nomadic ancestors of the Sumerians to settle in villages. The successful cultivation of wild grains took many hundreds of years, beginning in the seventh millennium of the Neolithic. Cultivation of a staple food necessitated settlement in one place for a period of time; this drastically changed the pattern of life from one of constant mobility to at least an extended period of living in one place. The miracle of a sustainable food source, the people believed, could only have come from the deities, and Nisaba, the grain goddess, was its origin and its guardian. Grain, like corn in the Americas, was central to the Sumerians' worldview. The cultivation of grain was a sacred task accompanied by ritual and prayer. The Sumerian calendar and the ritual year were organized around planting, cultivation, and harvest. Grain cultivation allowed for settlements to grow into cities and therefore for the development of an elaborate culture and a unique civilization. A royal hymn to Nisaba describes her sacred office as goddess of grain:

> Your growth is surely the furrow
> Your form is surely cereal
> Your features, all of them, are good
> Your figure is surely its grain[13]

From the beginning women were associated with grain and probably were its first cultivators. Grain was stored in the women's section of the local houses. In the temple, grain storage was in the gipar, the residence of the high priestess and her entourage. The gipar was originally a storehouse or granary. Early images of a reed-hut granary depict small animals eagerly waiting for their mothers to return. The storehouse was also a birth hut. Later it became the city treasury, storing as it did the city's reserve of wealth. Nisaba was praised for providing and protecting the storage of grain and was even addressed as the great storage room herself:

> Enlil is the king of all the lands
> You are his great storage room, you are his seal keeper . . .
> You bring riches into the storehouse[14]

An abundance of grain was essential to the survival of urban society. The royal hymn confirms this:

> Nisaba—the place which you do not establish
> [There,] mankind is not established, cities are not built.[15]

From a goddess of grain—the life-sustaining staple of the Sumerians' diet— Nisaba evolved into the goddess who created and supported urban civilization. She was the divine force that held urban civilization together, and, by association, the underpinning of all of its unique achievements, the invention of writing being the foremost. Writing strengthened a whole new world of scholarly pursuits, from the creative and intellectual achievements of literature and science to the practical recording of the elements of civil life. Nisaba was the archetypal scribe. In the first lines of one of the oldest pieces of literature, the Hymn to Kesh, Nisaba is named the one who wrote it down:

> establisher of the standard version thereof
>   was Nidaba
> she spun, as it were, a web
>   out of those words,
> and writing them down on a tablet
>   she laid them [ready] to hand.[16]

This description conveys the magical aura that surrounded the act of writing. Indeed, Nisaba is said to have written with a stylus of precious gold or silver, and the tablet itself was thought to be sacred, often described as made of the holy stone, lapis lazuli.

As goddess of creative thought, Nisaba came to be known as the wise woman, deity of wisdom. Sjöberg cites a text that describes her as geštù-ha-mun, 'an all comprehending wisdom.'[17] A hymn of King Lipit-Eshtar praises her as follows:

Nisaba, the woman radiant with joy
faithful woman, scribe, lady who knows everything
guided your fingers on the clay
embellished the writing on the tablets
made the hand resplendent with a golden stylus
the measuring rod, the gleaming surveyor's line,
the cubit ruler which gives wisdom
Nisaba lavishly bestowed on you[18]

In the Early Dynastic epic tale "Enmerkar and the Lord of Aratta," Nisaba uses her talent as one who stimulates creative mind and inspiration. In the tale, the lord of Aratta tried to outwit the lord of Uruk, Enmerkar, who wanted precious lapis lazuli found only in Aratta. In a bargain, the lord of Aratta offered the stone in exchange for grain from Uruk, with the stipulation that the grain had to be transported in open-net bags. How could Enmerkar possibly prevent the grain from spilling out of the net? He thought and thought, and in a moment of inspiration, born of divine Nisaba, he found a solution. He would soak the grain in water, making a malt that would not drop through the mesh of the nets. The tale describes Nisaba's visitation to Enmerkar:

Nidaba,
    the lady of vast intelligence,
opened for him
    her "Nidaba's holy house
    of understanding"[19]

Opening the "holy house / of understanding," creative inspiration, was the prerogative of Nisaba, goddess of creative mind.

Scholarly pursuits were valued in Sumer from the time of the first records. William Hallo calls Nisaba the "patron goddess of scholars."[20] Among the earliest tablets found were those that recorded extensive categorical lists, such as names of animals, plants, various products such as textiles, geographical names, and several lists of professions. Hallo says, "The organization of knowledge in lists was a characteristic medium for Mesopotamian learning from the beginning, and helped propagate and perpetuate the invention of written Sumerian in which all received wisdom was believed to be contained."[21] The lists provided an encyclopedic compendium, not only of knowledge, but of the given world. The lists encompassed Sumerian reality. In a third-millennium copy of the "Names and Professions" list from the Ur III period, which followed the Sargonic empire, Nisaba is named in the colophon, still praised as she had been for almost a thousand years, as the goddess of wisdom and of writing.

SHINING HOUSE OF STARS

In this final hymn to Nisaba at Eresh, Enheduanna appears in person. In a significant act, breaking the pattern she followed in all the preceding hymns, she drops the now-familiar colophon, "X goddess or god has built his/her house on your radiant site / and established his/her seat upon your dais." In a highly unusual signature, she writes instead,

> the person who bound this tablet together is Enheduanna
> my king something never before created
> did not this one give birth to it

Signing a personal name to a composition is unprecedented in Sumerian literature. We can infer her purpose in this unusually personal statement. She is presenting her composition to the king, her father, and this acknowledgment suggests that the piece will serve him. As we will see, the hymn itself reveals the relevance of the collection to the king. Then, she tells us that she has created a new piece of literature, never attempted before. Finally, in signing her name, she adds the prestige of her position as high priestess, saying she speaks with recognized authority. This is no ordinary group of hymns copied by an anonymous scribe. Far from being a casual exercise, the collection serves the purposes of the powerful king Sargon, who rules over every city in the collection: from ancient Eridu in the far south to the holy city of Nippur; from her familiar home in and around Ur to the ancient center on the Euphrates, Uruk; from cities on the Tigris near the southern gulf to others north along the river; cities in the fertile central plain between the two great rivers; cities east beyond the Tigris on the ancient passage into Iran; and finally to Sargon's newly built city of Akkad and its neighbors in the north, where the two rivers flow close to each other, almost closing the great oval their channels form to define the territory that is Sumer.

One by one, Enheduanna has described each city's primary temple and its deity, the temple that, more than any other feature, gives identity to the locale and its inhabitants. Each one is different. Even identical goddesses or gods appearing in more than one hymn display a cluster of unique aspects that belong to one temple, one city alone. The hymn to Nisaba tells us that citizens from these diverse cities with their separate local identities all come together under the roof of Eresh. Each locale is represented by the en-ul, the 'primeval lords,' who were the ancient mythological religious leaders of the first cities in the fertile crescent. Thus, from the beginning, Sumer has honored a great diversity, "a whole mix of peoples" who, despite their varying local beliefs and cultural practices, their geography, economics, ethnicity, even languages, are an identifiable people, held together in the land between the two rivers. This heritage, the hymn says, is recalled each month in her temple, suggesting that through a common religious practice, the people acknowledge their common origins. The Sumerian cities did celebrate in common certain monthly as well as seasonal rituals, and this uniformity may explain the monthly gathering the hymn implies. With her collection of Temple Hymns, Enheduanna assures the cities that even with the changes imposed by Sargon's conquest, their original identity, whose roots reach back thousands of years, has not been disturbed. The deities central to each community remain the same. Enheduanna reaffirms the well-known character of the primary goddess or god of every important city, and now, at Eresh, declares their common antiquity. Kings and rulers may come and go, but the deities of Sumer have provided a stable continuity from their most ancient origin, continuing until now and, implicitly, into the future.

Nisaba is the goddess who represents the defining cultural achievements that belong to all the cities. From her "shining house of stars" she counts the stars, applying her particular wisdom to the unfathomable celestial dome. She brings the authority of science to the culture by unlocking the mysteries of the cosmos.[22] She dares to "measure the heavens by cubits," and with her measuring rod she marks out the earth. These extraordinary powers she "brought down from heaven," and she "added her measure" to the powers already in the temple itself. Enki, apportioning powers to the deities in the myth "Enki and the World Order," gave the measuring rod to Nisaba, gave her the power of measurement.[23] In a later document she is recognized as "knowing the inmost (secrets) of numbers."[24] The hymn tells us that she brought these powers down from heaven, giving them earthly substance and accessibility and entrusting them to the safeguard of her temple. Nisaba, "giving strong council to all lands," disperses her wisdom and scholarly learning to all the cities. This period was a time of incremental advances in science and the arts. Enheduanna offers this hymn as the summation of her declaration that all the cities participate in this extraordinary culture.

Like Nisaba, Enheduanna as high priestess belonged to all the cities. With the Temple Hymns she, too, formulated with wisdom and visionary insight an overarching truth that connected the cities and held their diversity in a common identity. She must have looked to Nisaba for her own creative inspiration as she picked up her stylus, wrote hymn after hymn on the damp clay, each one uniquely suited to the primary temple and deity of a particular city. This one to Nisaba in Eresh extols the Sumerians' remarkable invention of writing and rightly links writing to wise council and to uncovering the secrets of the universe, secrets Nisaba, with her gift of measurement, inspired her followers to discover. The intellectual pursuits hinted at in the hymn, the pursuit of wisdom, the pursuit of knowledge, were to become the building blocks of modern civilization.

chapter 14

CONCLUSION: ENHEDUANNA'S GIFT

Enheduanna's poetry comes to us from a civilization of such antiquity that the sparse records reveal very little about the high priestess herself. For some specialists, claiming her as the author of the Temple Hymns and of the three devotional poems to Inanna is too great a presumption. To others, including myself, the consistent poetic voice in the work, along with several appearances of her actual name in the hymns and poems attributed to her, is evidence enough of her genuine authorship.

The voice we hear in the hymns is that of a gifted poet. Her compelling aesthetic in each hymn evokes a resonance in the reader. Enheduanna has almost perfect pitch in the daunting task of giving poetic life to temple after temple, to each one's awesome majesty or beauty or terrifying grandeur. Her voice is recognizable and unique. She was a scholar of the Sumerian religious tradition, in her lifetime already more that two thousand years old. Yet her hymns are anything but perfunctory reporting. Immersed as the high priestess was in Sumerian tradition, she dares to imagine what lies beyond human sight and knowledge. She describes with candor the everyday lives, cares, and inherent nature of the deities and their temples. She populates the entire surrounding cosmos with active, engaging, uncontrollable divine beings.

Consider the first hymn to Enki's temple in Eridu. Its dramatic beginning of thirteen lines swells to a climax, introducing the hymn, and indeed the entire collection, with compelling force. Creation happens in the first two lines when Enki's platform temple rises to split heaven and earth. This forceful act leaves in its wake elemental necessities—water, food, soap for ritual cleansing. Then, the crescendo of creation continues, accompanied by cosmic hymns. We see the grand surrounding wall and visit the holy of holies in the dark interior of the temple where the god lives. In a final chorus of two lines the hymn says this "firm-anchored house has a purity beyond measure."

This image of creation is Enheduanna's invention, not one borrowed from a known myth. In hymn after hymn, she embellishes familiar Sumerian mythic motifs with her rich imagery and poetic sense. After the explosive cosmic event of creation, Enheduanna calmly describes the everyday reality that occupies Enki's temple personnel. A human actor appears—the susbu priest. He makes plants grow. His cohorts bake bread and carry it to the inhabitants of the temple to eat. The process of creation makes clear that ordinary food and water have the same cosmic significance as wise Enki and his awesome abode.

Every hymn creates its own environment. In each one Enheduanna's intention is evident through her choice of content and description. Her perceptive involvement emerges as the reader is drawn into the compelling atmosphere of the poem. The main character in each hymn is the temple itself. Human activity is dwarfed by its awesome powers. At times the temple's powers seem to be greater than those of the deity who lives there. At the very least, the two, temple and divine personage, partake of the same otherworldly substance.

Enki's temple materializes out of the cosmic mist, causing the first separation of the two realms, heaven and earth. Asarluhi's hymn (TH 10) offers a more explicit description. Seven Wise Ones created his temple, "squeezed out of the abzu / like barley oil." The poet captures an image every Sumerian would understand, the daunting extraction process of squeezing precious oil from a tough, unyielding hull of barley. Asarluhi's hymn tells us that before creation the earth was "heavy with clouds," a "dense mist." The created temple becomes the "form-shaping place" (TH 7), the "navel of heaven and earth" (TH 2) that joins earth to heaven and to the underworld. The foundation of the temple is "the fifty abzus / the seven seas," a foundation that "plumbs the inner workings of the deities" (TH 8).

Temples exhibit a demeanor and character that correspond to their divine inhabitants. Thus the sun god Utu's temple (TH 13) is a "white-glowing house," whose "lustrous lapis beard hangs down in profusion," like Utu's sunbeams. Inanna's temples, like Inanna, are "grounded in desire" (TH 26) in their "irresistible ripeness." (TH 16). Each vibrant temple interacts with its resident deity in terms of mutual characteristics. Utu's temple lifts its "neck to the sky / close to Utu who tends you" (TH 13). The interior of the temple of the birth goddess Ninhursag "is a womb dark and deep" (TH 7), where she, "lady of molding /

works in your dark interior" (TH 39), giving birth to kings and to high priestesses. The temple of the underworld priest Ninazu (TH 14) spreads its shadow
"over / all the princes of the earth," just as Ninazu receives the dead, prince
and commoner alike. Enlil's temple (TH 2) exudes "measured reckoning" from
its top and "contemplation" from its base. Both aspects inform Enlil, "the fate
fixer," as he ponders his "divine decisions."

In their diversity the temples give order to life's mystery and fear, its terror and dread, beauty and desire. They and their divine residents provide a
container for the inevitable course of life from birth to death. With their cosmic dramas the divine personages cover all that can happen in the lives of the
worshipers, thus offering their subjects divine meaning and cosmic relevance
within the contained whole of the Sumerian religious tradition.

In spite of the temples' living presence, it is the deities themselves who
attract the affection, fear, respect, and awe of the individual Sumerians. Each
citizen has a personal deity whom he or she worships at an altar at home. The
deity, not the temple, receives their prayers. Whatever cosmic activity precipitated the temples' creation, it was ultimately channeled through an act of the
resident deity. The repeated colophon after each hymn reports that the deity
herself or himself built the temple and placed her or his seat on the honored
dais.

Female and male, the deities reflect human cares, fears, and longings. The
divine females possess some characteristics not found in their male counterparts, and vice versa, but there are many overlapping qualities common to
both. For example, only hymns to goddesses mention the arts of giving birth.
The female deities also are exclusively engaged in dream interpretation and
healing, both magical and medical. Only they have powers over desire, an
office mentioned in two of the hymns to Inanna. Flowers, joy, stars, the sea
and its dark waters occur almost exclusively in the hymns of goddesses. From
Shuzianna's temple (TH 6), "she sows flowers in profusion." Her hymn refers
to a cloistered residence for women. Other hymns mention the gipar, the
living quarters of Enheduanna in Ur, and also a residence for women in other
temples. No comparable habitation for men is known.

Enheduanna fully portrays the contradictory characteristics of the deities.
Some harbor the paradox of nature, as in these lines to Nanshe (TH 22):

> your lady Nanshe
>   a great storm   strong dark water
> born on the shore of the sea

laughing in the sea foam
playing playing in the waves

Only Inanna, among the goddesses (TH 40), is a fearsome warrior; spitting poison, "savage lion battering the wild bull," she "washes weapons in the blood of battle." These characteristics are far from those depicted in her description in Temple Hymn 16: "perfectly shaped fresh fruit / dazzling in your irresistible ripeness. . . . crowned with lapis lazuli desire," or as the evening star in TH 26, who "at twilight makes the firmament beautiful all on her own."

Nisaba, in the final hymn, displays an unusual universalism. From its beginning, she welcomes "a whole mix of people" into her temple, starting with the primeval lords. Nisaba opens her house to everyone and gives wise council to all lands. She is also unusual in her intellectual pursuits, writing and measurement. Her inclusiveness is in marked contrast to the division made in many of the hymns between the Sumerians and the "others," the enemy, the wicked, the evil ones.

On the other hand, male deities have almost exclusive claim to evil thwarting, weapons, and fighting. They are credited with making wise decisions and with reckoning. More males than females are accompanied by bulls and horns, lions and storms, as powerful aspects. Ningishzida (TH 15) travels a "mighty hair-raising path." His weapons are equally hair raising:

the neck-stock the fine-eyed net
the foot-shackling netherworld knot

Still, many of the males are gentle farmers or herdsmen. Nanna moon and Utu sun give precious light. Ishkur's rain creates abundance, moist wind, rainbow, and cloud. Three hymns mention the beauty of a god's long hair or beard. Shara (TH 25), hairdresser to Inanna, displays none of the typically male prowess. At his temple "graceful stone jars stand in the open air." He "keeps his eye on the wild cow," his mother, Inanna, and "offers sweet bread to eat."

The most powerful deities appear again and again in hymns to the other deities. Enlil, the ruling deity of this era, is called upon by lesser deities who rely on him for their status. Enki is invoked, particularly in relation to the moon god, Nanna, and to Asarluhi, his cohort in divination. An, in some myths the original creator deity of heaven, has no hymn of his own but is called upon or claimed as a father by lesser deities, male and female. Inanna appears in the hymn to her consort Dumuzi and her son, Shara, and is implied in other hymns in her role as sacred or taboo woman.

The Temple Hymns are among the archeological treasures dug out of Iraqi soil only in the past one hundred or so years. Their value, to use Enheduanna's words, "has a purity beyond measure." They are a direct link to the four-thousand-year-old cradle of Western civilization. They reveal a complexity of conceptual thought and a genius of poetic aesthetics we could never have imagined. Just as we are touched by ancient artistic relics from anonymous hands, so we are moved by the antiquity of this first poetry, the first ever from a known individual. The great civilization of the Sumerians, with their compulsion for records, their insistence on lists and catalogues and libraries, carefully preserved the lines of the Temple Hymns for us. We are grateful to these our ancestors for their gift of Enheduanna.

CHAPTER I

1. C. B. F. Walker, *Cuneiform* (Berkeley: University of California Press, 1987), 37. "Enheduanna, the daughter of Sargon I, and high priestess of the moon god Nanna at Ur, is one of the few female scribes known from Mesopotamia, and the earliest named author in history."

2. William W. Hallo, *Origins* (Leiden: E. J. Brill, 1996), 171.

3. Page du Bois, *Sappho Is Burning* (Chicago: University of Chicago Press, 1995), 6. "Homer the great poet, the first poet of the Western tradition whose work has come down to us, is now believed to have written or sung his epic poems in the eighth century B.C.E. . . . The world of Sappho, at least a century later, was a very different one."

4. Christophe Wall-Romana, "An Areal Location of Agade," *JNES* 49:3 (1990): 208. See also Douglas Frayne, *RIME*, vol. 2, *Sargonic and Gutian Periods* (Toronto: University of Toronto Press, 1993), 7.

5. Frayne, *RIME*, vol. 2, 7.

6. Hans J. Nissen, *The Early History of the Ancient Near East* (Chicago: University of Chicago Press, 1988), 167–168.

7. William W. Hallo and William Kelly Simpson, *The Ancient Near East: A History*, 2d ed. (Belmont, Calif.: Wadsworth/Thomas Learning, 1998), 53.

8. Nissen, *Early History*, 165.

9. Hallo and Simpson, *The Ancient Near East*, 51.

10. J. N. Postgate, "Royal Ideology and State Administration in Sumer and Akkad," in Jack M. Sasson, ed., *Civilizations of the Ancient Near East* (hereafter CANE) 1:401 (New York: Charles Scribner's Sons, 1995).

11. Penelope N. Weadock, "The *Giparu* at Ur," *Iraq* 37, no. 2 (1975): 103.

CHAPTER II

1. Guillermo Algaze, "Ancient Mesopotamia at the Dawn of Civilization—The Evolution of an Urban Landscape" (Department of Archeology, University of California San Diego, computer copy, 2006), 137.

2. Ibid.

3. Marc Van De Mieroop, *The Ancient Mesopotamian City* (Oxford: Oxford University Press, 1999), 36, 38.

4. Algaze, "Ancient Mesopotamia at the Dawn of Civilization," 157.

5. Ibid., 166.

6. Ibid., 157.

7. See, for example, A. Moortgat, *The Art of Ancient Mesopotamia* (London: Phaidon, 1969), 8–9; Nissen, *Early History,* 106.

8. Denise Schmandt-Besserat, "Images of Enship," in D. Schmandt-Besserat, ed., *The Legacy of Sumer* (Malibu: Undena Publications, 1976), 209.

9. The Uruk Vase was stolen from the Iraq Museum in Baghdad in 2003 during the looting following the U.S. invasion but was returned (slightly damaged) in the amnesty during the weeks following.

10. Krystyna Szarzyńska, *Sumerica* (Warszawa: Wydawnictwo Akademickie Dialog, 1997), 147.

11. Schmandt-Besserat, "Images of Enship," 213.

12. Piotr Steinkeller, "On Rulers, Priests and Sacred Marriage: Tracing the Evolution of Early Sumerian Kingship," in Kazuko Watanabe, ed., *Priests and Officials in the Ancient Near East* (Heidelberg: Universitatsverlag C. Winter, 1999), 113.

13. Ibid., 115.

14. Robert D. Biggs, *Inscriptions from Tell Abu Salabikh* (Chicago: University of Chicago Press, 1974), 45.

15. Steinkeller, "Rulers," 114.

16. F. A. M. Wiggerman, "Theologies, Priests, and Worship in Ancient Mesotamia," in CANE 3:1869.

17. Irene J. Winter, "Women in Public: The Disc of Enheduanna, the Beginning of the Office of En-Priestess, and the Weight of Visual Evidence," in Jean-Marie Durand, ed., *La Femme dans le proche orient antique* (Paris: Editions Recherche sur les Civilizations, 1987), 193–200.

18. Joan Goodnick Westenholz, "Enheduanna, En-Priestess, Hen of Nanna, Spouse of Nanna," in Hermann Behrens, Darlene Loding, and Martha Roth, eds., *DUMU-E₂-DUB-BA-A: Studies in Honor of Åke Sjöberg* (Philadelphia: University of Pennsylvania Museum, 1989), 544.

19. Ibid., 545.

20. Edmond Sollberger, "The Disc of Enheduanna," *Iraq* 22 (1960): 82.

21. Westenholz, "Enheduanna, En-Priestess," 539.

22. Dominique Collon, "Depictions of Priests and Priestesses in the Ancient Near East" in Kazuko Watanabe, ed., *Priests and Officials in the Ancient Near East* (Heidelberg: Universitatsverlag C. Winter, 1999), 20–21.

23. Weadock, "The *Giparu* at Ur," 106. Following the tradition of Assyriologists, words in the Akkadian language are written in italics.

24. When it is uncertain how a Sumerian sign is to be read, the words in transliteration are presented in capital letters.

25. Weadock, "The *Giparu* at Ur," 117.

26. C. J. Gadd, "En-an-e-du," *Iraq* 13 (1951): 33.

27. R. Caplice, É.NUN in Mesopotamian Literature," *Or* 42 (1973): 299.

28. Ibid., 118.

29. Ibid., 104.

30. Ibid.

31. Ibid., 109.

32. Stephanie Dalley et al., *The Legacy of Mesopotamia* (Oxford: Oxford University Press, 1998), 30.

33. Weadock, "The *Giparu* at Ur," 113.

CHAPTER III

1. Betty De Shong Meador, *Inanna—Lady of Largest Heart* (Austin: University of Texas Press, 2000), 94.

2. Ibid., 99.

3. Ibid., 100.

4. Hallo, *Origins*, 182. See also Sabina Franke, "Kings of Akkad," in CANE 2:835–836.

5. Meador, *Inanna*, 133.

6. Ibid., 134.

7. Ibid., 125.

8. Ibid., 175.

9. Ibid., 176.

10. Ibid.

11. Ibid.

12. Ibid., 101.

13. Ibid.

14. Ibid., 175.

15. Ibid., 134.

16. Ibid., 135.

17. Ibid., 125.

18. Jeremy Black, *Reading Sumerian Poetry* (Ithaca: Cornell University Press, 1998), 170.

19. Meador, *Inanna*, 134.

20. Hallo, *Origins,* 158.

21. Ibid.

22. Graham Cunningham, "In the Company of ni_2 'Self' and 'Fear(someness),'" in Jarle Ebeling and Graham Cunningham, eds., *Analysing Literary Sumerian—Corpus-based Approaches* (London: Equinox, 2007), 76.

23. Black, *Poetry*, 18.

24. Walter Benjamin, *Illuminations* (New York: Schocken Books, 1968), 14.

25. Black, *Poetry*, 6.

26. Ibid., 7.

27. Before his untimely death, Black supported a British group of storytellers of Mesopotamian works called "The Enheduanna Society."

28. Black, *Poetry*, 43.

29. Hallo, *Origins*, 171.

30. Gwendolyn Leick, *Mesopotamia* (London: Penguin Press, 2001), 120.

31. J. N. Postgate, *Early Mesopotamia* (London: Routledge, 1992), 26.

32. Black, *Poetry*, 44.

33. Piotr Michalowski, "Carminative Magic: Towards an Understanding of Sumerian Poetic," *ZA* 71/1 (1981): 2.

34. Black, *Poetry*, 43.

35. Annette Zgoll, *Der Rechtsfall der En-hedu-Ana im Lied nin-me-sara* (Munster: Ugarit-Verlag, 1997), 169. Unpublished translation by Tatjana Dorsch.

36. Ibid., 42.

37. Ibid., 158.

38. Ibid., 179.

39. Miguel Civil, "Les Limites de l'information textuelle," in M.-T. Barrelet, ed., *L'archeologie de l'Iraq du debut de l'epoque neolithique a 333 avant notre ere* (Paris: Colloques Internationaux de C.N.R.S., no. 580, 1980), 227:

> "D'habitude on attribue à Enheduanna, la fille de Sargon d'Akkad, tous les textes qui mentionnent son nom. Parmi ces textes se trouve l'hymne in-nin šà-gur₄-ra. . . . L'examen de sa langue et de son vocabulaire me fait soupçonner que le texte date de l'époque de Larsa. Si cette hypothèse est correcte, Enheduanna était à cette époc un nom générique pour désigner la prêtresse de Sin à Ur. Les implications de cet hymne seront très différentes selon qu'il se rapporte à une fille de Sargon ou à une fille de Rim-Sîn."

40. Weadock, "The *Giparu* at Ur," 109. See also C. J. Gadd, "En-an-e-du," *Iraq* 13 (1951): 27–39.

41. William W. Hallo and J. J. A. van Dijk, *The Exaltation of Inanna* (New Haven: Yale University Press, 1968).

42. Ibid., 1.

43. Hallo, *Origins,* 183. Hallo cites the recent discovery of a literary catalogue (Mark E. Cohen, *RA* 70 [1976]: 131f., lines 1–3) in which the three Inanna poems of Enheduanna are listed together at the beginning, "clarifying their relationship to each other and strengthening the case for attributing all three to Enheduanna," 265.

44. Ibid., 263.

45. William Hallo, "The Limits of Skepticism," *JAOS* 110/2 (1990): 191.

46. Ibid., 199.

47. Joan Goodnick Westenholz, "Enheduanna—Princess, Priestess, Poetess." Paper presented at the California Museum of Ancient Art, Los Angeles, California, May 1999, 17–20.

48. W. G. Lambert, "Ghost-writers?" in *N.A.B.U.* 2001, n. 3 (septembre).

49. Zgoll, *Der Rechtsfall der En-hedu-Ana im Lied nin-me-sara*, 181–182, citing C. Wilcke, "Der aktuelle Bezug der Sammlung der Sumerischen Templehymnen und en Fragment eines Klageliedes mit Anspielung auf sie," *ZA* 62 (1972): 35–61.

50. Ibid., 41.
51. Hallo and van Dijk, *Exaltation,* 2–3.
52. Westenholz, "Enheduanna, En-Priestess," 548.

CHAPTER IV

1. The Sumerian word múš that I have translated "radiant site" has several meanings. One corresponds to the Akkadian word *mātu,* meaning ground, territory, land. Another corresponds to the Akkadian *zīmu,* meaning appearance, glow, having to do with light. I have combined the two meanings into the phrase "radiant site."

2. As early as the fifth millennium Mesopotamian temples were built on raised platforms. The first ziggurats, built by the king Ur-Nammu in the period following that of the Akkadian empire, were larger, multiple-staged towers, a development from early platform temples.

3. William W. Hallo, "Antediluvian Cities," *JCS* 23/3 (1971): 66.

4. Ibid., 65.

5. Brian B. Schmidt, "Flood Narratives of Ancient Western Asia," in *CANE* 4:2341. Piotr Michalowski, "History as Charter: Some Observations on the Sumerian King List," *JAOS* 103/1 (1983): 239.

6. Herbert Sauren, "Nammu and Enki," in Mark E. Cohen, Daniel C. Snell, and David B. Weisberg, eds., *The Tablet and the Scroll* (Bethesda, Md.: CDL Press, 1993), 198. Sauren has separated forty-two lines from the beginning of the text "Enki and Ninmah" and argues that "this passage is a literary unit," calling this portion "Nammu and Enki." He states, "It seems that the mythology of Eridu is older than that of Nippur, but we are unable to indicate the date. We do not know if there was a pre-Sumerian name for Enki or if Nammu is of Sumerian origin," 204.

7. Ibid., 201.

8. Ibid.

9. Ibid., 203.

10. Ibid., 201–202.

11. William W. Hallo, "Enki and the Theology of Eridu," *JAOS* 116/2 (1996): 231–232.

12. Leick, *Mesopotamia,* 5–6.

13. Postgate, *Early Mesopotamia,* 23.

14. Seton Lloyd, *The Archaeology of Mesopotamia* (London: Thames and Hudson, 1978), 63.

15. Joan Oates, "Ur and Eridu, the Prehistory," *Iraq* 22 (1960): 35.

16. Ibid., 32.

17. Ibid., 45.

18. Ibid.

19. Ibid., 46.

20. Leick, *Mesopotamia,* 2–3.

21. H. L. J. Vanstiphout, "Why Did Enki Organize the World?" in I. L. Finkel and M. J. Geller, eds., *Sumerian Gods and Their Representations* (Groningen: Styx Publications, 1997), 120–121.

22. Oates, "Ur and Eridu, the Prehistory," 42.

23. Gwendolyn Leick, *Sex and Eroticism in Mesopotamian Literature* (London: Routledge, 1994), 70.

24. Mircea Eliade, *Myths, Dreams, and Mysteries* (New York: Harper and Row, 1957), 169.

CHAPTER V

1. John F. Robertson, "The Temple Economy of Old Babylonian Nippur: The Evidence for Centralized Management," in Maria de Jong Ellis, ed., *Nippur at the Centennial* (Philadelphia: University Museum, 1992), 177.

2. Biggs, *Inscriptions*, 46.

3. W. L. Lambert, "Nippur in Ancient Ideology," in Ellis, ed., *Nippur at the Centennial* (Philadelphia: University Museum, 1992), 119.

4. F. A. M. Wiggerman, "Theologies," 1869.

5. J. N. Postgate, "Royal Ideology," 399.

6. Ibid.

7. McGuire Gibson, "Patterns of Occupation at Nippur," in Ellis, ed., *Nippur at the Centennial* (Philadelphia: University Museum, 1992), 38.

8. Wiggerman, "Theologies," 1869.

9. Aage Westenholz, "Old Akkadian School Texts: Some Goals of Sargonic Scribal Education," *AfO* 25 (1974–1977): 95.

10. Ibid., 106.

11. Aage Westenholz, "The Early Excavators of Nippur," in Ellis, ed., *Nippur at the Centennial* (Philadelphia: University Museum, 1992), 291–292.

12. Ibid. 294.

13. Gibson, "Patterns," 38.

14. Lambert, "Nippur," 120.

15. Thorkild Jacobsen, *The Harps That Once . . .* (New Haven: Yale University Press, 1987), 169.

16. Piotr Michalowski, "The Unbearable Lightness of Enlil," in Jiri Prosecky, ed., *Intellectual Life of the Ancient Near East* (Prague: Oriental Institute, 1998), 242.

17. Leick, *Mesopotamia*, 152.

18. Ibid., 153.

19. Tikva Frymer-Kensky, *In the Wake of the Goddesses* (New York: Free Press, 1992), 224.

20. "Enlil and Ninlil" and "Enlil and Sud" in Black et al., The Electronic Text Corpus of Sumerian Literature [ETCSL] (Oxford: Oriental Institute, University of Oxford, 2005).

21. "Enlil and Ninlil," ETCSL.

22. Leick, *Sex*, 280.

23. Jacobsen, *Harps*, 167–180.

24. "Enlil and Ninlil," ETCSL.

25. Leick, *Sex*, 44–45.

26. "Enlil and Sud," ETCSL.

27. Sjöberg and Bergmann, "Temple Hymns," 59.

28. Mark Cohen, *The Cultic Calendars of the Ancient Near East* (Bethesda, Md.: CDL Press, 1993), 81.

29. Ibid.

30. Ibid., 107.

31. Ibid., paraphrasing J. J. A. van Dijk.

32. Ibid., 109.

33. Frymer-Kensky, *In the Wake of the Goddesses*, 21.

34. Jacobsen, *Harps*, 110.

35. Ibid., 173–174.

36. Walter Farber, "Witchcraft, Magic, and Divination in Ancient Mesopotamia," in CANE 1898.

37. Black and Green, *Gods, Demons and Symbols*, 155–156.

38. Ibid., 145.

39. A. R. George, *House Most High* (Winona Lake, Ind.: Eisenbrauns, 1993), 6.

40. Ibid., 124.

41. Ibid., 136.

42. Jacobsen, *Harps*, 107–108.

43. William W. Hallo, "Review of *The Return of Ninurta to Nippur*," *JAOS* 101/2 (1981): 254.

44. Ibid., 255.

45. Ibid., 253.

46. George, *House Most High*, 98, 132.

47. Åke W. Sjöberg, "Hymns to Ninurta with Prayers for Šūsîn of Ur and Būrsîn of Isin," in Barry L. Eichler, ed., *Kramer Anniversary Volume* (Kevelaer, Germany: Verlag Butzon and Bercker, 1976), 411.

48. McGuire Gibson, "Nippur 1990: Gula, Goddess of Healing, and an Akkadian Tomb," *Oriental Institute News and Notes*, 125 (September–October 1990): 125.

49. Jacobsen, *Harps*, 253.

50. Ibid., 254.

51. Sjöberg, "Ninurta," 417.

52. Jeremy Black, "The Sumerians in Their Landscape," in Tzvi Abusch, ed., *Riches Hidden in Secret Places* (Winona Lake, Ind.: Eisenbrauns, 2002), 52.

53. Cohen, *Calendars*, 84.

54. Sjöberg and Bergmann, "Sumerian Temple Hymns," 67.

55. George, *House Most High*, 86.

56. Meador, *Inanna*, 123–124.

57. Ibid., 123.

58. Ibid., 133.

59. George, *House Most High*, 86, 66.

60. Jacobsen, *Harps*, 157.

61. Richard A. Henshaw, *Female and Male: The Cultic Personnel* (Allison Park, Pa.: Pickwick Publications, 1994), 192.

62. Rivkah Harris, *Ancient Sippar* ([Istanbul]: Nederlands Historisch-Archaeologisch Instituut, 1975).

63. Ibid., 306.

64. Ibid., 308.

65. Ibid., 306.

66. George, *House Most High*, 117.

67. Ibid., 109.

68. Leick, *Sex*, 102, quoting E. Sollberger and J. R. Kupper, *Inscriptions Royales Sumeriennes et Akkadiennes* (Paris, 1971).

69. Thorkild Jacobsen, "Notes on Nintur," *Orientalia* 42/1–2 (1973): 283.

70. Thorkild Jacobsen, *Treasures of Darkness* (New Haven: Yale University Press, 1976), 108.

71. Rene Labat and Florence Malbran-Labat, *Manuel d'Epigraphie Akkadienne* (Paris: Librairie Orientaliste Paul Geuthner, 1995), 60. Jacobsen, *Treasures,* identifies the sign as "TU i.e.,tur$_5$," 250, n. 129.

72. Beatrice Laura Goff, *Symbols of Prehistoric Mesopotamia* (New Haven: Yale University Press, 1963), 62 and fig. 252.

73. Hallo and van Dijk, *Exaltation,* 53.

74. Biggs, *Inscriptions,* 31.

75. R. D. Biggs, "An Archaic Sumerian Version of the Kesh Temple Hymn from Tell Abu Salabikh," *ZA* 61/2 (1972): 196.

76. Gene B. Gragg, "The Kesh Temple Hymn," in A. Leo Oppenheim, ed., *Texts from Cuneiform Sources,* vol. 3 (Locust Valley, N.Y.: J. J. Augustin, 1969), 157.

77. Anne Draffkorn Kilmer, Appendix C: "The Brick of Birth," in G. Azarpey, "Proportional Guidelines in Near Eastern Art," *JNES* 46 (1987): 211.

78. Ibid., 212.

79. Ibid., 213.

80. Gragg, "The Kesh Temple Hymn," line 39, 169.

81. Ibid., line 90, 173.

82. Frymer-Kensky, *In the Wake of the Goddesses,* 20.

CHAPTER VI

1. David Rosenberg, *Abraham: The First Historical Biography* (New York: Basic Books, 2006), 63.

2. Ibid., 44.

3. Ibid., 42.

4. Ibid., 69.

5. Ibid., 51.

6. Ibid., 53.

7. See Temple Hymn 3.

8. Mark G. Hall, "A Study of the Sumerian Moon-God, Nanna/Suen" (Ph.D. diss., University of Pennsylvania, 1985), 107.

9. Frayne, "Inscriptions," 145–146.

10. Hildegard Lewy, "Assyria, c. 2600–1816 B.C.," in I. E. S. Edwards, C. J. Gadd, and N. G. L. Hammond, eds., *Cambridge Ancient History,* vol. 1, part 2 (Cambridge: Cambridge University Press, 1971), 736.

11. Ibid., 736.

12. Hall, "The Sumerian Moon-God, Nanna/Suen," 225.

13. Ibid. 464.

14. Cohen, *Cultic Calendars*, 3.

15. Ibid., 4.

16. Ibid., 401.

17. Lewy, "Assyria," 736.

18. Alexander Marschack, *The Roots of Civilization* (New York: McGraw-Hill, 1972), 136.

19. Judy Grahn, *Blood, Bread, and Roses: How Menstruation Created the World* (Boston: Beacon Press, 1993).

20. Chris Knight, *Blood Relations: Menstruation and the Origins of Culture* (New Haven: Yale University Press, 1991).

21. Among others offering a positive and substantive attitude toward menstruation and its relationship to the building of culture, Knight cites T. Buckley and A. Gottlieb, eds., *Blood Magic: The Anthropology of Menstruation* (Berkeley: University of California Press, 1988); E. Durkheim, "La prohibition de l'ineste et ses origines," in *Incest: The Nature and Origin of the Taboo*, trans. E. Sagarin (New York: Stuart Press, 1963 [1898]); J. G. Frazer, *The Golden Bough*, 2d ed., vol. 3 (London: Macmillan, 1900).

22. Knight, *Blood Relations*, 375.

23. Åke Sjöberg, "Miscellaneous Sumerian Hymns," za 63 (1973): 32.

24. Hall, "The Sumerian Moon-God, Nanna/Suen," 471–475, 728–730.

25. Sjöberg and Bergmann, *Hymns*, line 109, text C.

26. Ibid., 133–134.

27. Jacob Klein, "Shulgi of Ur: King of a Neo-Sumerian Empire," in cane 2:846.

28. Hall, "The Sumerian Moon-God, Nanna/Suen," 132.

29. Klein, "Shulgi," 846.

30. Ibid., 847.

31. Hall, "The Sumerian Moon-God, Nanna/Suen," 331.

32. Hallo, "Cities," 62.

33. Sir Max E. L. Mallowan, "The Early Dynastic Period in Mesopotamia" in I. E. S. Edwards, C. J. Gadd, and N. G. L. Hammond, eds., *Cambridge Ancient History*, vol. 1, part 2 (Cambridge: Cambridge University Press, 1971), 281–282.

34. Hall, "The Sumerian Moon-God, Nanna/Suen," 814–828.

35. Frymer-Kensky, *In the Wake of the Goddesses*, 43.

36. Leick, *Sex*, 196–197.

37. Jacobsen, *Harps*, 59.

38. George, *House Most High*, 64, 65, 107, 156.

39. Graham Cunningham, *Deliver Me from Evil: Mesopotamian Incantations, 2500–1500 B.C.* (Roma: Editrice Pontificio Instituto Biblioco, 1997), 77.

40. Black and Green, *Gods, Demons and Symbols*, 163.

41. Hall, "The Sumerian Moon-God, Nanna/Suen," 486.

42. Henshaw, *Female and Male*, 143–150.

43. George, *House Most High*, 97, 86.

44. Hall, "The Sumerian Moon-God, Nanna/Suen," 330.

45. Ibid., 327.

46. Cohen, *Cultic Calendars*, 400–401.

47. Ibid., 414.

48. Ibid., 401.

49. Ibid., 402.

50. Ibid., 409.

51. Ibid.

52. Ibid., 412.

53. Ibid., 404.

54. A. J. Ferrar, *Nanna-Suen's Journey to Nippur* (Rome: Biblical Institute Press, 1973), 1.

55. Ibid., 400.

CHAPTER VII

1. Piotr Steinkeller, "Archaic City Seals and the Question of Early Babylonian Unity," in Tzvi Abusch, ed., *Riches Hidden in Secret Places* (Winona Lake, Ind.: Eisenbrauns, 2002), 249–258.

2. Postgate, *Early Mesopotamia,* fig. 2:8, p. 33, #2.

3. Steinkeller, "Seals," 250.

4. Thorkild Jacobsen, "Early Political Development in Mesopotamia," ZA 52 (1957): 106–109.

5. J. L. Huot, "Larsa," in *Reallexikon du Assyriologie* (Berlin: Walter de Gruyter, 1983), 500–507.

6. Elizabeth C. Stone, "The Development of Cities in Ancient Mesopotamia," in *CANE* 1:239.

7. Rivkah Harris, *Gender and Aging in Mesopotamia* (Norman: University of Oklahoma Press, 2000), 109, quoting T. Jacobsen, "A Maidenly Inanna," in *JANES* 22 (1993): 63–68.

8. Wolfgang Heimpel, "The Sun at Night and the Doors of Heaven in Babylonian Texts," *Journal of Cuneiform Studies* 38 (1986): 143.

9. Black, *Poetry,* 179.

10. Ibid., 180.

11. Betty De Shong Meador, *Uncursing the Dark* (Chicago: Chiron Publications, 1992), 87.

12. Heimpel, "Sun," 151.

13. Ibid., 131.

14. Dina Katz, *The Image of the Netherworld in the Sumerian Sources* (Bethesda, Md.: CDL Press, 2003), 229.

15. Heimpel, "Sun," 149.

16. Black, *Poetry,* 180.

17. Heimpel, "Sun," 128.

18. Ibid., 129.

19. A. J. Ferrara, *Nanna-Suen's Journey to Nippur,* 91–92.

20. Cohen, *Cultic Calendars,* 466.

21. Volkert Haas, "Death and the Afterlife in Hittite Thought," in *CANE* 3:2021.

22. Katz, *Image of the Netherworld,* 101.

23. F. A. M. Wiggermann, "Transtigridian Snake Gods," in Finkel and Geller, eds., *Sumerian Gods,* 47–48.

24. Sjöberg and Bergmann, "Sumerian Temple Hymns," 88.

25. Haas, "Death and the Afterlife," 2021.

26. Cohen, *Cultic Calendars*, 470.

27. Jacobsen, *Harps*, 59.

28. Ibid.

29. Frymer-Kensky, *In the Wake of the Goddesses*, 111.

30. The word for the harp, *zannaru*, is an Akkadian word for an ear-shaped harp. Personal communication from Anne D. Kilmer.

31. Henshaw, *Female and Male*, 34. Henshaw places the shita officials among the highest ranking cult personnel in the temples.

32. E. Douglas Van Buren, "The God Ningizzida," *Iraq* 1 (1934): 65.

33. Jacobsen, *Harps*, 56.

34. W. G. Lambert, "A New Babylonian Descent to the Netherworld," in Tiva Abusch, John Huehnergard, and Piotr Steinkeller, eds., *Lingering Over Words* (Atlanta: Scholars Press, 1990), 289–300.

35. Jacobsen, *Harps*, 80–83.

36. Lambert, "New Descent," 295.

37. Jo Ann Scurlock, "Death and the Afterlife in Ancient Mesopotamian Thought" in CANE 3:1888.

38. Jacobsen, *Harps*, 59.

39. Lambert, "New Descent," 300.

40. Wiggerman, "Snake Gods," 48.

41. Ibid.

42. Hallo and van Dijk, *Exaltation*, 8.

43. Meador, *Inanna*.

44. Harris, *Gender*, 158–159.

45. Ibid.

46. H. L. J. Vanstiphout, "Inanna/Ishtar as a Figure of Controversy," in H. G. Kippenberg, ed., *Struggles of Gods* (Berlin: Mouton, 1984), 232–233.

47. Harris, *Gender*, 167–168, citing Anne Kilmer, "An Oration on Babylon," *Altorientalische Forschungen* 18 (1991): 9–22.

48. Jacobsen, *Treasures*, 135ff.

49. Harris, *Gender*, 158, citing J. Bottéro, "La femme, l'amour et la guerre en Mesopotamie ancienne," in *Poikilia etudes offerts a Jean-Pierre Vernan* (Paris: Editions de L'ecole des Hautes Etudes, 1987), 165–183.

50. Meador, *Inanna*, 179.

51. Ibid., 171.

52. Ibid., 134–135.

53. Szarzyńska, *Sumerica*, 39, 141, 146.

54. Meador, *Inanna*, 118.

55. See Yitzchak Sefati, *Love Songs in Sumerian Literature* (Jerusalem: Bar-Ilan University Press, 1998).

56. Meador, *Inanna*, 19–20.

57. Leick, *Sex*, 53, citing myth translation from S. Dalley, *Myths from Mesopotamia* (Oxford: Oxford University Press, 1989), 79.

58. Ibid.

59. Meador, *Inanna*, 179.

60. Ibid., 127–128.

61. Guillermo Algaze, *The Uruk World System*, 2d ed. (Chicago: University of Chicago Press, 2005), 2.

62. Ibid., 6.

63. Leick, *Mesopotamia*, 33.

64. Meador, *Inanna*, 177.

65. Ibid., 171–180.

66. Ibid., 117.

67. Simo Parpola, *Assyrian Prophecies* (Helsinki: Helsinki University Press, 1997), xxi.

68. Thorkild Jacobsen, "Toward the Image of Tammuz," in William L. Moran, ed., *Toward the Image of Tammuz and Other Essays on Mesopotamian History and Culture* (Cambridge: Harvard University Press, 1970), 28–29.

69. The Sumerian King List, compiled at the beginning of the second millennium, is a largely fictional account of the succession of kings, all purported to have been appointed in heaven.

70. Raphael Kutscher, "The Cult of Dumuzi/Tammuz" in Jacob Klein and Aaron Skaist, eds., *Bar-Ilan Studies in Assyriology*, (Ramat Gan, Israel: Bar-Illan University, 1990), 32.

71. Jerrold S. Cooper, "Gendered Sexuality in Sumerian Love Poetry," in Finkel and Geller, eds., *Sumerian Gods*, 86.

72. Sefati, *Love Songs*, 33.

73. Cooper, "Gendered Sexuality," 87.

74. Ibid., 88.

75. Meador, *Inanna*, 11.

76. Leick, *Sex*, 71.

77. Jacobsen, *Harps*, 50. For this text, "Dumuzi's Dream," and others, see "Dumuzi Texts," in *Harps*, 1–84.

78. *The Holy Bible: Revised Standard Version* (New York: Thomas Nelson and Sons, 1952), 867.

79. Alasdair Livingstone, "How the Common Man Influences the Gods of Sumer," in Finkel and Geller, eds., *Sumerian Gods*, 220.

80. Cooper, "Gendered Sexuality," 97.

81. Kutscher, "Dumuzi/Tammuz," 44.

82. Jacobsen, *Harps*, 24–25.

83. Ibid., 27.

84. Leick, *Sex*, 100.

85. Ibid., 101.

86. Katz, *Image of the Netherworld*, 386, n. 10, citing Gebhard Selz, *Untersuchungen zur Götterwelt des altsumerischen Stadtstaates von Lagash* (Philadelphia, 1995), 132.

87. Katz, *Image of the Netherworld*, 176.

88. Ibid.

89. Meador, *Uncursing*, 22.

90. Frymer-Kensky, *In the Wake of the Goddesses*, 37.

91. Wolfgang Heimpel, "The Lady of Girsu," in Tzvi Abusch, ed., *Riches Hidden in Secret Places* (Winona Lake, Ind.: Eisenbrauns, 2002), 156.

92. Ibid.

93. Ibid.

94. Graham Cunningham, *'Deliver Me from Evil,'* 51.

95. Ibid.

96. Frymer-Kensky, *In the Wake of the Goddesses,* 43.

97. Cunningham, *'Deliver Me from Evil,'* 14.

98. Henshaw, *Female and Male,* 145.

99. Frymer-Kensky, *In the Wake of the Goddesses,* 35–36.

100. Robert Biggs, "Pre-Sargonic Riddles" *JNES* 32/1 (1973): 28–29.

CHAPTER VIII

1. Hallo, "Return of Ninurta," 255.

2. Harriet Crawford, *Sumer and the Sumerians,* 2d ed. (Cambridge: Cambridge University Press, 2004), 10.

3. Postgate, *Early Mesopotamia,* 32.

4. Postgate, "Royal Ideology," 397.

5. Hallo, "Enki," 231. Hallo calls Lagash "a leading actor in the outgoing Early Dynastic Period and once again in the late Sargonic Period. Lagash was dormant, if not actually suppressed, in the Ur III and early Isin Periods but surfaced once more under the Dynasty of Larsa and thereafter."

6. Jacobsen, *Treasures,* 80.

7. See Black and Green, *Gods, Demons and Symbols,* 138; Jacobsen, *Harps,* 234; Hallo, "Return of Ninurta," 254; W. G. Lambert, "The Historical Development of the Mesopotamian Pantheon: A Study in Sophisticated Polytheism," in Hans Goedicke and J. J. M. Roberts, eds., *Unity and Diversity* (Baltimore: Johns Hopkins University Press, 1975), 193.

8. Hallo, "Return of Ninurta," 255.

9. Heimpel, "Lady of Girsu," 155.

10. Ibid., 158. See also Steinkeller, "On Rulers," 113.

11. Ibid., 160.

12. Frymer-Kensky, *In the Wake of the Goddesses,* 70.

13. William W. Hallo, "The Limits of Skepticism," 198.

14. Postgate, *Early Mesopotamia,* 269.

15. Hallo, *Origins,* 332.

16. Black and Green, *Gods, Demons and Symbols,* 107; Donald P. Hansen, "Art of the Akkadian Dynasty," in Joan Aruz, ed., *Art of the First Cities* (New York: Metropolitan Museum of Art, 2003), 190, 191.

17. Gebhard J. Selz, "The Holy Drum, the Spear, and the Harp," in I. L. Finkel and M. J. Geller, eds., *Sumerian Gods and Their Representations* (Styx Publications: Groningen, 1997), 174.

18. Irene Winter, "Aesthetics in Ancient Mesopotamian Art" in CANE 4:2577.

19. Ibid.

20. Cohen, *Cultic Calendars,* 9.

21. Ibid., 37.

22. Ibid., 470.

23. S. N. Kramer, *The Sumerians* (Chicago: University of Chicago Press, 1963), 64.

24. Ibid.

25. Jacobsen, *Harps*, 387.

26. Heimpel, "Lady of Girsu," 159.

27. George, *House Most High*, 157.

28. Sjöberg and Bergmann, "Sumerian Temple Hymns," 104.

29. Jeremy Black et al., ETCSL, line 263; Sjöberg and Bergmann, "Sumerian Temple Hymns," 104.

30. Leick, *Sex*, 132, citing W. H. P. Römer, *Sumerische 'Konigshymnen' der Isin-Zeit* (Leiden, 1965), 238.

31. Ibid., 84, citing T. Jacobsen, *Harps*, 18.

32. Ibid., 132.

33. Sjöberg and Bergmann, "Sumerian Temple Hymns," 105.

34. Postgate, *Early Mesopotamia*, 132.

35. Frymer-Kensky, *In the Wake of the Goddesses*, 37.

36. Sjöberg and Bergmann, "Sumerian Temple Hymns," 105.

37. Postgate, *Early Mesopotamia*, 186.

38. Ibid.

39. George F. Bass, "Sea and River Craft in the Ancient Near East" in CANE 3:1421.

40. Postgate, *Early Mesopotamia*, 115.

41. Ibid., 61–62.

42. Ibid., 26. Postgate omits line 266 of the hymn: "Etarsirsir—divine decision and me devising" (my translation).

43. Franz Wiggermann, "Scenes from the Shadow Side," in M. E. Vogelzang and H. L. J. Vanstiphout, eds., *Mesopotamian Poetic Language* (Groningen: Styx Publications, 1996), 209.

44. Ibid.

45. Vanstiphout, "Enki Organize," 117.

46. Ibid., 121.

47. Ibid., 127.

48. Leo Oppenheim, *The Interpretation of Dreams in the Ancient Near East* (Philadelphia: American Philosophical Society, 1956), 237.

49. Jacobsen, *Harps*, 389. Siratr was Nanshe's temple in Ninâ.

50. Miguel Civil, "The Song of the Plowing Oxen," in Eichler, ed., *Kramer Anniversary Volume*, 83.

51. Ibid., 84.

52. Ibid.

53. Ibid., 87.

54. Oppenheim, *Dreams*, 237.

55. Ibid., 301.

56. Meador, *Inanna*, 178.

57. Julia M. Asher-Greve, "The Oldest Female Oneiromancer," in Jean-Marie

Durand, ed., *La Femme dans le Proche-Orient Antique* (Paris: Editions Recherche sur les Civilisations, 1987), 32.

58. Wolfgang Heimpel, "The Nanshe Hymn," *JCS* 33/2 (1981): 83.

59. Ibid., 68.

60. Jacobsen, *Harps*, 68.

61. Sjöberg and Bergman, "Sumerian Temple Hymns," line 290, 109.

62. Selz, "The Holy Drum," 175 and fn. 179.

63. Meador, *Inanna*, 123, 133.

64. Harris, *Gender*, 53, 90.

65. Postgate, *Early Mesopotamia*, 235.

66. Ibid.

67. Cohen, *Cultic Calendars*, 60.

68. Jacobsen, *Harps*, 450.

69. Kutscher, "Dumuzi/Tammuz," 37.

70. Sjöberg and Bergman, "Sumerian Temple Hymns," 110.

CHAPTER IX

1. Meador, *Inanna*, 179.

2. Jacobsen, *Harps*, 330. See further evidence in Laura D. Steele, "Review of D. Bolger and N. Serwint, eds., *Engendering Aphrodite: Woman and Society in Ancient Cyprus,*" *Nin* 4 (2003): 125.

3. Meador, *Dark*, 84.

4. Meador, *Inanna*, 176.

5. Henshaw, *Female and Male*, 228. See also Martha T. Roth, "Marriage, Divorce, and the Prostitute in Ancient Mesopotamia," in Christopher A. Faraone and Laura K. McClure, eds., *Prostitutes and Courtesans in the Ancient World* (Madison: University of Wisconsin Press, 2006), 21–39. Roth says, "It is clear that, other than this highly restricted and structured 'sacred marriage,' there was no ritualized or institutionalized sexual intercourse associated with Mesopotamian religions or temples," 23.

6. Ibid., 233.

7. Ibid., 206–215.

8. Sjöberg and Bergman, "Sumerian Temple Hymns," 123.

9. Aruz, *Art of the First Cities*, 78.

10. Hans J. Nissen, "Western Asia before the Age of Empires," in CANE 2:804–805.

11. Cohen, *Cultic Calendars*, 84.

12. Ibid., 161–178.

13. Aruz, *Art of the First Cities*, 50.

14. Szarzynska, *Sumerica*, 40.

15. Selz, "Holy Drum," 187n26. Selz says, "There can be little doubt that the astral aspects of Inanna go back as far as Uruk IV" (3300–3100 BCE).

16. Bendt Alster, "Early Patterns in Mesopotamian Literature," in Barry L. Eichler, ed., *Kramer Anniversary Volume* (Kevelaer, Germany: Verlag Butzon and Bercker, 1976), 15.

17. Ibid., 20.

18. Ibid., 19.

19. Ibid., 63.

20. Szarzynska, *Sumerica*, 142.

21. Lloyd, *Archeology of Mesopotamia*, 63.

22. Alster, "Early Patterns," 17.

23. Szarzynska, *Sumerica*, 142.

24. Ibid., 115.

25. Biggs, *Inscriptions*, 47.

26. Szarzynska, *Sumerica*, 109.

27. Ibid., 111–112.

28. Sarzynska, *Sumerica*, 129, n. 1, explains, "The word hud$_2$ means literally 'bright, shine,' and it is expressed in writing with the pictogram UD which appears as the sun rising in the morning. The word sig is expressed with the same pictogram, only in the rotated position, thus showing the sun setting in the evening."

29. Alster, "Early Patterns," 16.

30. Kramer, *Sumerians*, 173.

31. Jacobsen, *Harps*, 332.

32. Ibid., 314–315.

33. W. G. Lambert, "Sumerian Gods: Combining the Evidence of Texts and Art," in I. L. Finkel and M. J. Geller, eds., *Sumerian Gods and Their Representations* (Groningen: Styx Publications, 1997), 7.

34. D. R. Frayne, *The Early Dynastic List of Geographical Names* (New Haven: American Oriental Society, 1992), 37. Citing Robert McC. Adams, *The Heartland of Cities* (Chicago: University of Chicago Press, 1981).

35. Idem.

36. William L. Moran, "The Keš Temple Hymn and the Canonical Temple List," in Barry L. Eichler, ed., *Kramer Anniversary Volume* (Kevelaer, Germany: Verlag Butzon and Bercker, 1976), 338.

37. Ibid., 338, n. 32.

38. Jacobsen, "Nintur," 293.

39. Ibid., 285.

40. Frymer-Kensky, *In the Wake of the Goddesses*, 223.

41. Sjöberg and Bergmann, "Sumerian Temple Hymns," 71–73.

42. Gragg, "The Kesh Temple Hymn," 161.

43. Ibid., 160.

44. Sjöberg and Bergmann, "Sumerian Temple Hymns," 120.

45. Aruz, *Art of the First Cities*, 63–64.

46. Biggs, "Kesh Temple Hymn," 200.

47. Jacobsen says in "Nintur," 384, her daughter is Lisin, but in *Harps*, 60, he states that Lulil is the son of Ninhursag of Adab: "Lulil we know to have been a dying god. His mother was Ninhursaga in Adab, and laments for him survive."

48. Aruz, *Art of the First Cities*, 54.

49. Dietz Otto Edzard, "The Names of the Sumerian Temples," in I. L. Finkel and J. J. Geller, eds., *Sumerian Gods and Their Representations* (Groningen: Styx Publications, 1997), 162. Edzard translates the name of the temple as "Huge Palace."

50. Kramer, *Sumerians*, 206.

51. Frymer-Kensky, *In the Wake of the Goddesses*, 49.

52. Asher-Greve, "The Oldest Female Oneiromancer," 30.

53. Hallo, "Theology of Eridu," 233.

54. Robert D. Biggs, "Medicine, Surgery, and Public Health in Ancient Mesopotamia," in *CANE* 3:1918.

55. Vanstiphout, "Enki," 125–126.

56. Meador, *Inanna*, 133.

57. Joan G. Westenholz, "Metaphorical Language in the Poetry of Love in the Ancient Near East," in *Proceedings 38th RAI* (Paris, 1992), 381–387.

58. See the remarks on hierodule in the discussion of Temple Hymn 25.

59. Sjöberg and Bergmann, "Sumerian Temple Hymns," 123.

60. Meador, *Dark*, 60.

61. Frayne, *Sargonic and Gutian Periods*, 80.

62. Hallo, *Origins*, 233.

63. Crawford, *Sumer and the Sumerians*, 47.

64. Cohen, *Cultic Calendars*, 188.

CHAPTER X

1. Frayne, *Geographical Names*, 51.

2. Ibid., 5, 8; Dominique Charpin, "L'énumération des villes dans le prologue du <Code de Hammurabi>," *N.A.B.U.* 1 (mars 2003): 2–3.

3. Åke W. Sjöberg, "Hymn to Numušda with a Prayer for King Siniqišam of Larsa and a Hymn to Ninurta," *Orientalia Suecana* 22 (1973): 110.

4. Ibid., 111.

5. Ibid., 119.

6. Samuel Noah Kramer, "The Marriage of Martu," in Jacob Klein and Aaron Skaist, eds., *Bar-Ilan Studies in Assyriology* (Ramat Gan, Israel: Bar-Ilan University, 1990), 11–22; Jacob Klein, "The God Martu in Sumerian Literature," in I. L. Finkel and M. J. Geller, eds., *Sumerian Gods* (Groningen: Styx Publications, 1997), 99–116.

7. Klien, "Martu," 116.

8. Ibid., 102.

9. Ibid., 113.

10. Ibid.

11. *Repertoire Geographique des Textes Cuneiformes*, Vol. 1: *Presargonic and Sargonic*, 1977, 114.

12. Sjöberg and Bergmann, "Sumerian Temple Hymns," 127.

CHAPTER XI

1. Algaze, *Uruk World*, 111.

2. Ibid., 45.

3. Postgate, *Early Mesopotamia*, 7–8.

4. Ibid., 7.

5. Wiggerman, "Snake Gods," 48.

6. Ibid., 43. Wiggerman cites this passage from the *Stele of the Vultures,* a prescribed punishment for one who breaks an oath.

7. Ibid.

8. Ibid., fig. 4/d, 53.

9. Ibid., 37, n. 40.

10. Ibid., 43, n. 89.

11. Jacobsen, *Harps,* 53.

12. Ibid., 61.

13. Wiggerman, "Snake Gods," 44.

14. Ibid., 48.

15. Algaze, *Uruk World,* 14.

16. Wiggerman, "Snake Gods," 48.

17. Ibid., 35.

18. Ibid.

19. Ibid., 48.

20. Postgate, *Early Mesopotamia,* 7.

21. Hallo, "Antediluvian Cities," 60.

22. Robert McC. Adams, *The Land Behind Baghdad* (Chicago: University of Chicago Press, 1965), 145–46.

23. Wiggerman, "Snake Gods," 38, 52, fig. 3c.

24. Ibid., 37.

25. Sabina Franke, "The Kings of Akkad," 832.

CHAPTER XII

1. Katz, *The Image of the Netherworld,* 52–53.

2. Nissen, *Early History,* 145.

3. Postgate, *Early Mesopotamia,* 137.

4. Ibid.

5. Crawford, *Sumer and the Sumerians,* 85.

6. Wall-Romana, "An Areal Location of Agade," 208.

7. Hallo and Simpson, *The Ancient Near East,* 53.

8. Jack M. Sasson, "King Hammurabi of Babylon," in CANE 2:912.

9. Wiggerman, "Snake Gods," 36.

10. Selz, "Holy Drum," 171, n. 72.

11. Harris, *Gender,* 129. See also Erica Reiner, *Your Thwarts in Pieces Your Mooring Rope Cut* (Detroit: Horace H. Rackham School of Graduate Studies at the University of Michigan, 1985), 50–59.

12. Scurlock, "Death and the Afterlife," CANE 3:1887.

13. Black et al., "Enlil and Ninlil," ETCSL.

14. Katz, *The Image of the Netherworld,* 411.

15. Ibid., 416.

16. Scurlock, "Death and the Afterlife," CANE 3:1887.

17. Jean Bottéro, *Religion in Ancient Mesopotamia* (Chicago: University of Chicago Press, 2001), 211.

18. Frayne, *Early Names,* 13.

19. Postgate, *Early Mesopotamia*, 306, n. 32.

20. Frayne, *Early Names*, 14.

21. See Zgoll, 181-182, *Der Rechtsfall der En-hedu-Ana im Lied nin-me-sara*, citing C. Wilcke (see n. 49, chapter 3).

22. Meador, *Inanna*, 89.

23. Donald Matthews, "Legal and Social Institutions of Ancient Mesopotamia," in CANE 1:471.

24. Lambert, "Pantheon," 193.

25. The emphasis on law and justice throughout Mesopotamian history, both north and south, is in contrast to the biblical report in II Kings 17/31, where the "Sepharvites burned their children in the fire to . . . the gods of Sepharvaim." The king of Assyria, in this account, brought people from "Sepharvaim," thought to be Sippar, to occupy Sumaria, a territory on the Mediterranean, where they worshiped their own gods, not the god of Israel.

26. Postgate, *Early Mesopotamia*, 253.

27. Leick, *Cities*, 169.

28. Postgate, *Early Mesopotamia*, 267.

29. Frayne, *Inscriptions*, 157.

30. Franke, "Kings of Akkad," 831-832.

31. Leick, *Mesopotamia*, 168.

32. Ibid.

33. Harris, *Gender*, 152.

34. Postgate, *Early Mesopotamia*, 131.

35. Harris, *Ancient Sippar*, 304.

36. Postgate, *Early Mesopotamia*, 131.

37. Ibid.

38. Irene J. Winter, "Women in Public," 200-201.

39. Meador, *Inanna*, 123-124.

40. Ibid., 133.

41. Jacobsen, "Nintur," 293-295.

42. Wall-Romana, "An Areal Location of Agade," 218-221.

43. Ibid., 282.

44. Ibid., 283.

45. Sjöberg and Bergmann, "Sumerian Temple Hymns," 72-73; Jacobsen, "Nintur," 285.

46. Jacobsen, "Nintur," 280.

47. Ibid., 294.

48. Ibid.

49. Ibid., 292.

50. Wall-Romana, "An Areal Location of Agade," 218.

51. Gùb-ZU in hymn 40 refers to the left (side); á-zi-da in hymn 41 is often translated as "right arm," but the parallel in the two hymns from the same city suggests location, left and right. Á-zi-da occurs as an epithet of temples, meaning right arm of the deity occupant of the temple.

52. A similar line (#143) occurs in Temple Hymn 10 to Asarluhi in Kuar re "traitors": "he spits all over them."

53. Meador, *Inanna*, 91, 117, 171.

54. Ibid., 117, 118.

55. Ibid., 99.

56. Dominique Charpin, "The History of Ancient Mesopotamia: An Overview," in CANE 2:810.

57. Leick, *Mesopotamia*, 97.

58. Postgate, *Early Mesopotamia*, 78, quoting J. S. Cooper, *The Curse of Agade* (Baltimore: Johns Hopkins University Press, 1983), 50–51.

59. Charpin, "History," CANE 2:810.

60. Postgate, *Early Mesopotamia*, 267.

61. Harvey Weiss, "Kish, Akkad and Agade," *JAOS* 95/3 (1975): 446.

62. Ibid., 447.

63. Ibid., 451.

64. Ibid., 434.

65. Leick, *Mesopotamia*, 108.

66. Wall-Romana, "An Areal Location of Agade," 209.

67. Ibid., 207.

68. Ibid., 209.

69. Ibid., 238.

70. Ibid., 243.

71. Ibid., 244.

72. Black and Green, *Gods, Demons and Symbols*, 106–107.

73. Sjöberg and Bergman, "Sumerian Temple Hymns," 146.

74. Ibid.

CHAPTER XIII

1. Miguel Civil, "Enlil and Ninlil: The Marriage of Sud," *JAOS* 103/1 (1983): 45.

2. Ibid.; Frayne, *List*, 98.

3. Saba is also the name of the city in southwest Iran where soapwort grows.

4. Algaze, *The Uruk World System*, 16; see also the discussion of Temple Hymn 1.

5. Ibid., 4.

6. Ibid., 6.

7. Leick, *Cities*, 34–35.

8. Denise Schmandt-Besserat, *Before Writing*, vol. 1, *From Counting to Cuneiform* (Austin: University of Texas Press, 1992), 17–48 and throughout.

9. Leick, *Cities*, 66–67.

10. Harriet P. Martin et al., *The Fara Tablets* (Bethesda, Md.: CDL Press, 2001), vii.

11. Ibid., 15.

12. Biggs, *Inscriptions*, 28.

13. Daniel Reisman, "A 'Royal' Hymn of Isib-Erra to the Goddess Nisaba," in Barry Eichler, ed., *Kramer Anniversary Volume*, 362.

14. Ibid., 361.

15. Ibid., 359.

16. Jacobsen, *Harps*, 378–79. Nidaba is another way of writing Nisaba.

17. Sjöberg and Bergmann, "Sumerian Temple Hymns," 84.

18. Frymer-Kinsky, 39–40 quoting H.L.J. Vanstiphout, "Lipit-Eshtar's Praise in the Edubba," *JCS* 30 (1978):33–61.

19. Jacobsen, *Harps,* 301.

20. Hallo, *Origins,* 87.

21. Ibid.

22. Alster, "Early Patterns," p. 17; Sjöberg and Bergmann, "Sumerian Temple Hymns," 148, line 140.

23. Vanstiphout, "Enki," 126.

24. Jacobsen, *Harps,* 412.

Abusch, Tzvi, ed. *Riches Hidden in Secret Places: Ancient Near Eastern Studies in Memory of Thorkild Jacobsen*. Winona Lake, Ind.: Eisenbrauns, 2002.

Abusch, Tzvi, John Huehnergard, Piotr Steinkeller, eds. *Lingering Over Words*. Atlanta: Scholars Press, 1990.

Adams, Robert McC. *The Land Behind Baghdad*. Chicago: University of Chicago Press, 1965.

———. *The Heartland of Cities*. Chicago: University of Chicago Press, 1981.

Algaze, Guillermo. *The Uruk World System, Second Edition*. Chicago: The University of Chicago Press, 2005.

Algaze, Guillermo. "Ancient Mesopotamia at the Dawn of Civilization: The Evolution of an Urban Landscape." Department of Archeology, University of California, San Diego. Computer copy, 2006.

Alster, Bendt. "Early Patterns in Mesopotamian Literature." In *Kramer Anniversary Volume*, edited by Berry L. Eichler. Kevelaer, Germany: Verlag Butzon and Bercker, 1976.

———. "Interaction of Oral and Written Poetry in Early Mesopotamian Literature." In *Mesopotamian Epic Literature*, edited by Marianna E. Vogelzang and Herman L. J. Vanstiphout. Lewiston, N.Y.: Edwin Mellen Press, 1992.

Aruz, Joan, ed. *Art of the First Cities*. New York: Metropolitan Museum of Art, 2003.

Asher-Greve, J. M. "The Oldest Female Oneiromancer." In *La Femme dans le Proche-Orient Antique*, edited by Jean-Marie Durand. Paris: Editions Recherche sur les Civilisations, 1987.

Bahrani, Zainab. *Women of Babylon*. London: Routledge, 2001.

Bass, George F. "Sea and River Craft in the Ancient Near East." In CANE 3:1421.

Benjamin, Walter. *Illuminations*. New York: Schocken Books, 1968.

Biggs, Robert D. "An Archaic Sumerian Version of the Kesh Temple Hymn from Tell Abu Salabikh." ZA 61/2 (1972): 193-207.

————. "Pre-Sargonic Riddles from Lagash." *JNES* 32/1 (1973).

————. *Inscriptions from Tell Abu Salabikh*. Chicago: University of Chicago Press, 1974.

————. "Medicine, Surgery, and Public Health in Ancient Mesopotamia." In CANE 3:1911–1924.

Black, Jeremy. *Reading Sumerian Poetry*. Ithaca: Cornell University Press, 1998.

————. "The Sumerians in Their Landscape." In *Riches Hidden in Secret Places*, edited by Tzvi Abusch. Winona Lake, Ind.: Eisenbrauns, 2002.

————. "En-hedu-ana Not the Composer of the Temple Hymns." *N.A.B.U.*, no. 1 (March 2002).

Black, Jeremy, G. Cunningham, E. Fluckiger-Hawker, E. Robson, and G. Zólyomi. The Electronic Text Corpus of Sumerian Literature. Available: http://www-etcsl.orient .ox.ac.uk/. Oxford: Oxford University, 2004.

Black, Jeremy, and Anthony Green. *Gods, Demons and Symbols of Ancient Mesopotamia*. Austin: University of Texas Press, 1995.

Bottéro, Jean. "La femme, l'amour et la guerre en Mesopotamie ancienne." In *Poikilia études offertes à Jean-Pierre Vernand*. Paris: Éditions de l'École des Hautes Études, 1987.

————. *Religion in Ancient Mesopotamia*. Chicago: University of Chicago Press, 2001.

Braidwood, R. J., and B. Howe et al. *Prehistoric Investigations in Iraqi Kurdistan*. Oriental Institute Publication no. 31. Chicago: University of Chicago Press, 1960.

Burns, A. R. *The Lyric Age of Greece*. Glasgow: Minerva Press, 1968.

Caplice. R. É.NUN in Mesopotamian Literature." *Or* 42 (1973): 299–305.

Charpin, Dominique, "The History of Ancient Mesopotamia: An Overview." In CANE 2:807–829.

————. "L'énumération des villes dans le prologue du <Code de Hammurabi>. *N.A.B.U.*, no. 1 (March 2003): 2–3.

Civil, Miguel. "The Song of the Plowing Oxen." In *Kramer Anniversary Volume*, edited by Barry L. Eichler. Kevelaer, Germany: Verlag Butzon and Bercker, 1976.

————. "Les limites de l'information textuelle." In *L'archeologie de l'Iraq du debut de l'epoque neolithique a 333 avant notre ere*, edited by M.-T. Barrelet. Paris: Colloques Internationaux de C.N.R.S., no. 580, 1980.

————. "Enlil and Ninlil: The Marriage of Sud. *JAOS* 103/1, 1983.

————. "Ancient Mesopotamian Lexicography." In CANE 4:2305–2314.

Cohen, Mark. *The Cultic Calendars of the Ancient Near East*. Bethesda, Md.: CDL Press, 1993.

Cohen, Sol. "Enmerkar and the Lord of Aratta." Ph.D. diss. University of Pennsylvania, 1973.

Collon, Dominique. "Depictions of Priests and Priestesses in the Ancient Near East." In *Priests and Officials in the Ancient Near East*, edited by Kazuko Watanabe. Heidelberg: Universitatsverlag C. Winter, 1999.

Cooper, J. S. *The Curse of Agade*. Baltimore: Johns Hopkins University Press, 1983.

————. "Enki's Member: Eros and Irrigation in Sumerian Literature." In *Dumu-é-dub-ba-a: Studies in Honor of Åke W. Sjöberg*, edited by Hermann Behrens, Darlene Loding, Martha T. Roth. Philadelphia: Samuel Noah Kramer Fund, University Museum, 1989.

————. "Babbling On: Recovering Mesopotamian Orality." In *Mesopotamian Epic Literature*, edited by Marianna E. Vogelzang and Herman L. J. Vanstiphout. Lewiston, N.Y.: Edwin Mellen Press, 1992.

————. "Gendered Sexuality in Sumerian Love Poetry." In *Sumerian Gods and Their Representations*, edited by I. L. Finkel and M. J. Geller. Gronigen: Styx Publications, 1997.

Crawford, Harriet. *Sumer and the Sumerians*. 2d ed. Cambridge: Cambridge University Press, 2004.

Cunningham, Graham. *Deliver Me from Evil: Mesopotamian Incantations, 2500–1500 B.C.* Roma: Editrice Pontificio Instituto Biblico, 1997.

————. "In the Company of ni_2 'Self' and 'Fear(someness).'" In *Analysing Literary Sumerian: Corpus-Based Approaches*, edited by Jarle Ebeling and Graham Cunningham. London: Equinox, 2007.

Dalley, Stephanie. *Myths from Mesopotamia*. Oxford: Oxford University Press, 2000.

Dalley, Stephanie, et al. *The Legacy of Mesopotamia*. Oxford: Oxford University Press, 1998.

du Bois, Page. *Sappho Is Burning*. Chicago: University of Chicago Press, 1995.

Ebeling, Jarle, and Graham Cunningham. *Analysing Literary Sumerian*. London: Equinox, 2007.

Edzard, Dietz Otto. "The Names of the Sumerian Temples." In *Sumerian Gods and Their Representations*, edited by I. L. Finkel and M. J. Geller. Groningen: Styx Publications, 1997.

Edzard, Dietz Otto, Gertrud Farber, and Edmond Sollberger. *Die Orts-und Gewassernamen der prasargonischen und sargonischen Zeit. Répertoire Géographique des Textes Cunéiformes*, volume 1 (Wiesbaden: L Reichert, 1977).

Eliade, Mircea. *Myths, Dreams, and Mysteries*. New York: Harper and Row, 1957.

Ellis, Maria de Jong, ed. *Nippur at the Centennial*. Philadelphia: University Museum, 1992.

Eichler, Barry L., ed. *Kramer Anniversary Volume*. Kevelaer, Germany: Verlag Butzon and Bercker, 1976.

Falkenstein, Adam. "Enheduʿanna, Die Tochter Sargons von Akkade." *Revue d'Assyriologie* 52 (1975): 129–131.

Farber, Walter. "Witchcraft, Magic, and Divination in Ancient Mesopotamia." In CANE 3:1895–1909.

Ferrara, A. J. *Nanna-Suen's Journey to Nippur*. Rome: Biblical Institute Press, 1973.

Finkel, I. L. and M. J. Geller, eds. *Sumerian Gods and Their Representations*. Groningen: Styx Publications, 1997.

Foster, Benjamin R. "On Authorship in Akkadian Literature." *Annali* 51 (1991): 17–32.

Franke, Sabina, "The Kings of Akkad: Sargon and Naram-Sin." In CANE 2:831–842.

Frayne, D. R. *The Early Dynastic List of Geographical Names*. New Haven: American Oriental Society, 1992.

————. *Royal Inscriptions of Mesopotamia: Early Periods*, volume 2, *Sargonic and Gutian Periods (2334–2113 B.C.)*. Toronto: University of Toronto Press, 1993.

Frymer-Kensky, Tikva. *In the Wake of the Goddesses*. New York: Free Press, 1992.

Gadd, C. J. "En-an-e-du." *Iraq* 13 (1951): 27–39.

George, A. R. *House Most High: The Temples of Ancient Mesopotamia*. Winona Lake, Ind.: Eisenbrauns, 1993.

Gibson, McGuire. "Nippur 1990: Gula, Goddess of Healing, and an Akkadian Tomb." *The Oriental Institute News and Notes*. September–October, 1990.

———. "Patterns of Occupation at Nippur." In *Nippur at the Centennial*, edited by Maria de Jong Ellis. Philadelphia: University Museum, 1992.

Goedicke, Hans, and J. J. M. Roberts. *Unity and Diversity*. Baltimore: Johns Hopkins University Press, 1975.

Goff, Beatrice Laura. *Symbols of Prehistoric Mesopotamia*. New Haven: Yale University Press, 1963.

Gragg, Gene B. "The Keš Temple Hymn." In *Texts from Cuneiform Sources*. Volume 3. Edited by A. Leo Oppenheim. Locust Valley, N.Y.: J. J. Augustin, 1969.

Grahn, Judy. *Blood, Bread, and Roses: How Menstruation Created the World*. Boston: Beacon Press, 1993.

Green, Anthony. "Myths in Mesopotamian Art." In *Sumerian Gods and Their Representations*, edited by I. L. Finkle and M. J. Geller. Gronigen: Styx Publications, 1997.

Haas, Volkert. "Death and the Afterlife in Hittite Thought." In CANE 3:2021.

Hall, Mark G. "A Study of the Sumerian Moon-God, Nanna/Suen." Ph.D. dissertation, University of Pennsylvania, 1985.

Hallo, William W. "Antediluvian Cities," *JCS* 23/3 (1971): 57–67.

———. "Toward a History of Sumerian Literature." In *Sumerological Studies in Honor of Thorkild Jacobsen*, edited by S. J. Lieberman. Chicago: University of Chicago Press, 1975.

———. "Review of *The Return of Ninurta to Nippur*." *JAOS* 101/2 (1981).

———. "The Limits of Skepticism." *JAOS* 110/2 (1990).

———. "Enki and the Theology of Eridu." *JAOS* 116/2 (1996): 231–235.

———. *Origins*. Leiden: E. J. Brill, 1996.

Hallo, William W., and William Kelly Simpson. *The Ancient Near East: A History*. 2d ed. Belmont, Calif.: Wadsworth/Thomson Learning, 1998.

Hallo, William W., and J. J. A. van Dijk. *The Exaltation of Inanna*. New Haven: Yale University Press, 1968.

Hansen, Donald P. "Art of the Akkadian Dynasty." In *Art of the First Cities*, edited by Joan Aruz. New York: Metropolitan Museum of Art, 2003.

Harris, Rivkah. *Ancient Sippar*. Te Istanbul: Nederlands Historisch-Archaeologisch Institut, 1975.

———. *Gender and Aging in Mesopotamia*. Norman: University of Oklahoma Press, 2000.

Heimpel, W. "The Nanshe Hymn." *JCS* 33/2 (1981).

———. "The Sun at Night and the Doors of Heaven in Babylonian Texts." *JCS* 38 (1986): 143.

———. "The Lady of Girsu." In *Riches Hidden in Secret Places*, edited by Tvzi Abusch. Winona Lake, Ind.: Eisenbrauns, 2002.

Helbaek, Hans. "Ecological Effects of Irrigation in Ancient Mesopotamia." *Iraq* 22 (1960): 186–199.

Henshaw, Richard A. *Female and Male: The Cultic Personnel*. Allison Park, Penn.: Pickwick Publications, 1994.

The Holy Bible: Revised Standard Version. New York: Thomas Nelson & Sons, 1952.

Huot, J. L. "Larsa." In *Reallexikon der Assyriologie.* Berlin: Walter de Gruyter, 1983.

Jacobsen, Thorkild. "Early Political Development in Mesopotamia." *ZA* 52 (1957).

——. "Some Sumerian City-Names." *JCS* 21 (1967): 101–103.

——. "Toward the Image of Tammuz." In *Toward the Image of Tammuz and Other Essays on Mesopotamian History and Culture,* edited by William L. Moran. Cambridge: Harvard University Press, 1970.

——. "Notes on Nintur." *Orientalia* 42/1–2 (1973): 274–298.

——. *Treasures of Darkness.* New Haven: Yale University Press, 1976.

——. *The Harps that Once . . .* New Haven: Yale University Press, 1987.

——. "A Maidenly Inanna." *JANES* 22 (1993): 63–68.

Jawad, Abdul Jalil. *The Advent of the Era of Townships in Northern Mesopotamia.* Leiden: E. J. Brill, 1965.

Katz, Dina. *The Image of the Netherworld in the Sumerian Sources.* Bethesda, Md.: CDL Press, 2003.

Kilmer, Anne Draffkorn. "Appendix C: The Brick of Birth." In G. Azarpay, "Proportional Guidelines in Near Eastern Art." *JNES* 46 (1987): 211–213.

——. "An Oration on Babylon." *Altorientalische Forschungen* 18 (1991): 9–22.

Kippenberg, H. G., ed. *Struggles of Gods.* Berlin: Mouton, 1984.

Klein, Jacob. "Shulgi of Ur: King of a Neo-Sumerian Empire." In *CANE* 2:843–857.

——. "The God Martu in Sumerian Literature." In *Sumerian Gods and Their Representations,* edited by I. L. Finkel and M. J. Geller. Groningen: Styx Publications, 1997.

Klein, Jacob, and Aaron Skaist, eds. *Bar-Ilan Studies in Assyriology.* Ramat Gan, Israel: Bar-Ilan University, 1990.

Knight, Chris. *Blood Relations: Menstruation and the Origins of Culture.* New Haven: Yale University Press, 1991.

Kramer, S. N. *The Sumerians.* Chicago: University of Chicago Press, 1963.

——. "Poets and Psalmists." In *The Legacy of Sumer,* edited by D. Schmandt-Besserat. Malibu, Calif.: Undena Press, 1976.

——. "The Marriage of Martu." In *Bar-Ilan Studies in Assyriology,* edited by Jacob Klein and Aaron Skaist. Ramat Gan, Israel: Bar-Ilan University, 1990.

Kramer, S. N., and John Maier. *Myths of Enki, the Crafty God.* New York: Oxford University Press, 1989.

Kutscher, Raphael. "The Cult of Dumuzi/Tammuz." In *Bar-Ilan Studies in Assyriology,* edited by Jacob Klein and Aaron Skaist. Ramat Gan, Israel: Bar-Ilan University, 1990.

Labat, Rene, and Florence Malbran-Labat. *Manuel d'Epigraphie Akkadienne.* Paris: Librairie Orientaliste Paul Geuthner, 1995.

Lambert, W. G. "The Historical Development of the Mesopotamian Pantheon: A Study in Sophisticated Polytheism." In *Unity and Diversity,* edited by Hans Goedicke and J. J. Roberts. Baltimore: Johns Hopkins University Press, 1975.

——. "The Cult of Ištar of Babylon." In *Le Temple et Le Cult: Compte Rendu de la Vingtiéme Rencontre Assyriologique Internationale.* Te Istanbul: Nederlands Historisch-Archeologisch Institute, 1975.

————. "A New Babylonian Descent to the Netherworld." In *Lingering over Words*, edited by Tiva Abusch, John Huehnergard, and Piotr Steinkeller. Atlanta: Scholars Press, 1990.

————. "Nippur in Ancient Ideology." In *Nippur at the Centennial*, edited by Maria de Jong Ellis. Philadelphia: University Museum, 1992.

————. "Myth and Mythmaking in Sumer and Akkad." In CANE 3:1825–1835.

————. "Sumerian Gods: Combining the Evidence of Texts and Art." In *Sumerian Gods and Their Representations*, edited by I. L. Finkel and M. J. Geller. Groningen: Styx Publications, 1997.

————. "Ghost-writers?" *N.A.B.U.* 3 (September), 2001.

Legrain, L. *Archaic Seal-Impressions*. London/Philadelphia: Ur Excavations 3, 1936.

Leick, Gwendolyn. *Sex and Eroticism in Mesopotamian Literature*. London: Routledge, 1994.

————. *Mesopotamia: The Invention of the City*. London: Penguin Press, 2001.

Lewy, Hildegard. "Assyria, c. 2600–1816 B.C." In *Cambridge Ancient History*, volume 1, part 2, edited by I. E. S. Edwards, C. J. Gadd, and N. G. L. Hammond. Cambridge: Cambridge University Press, 1971.

Lieberman, Stephen J. "Nippur: City of Decisions." In *Nippur at the Centennial*, edited by Maria de Jong Ellis. Philadelphia: University Museum, 1992.

Livingstone, Alasdair. "How the Common Man Influences the Gods of Sumer." In *Sumerian Gods and Their Representations*, edited by I. L. Finkel and M. J. Geller. Gronigen: Styx Publications, 1997.

Lloyd, Seton. "Ur, Al 'Ubaid, 'Uqair and Eridu." *Iraq* 22 (1960).

————. *The Archaeology of Mesopotamia*. London: Thames and Hudson, 1978.

Mallowan, Sir Max E. L. "The Early Dynastic Period in Mesopotamia." In *Cambridge Ancient History*, volume 1, part 2, edited by I. E. S. Edwards, C. J. Gadd, and N. G. L. Hammond. Cambridge: Cambridge University Press, 1971.

Marschack, Alexander. *The Roots of Civilization*. New York: McGraw-Hill, 1972.

Martin, Harriet P., Francesco Pomponio, Giuseppe Visicato, and Aage Westenholz. *The Fara Tablets*. Bethesda, Md.: CDL Press, 2001.

Matthews, Donald. "Legal and Social Institutions of Ancient Mesopotamia." In CANE 1:455–468.

Meador, Betty De Shong. *Uncursing the Dark*. Chicago: Chiron Publications, 1992.

————. *Inanna—Lady of Largest Heart*. Austin: University of Texas Press, 2000.

Michalowski Piotr. "Sailing to Babylon, Reading the Dark Side of the Moon." In *The Study of the Ancient Near East in the Twenty-First Century*, edited by Jerrold S. Cooper and Glenn M. Schwartz. Winona Lake, Ind.: Eisenbrauns, 1966.

————. "Carminative Magic: Towards an Understanding of Sumerian Poetics." ZA 71/1 (1981).

————. "History as Charter: Some Observations on the Sumerian King List." JAOS 103/1 (1983).

————. "Early Communicative Systems: Art, Literature and Writing." In *Investigating Artistic Environments in the Ancient Near East*, edited by Ann C. Gunter: Washington: Smithsonian Institution Press, 1990.

————. "Charisma and Control: On Continuity and Change in Early Mesopotamian Bureaucratic Systems." In *The Organization of Power: Aspects of Bureaucracy in the*

ANE, edited by McGuire Gibson and Robert D. Biggs, 2d ed. *SAOC* 46. Chicago: Oriental Institute of the University of Chicago, 1991.

————. "The Unbearable Lightness of Enlil." In *Intellectual Life of the Ancient Near East*, edited by Jiří Prosecky. Prague: Oriental Institute, 1998.

Mitchell, Stephen. *Gilgamesh, a New English Version*. New York: Free Press, 2004.

Moortgat, Anton. *The Art of Ancient Mesopotamia*. London: Phaidon, 1969.

Moran, William L. "The Keš Temple Hymn and the Canonical Temple List." In *Kramer Anniversary Volume*, edited by Barry L. Eichler. Kevelaer, Germany: Verlag Butzon and Bercker, 1976.

————, ed. *Towards the Image of Tammuz*. Cambridge: Harvard University Press, 1970.

Nissen, Hans J. *The Early History of the Ancient Near East*. Chicago: University of Chicago Press, 1988.

————. "Western Asia Before the Age of Empires." In *CANE* 2:701–806.

Oates, Joan, "Ur and Eridu, the Prehistory." *Iraq* 22 (1960): 32–50.

Oppenheim, A. Leo. *The Interpretation of Dreams in the Ancient Near East*. Philadelphia: American Philosophical Society, 1956.

————. *Ancient Mesopotamia*. Chicago: University of Chicago Press, 1977.

————, ed. *Texts from Cuneiform Sources*. Volume 3. Locust Valley, N.Y.: J. J. Augustin, 1969.

Parpola, Simo. *Assyrian Prophecies*. Helsinki: Helsinki University Press, 1997.

Postgate, J. N. *Early Mesopotamia*. London: Routledge, 1992.

————. *Texts from Cuneiform Sources*. Volume 3. Locust Valley, N.Y.: J. J. Augustin, 1969.

————. "Royal Ideology and State Administration in Sumer and Akkad." In *CANE* 1:395–411.

Reiner, Erica. *Your Thwarts in Pieces Your Mooring Rope Cut*. Detroit: Horace H. Rackham School of Graduate Studies at the University of Michigan, 1985.

————. "Why Do You Cuss Me?" *Procedures of the American Philosophical Society* 130 (1986): 1–6.

Reisman, Daniel. "A 'Royal' Hymn of Isib-Erra to the Goddess Nisaba." In *Dramer Anniversary Volume*, edited by Barry Eichler. Kevelaer, Germany: Verlag Butzon and Bercker, 1976.

Répertoire Géographique des Textes Cunéiformes, volume 1, "Presargonic and Sargonic," 1977.

Rexroth, Kenneth. "The Poet as Translator." In *The Craft and Context of Translation*. Austin: University of Texas Press, 1961.

Roberts, J. J. M. "Divine Freedom and Cultic Manipulation in Israel and Mesopotamia." In *Unity and Diversity*, edited by Hans Goedeke and J. J. M. Roberts. Baltimore: Johns Hopkins University Press, 1975.

Robertson, John F. "The Temple Economy of Old Babylonian Nippur: The Evidence for Centralized Management." In *Nippur at the Centennial*, edited by Maria de Jong Ellis. Philadelphia: University Museum, 1992.

Robson, Eleanor. "Bird and Fish in the OB Sumerian Literary Catalogues." *N.A.B.U.*, no. 3 (September), 2003.

Römer, W. H. P. *Sumerische 'Konighymnen' der Isin-Zeit*. Leiden, 1965.

Rosenberg, David. *Abraham: The First Historical Biography*. New York: Basic Books, 2006.

Roth, Martha T. "Marriage, Divorce, and the Prostitute in Ancient Mesopotamia." In *Prostitutes and Courtesans in the Ancient World*, edited by Christopher A. Faraone and Laura K. McClure. Madison: University of Wisconsin Press, 2006.

Sasson, Jack M. "King Hammurabi of Babylon." In CANE 2:901–915.

———, ed. *Civilizations of the Ancient Near East*. 4 vols. New York: Charles Scribner's Sons, 1995.

Sauren, Herbert. "Nammu and Enki." In *The Tablet and the Scroll: Near Eastern Studies in Honor of William W. Hallo*, edited by Mark E. Cohen, Daniel C. Snell, and David B. Weisberg. Bethesda, Md.: CDL Press, 1993.

Schmandt-Besserat, Denise. "Images of Enship." In *The Legacy of Sumer*, edited by Denise Schmandt-Besserat. Malibu, Calif.: Undena Publications, 1976.

———. *Before Writing*, volume 1, *From Counting to Cuneiform*. Austin: University of Texas Press, 1992.

———, ed. *The Legacy of Sumer*. Malibu, Calif: Undena Publications, 1976.

Scurlock, JoAnn. "Death and the Afterlife in Ancient Mesopotamian Thought." In CANE 3:1883–1893.

Sefati, Yitschak. *Love Songs in Sumerian Literature*. Ramat Gan, Israel: Bar-Ilan University, 1998.

Selz, Gebhard J. "The Holy Drum, the Spear, and the Harp." In *Sumerian Gods and Their Representations*, edited by I. M. Finkel and M. J. Geller. Groningen: Styx Publications, 1997.

———. *Untersuchungen zur Göotterwelt des altsumerischen Stadtstaates von Lagaš*. Philadelphia, 1995.

Sjöberg, Åke W. "Hymn to Numušda with a Prayer for King Siniqišam of Larsa and a Hymn to Ninurta." *Orientalia Suecana* 22 (1973).

———. "Miscellaneous Sumerian Hymns." ZA 63 (1973).

———. "Hymns to Ninurta with Prayers for Šūsîn of Ur and Bursîn of Isin." In *Kramer Anniversary Volume*, edited by Barry L. Eichler. Kevelaer, Germany: Verlag Butzon and Bercker, 1976.

Sjöberg, Åke W., and Eugen Bergmann S.J. "The Collection of the Sumerian Temple Hymns." In *Texts from Cuneiform Sources*, volume 3, edited by A. Leo Oppenheim. Locust Valley, N.Y.: J. J. Augustin, 1969.

Sollberger, Edmond. "The Disc of Enheduanna." *Iraq* 22 (1960): 75–86.

———. "The Temple in Babylonia." In *Le Temple et le Cult: Compte Rendu de la Vingtième Rencontre Assyriologique Internationale*. Te Istambul: Nederlands Historisch-Archeologisch Institute, 1975, 31–34.

Sollberger, Edmond, and J. R. Kupper. *Inscriptions Royales Sumeriennes et Akkadiennes*. Paris, 1971.

Steele, Laura D. "Review of D. Bolger and N. Serwint, eds., *Engendering Aphrodite: Woman and Society in Ancient Cyprus*." *Nin* 4 (2003).

Steinkeller, Piotr. "On Rulers, Priests and Sacred Marriage." In *Priests and Officials in the Ancient Near East*, edited by Kazuko Watanabe. Heidelberg: Universitatsverlag C. Winter, 1999.

———. "Archaic City Seals and the Question of Early Babylonian Unity." In *Riches*

Hidden in Secret Places, edited by Tzvi Abusch. Winona Lake, Ind.: Eisenbrauns, 2002.

Stone, Elizabeth C. "The Development of Cities in Ancient Mesopotamia." In CANE 1:235–248.

Szarzyńska, Krystyna. *Sumerica.* Warszawa: Wydawnictwo Akademickie Dialog, 1997.

Teissier, Beatrice. *Ancient Near Eastern Cylinder Seals: From the Marcopoli Collection.* Berkeley: University of California Press, 1984.

Teubal, Savina J. *Sarah the Priestess.* Athens, Ohio: Swallow Press, 1984.

Van Buren, E. Douglas. "The God Ningizzida." *Iraq* 1 (1934): 60–89.

Van De Mieroop, Marc. *The Ancient Mesopotamian City.* Oxford: Oxford University Press, 1999.

Vanstiphout, H. L. J. "Lipit-Eshtar's Praise in the Edubba." *JCS* 30 (1978): 33–61.

———. "Inanna/Ishtar as a Figure of Controversy." In *Struggles of Gods,* edited by H. G. Kippenberg. Berlin: Mouton, 1984.

———. "Why Did Enki Organize the World?" In *Sumerian Gods and Their Representations,* edited by I. L Finkel and M. J. Geller. Gronigen: Styx Publications, 1997.

Vogelzang, M. E., and Vanstiphout, H. L. J., eds. *Mesopotamian Poetic Language.* Gronigen: Styx Publications, 1996.

Walker, C. B. F. *Cuneiform.* Berkeley: University of California Press, 1987.

Wall-Romana, Christophe. "An Aerial Location of Agade." *JNES* 49 (1990): 205–245.

Weadock, Penelope N. "The *Giparu* at Ur." *Iraq* 37, no. 2 (1975): 101–128.

Weiss, Harvey, "Kish, Akkad and Agade," *JAOS* 95.3 (1975): 434–453.

Westenholz, Aage, "Old Akkadian School Texts: Some Goals of Sargonic Scribal Education." *AfO* 25 (1974–1977): 95–112.

———. "The Early Excavators of Nippur." In *Nippur at the Centennial,* edited by Maria de Jong Ellis. Philadelphia: University Museum, 1992.

Westenholz, Joan Goodnick, "Enheduanna, En-Priestess, Hen of Nanna, Spouse of Nanna." in *Dumu é.dub.ba.a: Studies in Honor of Åke Sjöberg,* edited by Hermann Behrens, Darlene Loding, and Martha Roth. Philadelphia: University of Pennsylvania Museum, 1989.

———. "Metaphorical Language in the Poetry of Love in the Ancient Near East." In *Proceedings 38th RAI.* Paris 1992, 381–387.

———. "Oral Traditions and Written Texts in the Cycle of Akkade." In *Mesopotamian Epic Literature,* edited by Marianna E. Vogelzang and Herman L. J. Vanstiphout: Lewiston, N.Y.: Edwin Mellen Press, 1992.

———. "Nanaya: Lady of Mystery." In *Sumerian Gods and Their Representations,* edited by I. L. Finkel and M. J. Geller. Groningen: Styx Publications, 1997.

———. "Enheduanna—Princess, Priestess, Poetess." Paper presented at the California Museum of Ancient Art, Los Angeles, California, May 1999.

Wiggermann, F. A. M. "Transtigridian Snake Gods." In *Sumerian Gods and Their Representations,* edited by I. L. Finkel and M. J. Geller. Groningen: Styx Publications, 1997.

———. "Theologies, Priests, and Worship in Ancient Mesopotamia." In CANE 3:1857–1870.

———. "Scenes from the Shadow Side." In *Mesopotamian Poetic Language: Sumerian and Akkadian,* edited by M. E. Vogelzang and H. L. J. Vanstiphout. Groningen: Styx Publications, 1996.

Winter, Irene J. "Women in Public: The Disc of Enheduanna, the Beginning of the Office of En-Priestess, and the Weight of Visual Evidence." In *La Femme dans le Proche-Orient antique,* edited by Jean-Marie Durand. Paris: Editions Recherché sur les Civilizations, 1987.

———. "Aesthetics in Ancient Mesopotamian Art." In CANE 4:2569–2582.

Wolkstein, Diane, and Samuel Noah Kramer. *Inanna—Queen of Heaven and Earth.* New York: Harper and Row, 1983.

Woolley, Sir Leonard. *Excavations at Ur.* London: Ernest Been, 1954.

Zgoll, Annette. *Der Rechtsfall der En-hedu-Ana im Lied nin-me-šara.* Münster: Ugarit-Verlag, 1997.

Note: *Words in the Akkadian language are set in italics. The Sumerian word* **me** *is set in boldface type; some signs in the Sumerian language are set in caps where it is uncertain how they are to be read; otherwise, Sumerian words are set in roman type. Page references in italics denote illustrations; page references in boldface denote the texts of the Temple Hymns.*

Lightning Source UK Ltd.
Milton Keynes UK
UKHW010051230421
382481UK00001B/10